The Wonder that is Sanskrit

The Wonder that is Sanskrit

Sampad & Vijay

Sri Aurobindo Society, Pondicherry
in association with
Mapin Publishing, Ahmedabad

First published in India in 2002 by
Sri Aurobindo Society, Pondicherry
email: mother@sriaurobindosociety.org.in
www.sriaurobindosociety.org.in
in association with
Mapin Publishing Pvt. Ltd.
Ahmedabad 380013, India
Tel : 79-755 1833
Fax: 79-755 0955
email: mapin@icenet.net
www.mapinpub.com

Simultaneously published in the United States of America in 2002 by
Grantha Corporation
80 Cliffedgeway, Middletown, NJ 07701

Researched by
Sri Aurobindo Institute of Research in Social Sciences, a unit of Sri Aurobindo Society, Pondicherry-605002

ISBN: 81-88204-08-0 (Mapin)
ISBN: 1-890206-50-4 (Grantha)
ISBN: 81-7060-182-7 (Sri Aurobindo Society)
LC : 2002101938

Processed and Printed by
Sudarsan Graphics, Chennai

Printed in INDIA

Distributed in North America by
Antique Collectors' Club
Market Street Industrial Park
Wappingers' Falls, NY 12590
Tel: 800-252 5321
Fax: 845-297 0068
email: info@antiquecc.com
www.antiquecc.com

Distributed in the United Kingdom & Europe by
Art Books International
Unit 14 Groves Business Centre
Shipton Road
Milton-under-Wychwood
Chipping Norton
Oxon OX7 6JP UK
Tel: 1993 830000
Fax: 1993 830007
email: sales@art-bks.com
www.artbooksinternational.co.uk

Distributed in Asia by
Hemisphere Publication Services
240 MacPherson Road
#08-01 Pines Industrial Building
Singapore
Tel: 65-741 5166
Fax: 65-742 9356
email: info@hemisphere.com.sg

Contents

An Explanatory Note

This is a book on Sanskrit. Hence there are many original texts and words from Sanskrit which have been given here in the *Devanagari* script. For those who cannot read *Devanagari*, these have also been provided in the Roman script with diacritical marks to facilitate the correct pronounciation. For the words and phrases which are part of the English text, the transliteration comes immediately after the Sanskrit words. For the *shlokas*, the transliterations are given as a special appendix at the end. We have explained the system of transliteration that has been followed.

There is also a detailed glossary of Sanskrit names and terms, a bibliography and an index.

Acknowledgements

There are many persons who have contributed in making this journey into Sanskrit very fulfilling and satisfying and who have revealed to me its hidden wonders. I would first like to thank all the authors and publishers from whose writings we have quoted freely and extensively. In most cases the references are given but some times the sources could not be traced.

A very important contribution has been of Sampad who untiringly did the research and patiently explained to me the intricate details. The final form and presentation owe a lot to Shonar who carefully went through the entire manuscript and gave her frank and valuable suggestions. Gita, Sushanto, Debajyoti, Krishna, Prashanti, Shivakumar and Swami Vishwanath have helped in the designing, typesetting, formatting and proof-reading.

The quality of the type-setting, formatting and printing is due to the great care taken by Sudarsan Graphics and Kolam Information Services Pvt. Ltd.

I am specially grateful to Prof. Kutumba Sastri who encouraged us and was always available for guidance with his vast knowledge of Sanskrit.

Finally I would like to thank the Tirumala Tirupati Devasthanam and the Manidevi Charitable Trust for their help and support in preparing and printing this book.

Vijay

System of Transliteration

VOWELS

Devanāgarī letter	*English equivalent*	*Pronounce as in*	*Devanāgarī letter*	*English equivalent*	*Pronounce as in*
अ	*a*	rur*a*l	ऌ	*l̥r*	revel*ry*
आ	*ā*	f*a*ther	ए	*e*	th*e*y
इ	*i*	f*i*ll	ऐ	*ai*	*ai*sle
ई	*ī*	pol*i*ce	ओ	*o*	g*o*
उ	*u*	f*u*ll	औ	*au*	H*au*s (German)
ऊ	*ū*	r*u*de			
ऋ	*ṛ*	mer*ri*ly	अं	*ṁ*	(the *anusvāra*)[1]
ॠ	*ṝ*	ma*ri*ne	अः	*ḥ*	(the *visarga*)[2]

CONSONANTS

क्	*k*	*k*ill	त्	*t*	Similar to the previous five but with the tongue against the teeth as in the French dentals.
ख्	*kh*	in*kh*orn	थ्	*th*	
ग्	*g*	*g*et	द्	*d*	
घ्	*gh*	lo*g-h*ut	ध्	*dh*	
ङ्	*ṅ*	si*n*g	न्	*n*	
च्	*c*	*ch*urch	प्	*p*	*p*ut
छ्	*ch*	hit*chh*ike	फ्	*ph*	u*ph*ill
ज्	*j*	*j*et	ब्	*b*	*b*ear
झ्	*jh*	hed*geh*og	भ्	*bh*	a*bh*or
ञ्	*ñ*	si*n*ge	म्	*m*	*m*ap
ट्	*ṭ*	*t*rue	य्	*y*	*y*ear
ठ्	*ṭh*	an*th*ill	र्	*r*	*r*ed
ड्	*ḍ*	*d*rum	ल्	*l*	*l*ull
ढ्	*ḍh*	red*h*ead	ळ्	*ḷ*	often for *ḍ* in Veda.
ण्	*ṇ*	tour*n*ament	व्	*v*	*ivy* (but like *w* after consonants)
श्	*ś*	*s*ure	क्ष्	*kṣ*[3]	
ष्	*ṣ*	*sh*un	त्र्	*tr*	
स्	*s*	*s*aint	ज्ञ्	*jñ*	
ह्	*h*	*h*ear	ॐ	*om*	

1. A nasal sound, sometimes pronounced like *n* (as in *haṁsa*), sometimes representing a final *m*. The *anusvāra* has been transliterated *ṅ ñ ṇ n* or *ṁ* according to the phonetic group of the following letter with which it coalesces.
2. An "h"-like aspiration at the end (*anityaḥ*) or occasinally in the middle (*duḥkha*) of a word.
3. These are the special conjunct consonant letters used in sanskrit.

introduction

Introduction

Let it be known right at the outset that this book is not written by a scholar and furthermore is not meant for scholars. I have never studied Sanskrit in a systematic manner or in great depth, but it has always held a strange fascination for me. I have enjoyed listening to its sound, for even if one does not understand Sanskrit, it compels one to pay attention and often brings an inexplicable joy. I wondered why it was so and how Sanskrit came to acquire such a power. Not only was it a mantric lure, I also felt that if one truly wants to understand India, its culture and ethos, a knowledge of Sanskrit is essential.

On the other hand, I too surrendered to the stereotype of Sanskrit being a very difficult language to learn and grasp, something very alien and distant from our usual spoken and written languages, meant only for the scholars, perhaps even a dead language. Though there was an attraction, with such an in-built bias there was also a strong resistance to make the effort to study it in greater depth.

However, certain circumstances intervened and compelled me to do so. We took up a project called 'Resurgent India', where our endeavour was to discover the greatest and highest achievements of India in every field. While identifying these peaks in the field of language, it was inevitable for us to turn to Sanskrit, one of the oldest and richest languages of the world.

What resulted was an enthralling and fulfilling experience. The deeper we went into it, the more amazed we were by the beauty and perfection of this language. Whichever aspect we explored, there seemed to be no limit to its treasures and wonders.

It was veritably the experience of entering an ancient Indian temple, huge, majestic and mighty, yet with each facet intricately carved and planned to precision. The human mind, once awakened and made aware, knows no rest until it is completely satisfied. It was only natural that a multitude of questions should have arisen and demanded further research and explanation.

An Extraordinary Language

What is language? What is its purpose? How does it communicate? What are the challenges and difficulties it faces? What is the role of grammar, of phonetics? How do they originate? What are the basic fundamental sounds? How do the vocal chords produce them and how does one organise and arrange these sounds in a systematic manner?

We have all learnt our alphabets, our grammars and our languages from early childhood. But rarely does one bother to ask such questions. However, here the questions were raised by Sanskrit itself and we were wonder-struck by the manner in which Sanskrit had answered them.

Sanskrit is a "most wonderful language."[1] One would imagine such a statement to be mere sales talk, the label 'most wonderful' being placed on practically everything in modern times. What it is, in actuality, is a very well researched and deduced summation by the renowned German Indologist, Max Mueller. But lest this be considered the personal assessment of one scholar, let us see what Professor Friedrich Schlegel, writer and critic, who established the first chair of Indology in Germany at Hanmoben, has to say: "Justly it is called Sanskrit, that is, 'perfect, finished'. Sanskrit combines these various qualities possessed separately by other tongues: Grecian copiousness, deep-tone Roman force, the divine afflatus characterising the Hebrew tongues. Judged by an organic standard of the principal elements of language, Sanskrit excels in grammatical structure and is indeed the most perfectly developed of all idioms, not excepting Greek and Latin."[2]

This was only one aspect of our discovery. A language derives its value not merely from its logical and grammatical structure but from the manner in which it has been used and the richness of its literature. Whether we looked at the simple, unsophisticated folk style found in fable-books like the *Pañcatantra* and the *Hitopadeśa*, or the practical and scientific writings in the various *Śāstras* like the *Arthaśāstra*, *Nāṭyaśāstra*, *Āyurveda* or *Jyotiṣa*; whether we delved into the rich, highly developed literary style that expressed itself through the poetry, the dramas and the prose romances of Kalidasa, Bhavabhuti and Magha; whether we turned to the thousands of *Subhāṣitas* (reflective and didactic stanzas), as in the *Nītiśataka* of Bhartrihari, or we studied the great philosophies and learned commentaries of Kapila or Panini; whether we read the well-known epics, the *Mahābhārata* and the *Rāmāyaṇa*, which are an entire world in themselves; whether we sought for the principles of yoga in the *Yogasūtras* of Patanjali, or scaled the highest peaks of spiritual poetry through the *Vedas*, the *Upaniṣads* and the *Gītā* – there was no limit to the treasures that awaited us.

And it was not just a question of a phenomenal quantity and variety but also of the highest quality. Says W.C. Taylor, an American Indologist, "It was an astounding discovery that Hindustan possessed, in spite of the changes of realms and changes of time, a language of unrivalled richness and variety…a philosophy compared with which, in point of age, the lessons of Pythagoras are but of yesterday, and in point of daring speculation Plato's boldest efforts were tame and commonplace. This literature, with all its colossal proportions – which can scarcely be described without the semblance of bombast and exaggeration – claimed, of course, a place for itself. It stood alone and it was able to stand alone."[3]

It is therefore not without reason that the well-known historian Will Durant, while writing about India and Sanskrit, affirms: "India was the motherland of our race and Sanskrit the mother of Europe's languages; she was the mother of our philosophy, mother, through the Arabs, of much of our mathematics; mother, through the Buddha, of the ideals embodied in Christianity; mother through the village community, of self-government and democracy. Mother India is in many ways the mother of us all."[4]

The Importance of Sanskrit

In a certain sense all language is an attempt to find the perfect unity of the word, the sound and the meaning. And perhaps this has never been achieved as perfectly and harmoniously as in the Sanskrit language. In this book, we have tried to share the thrill experienced on coming into contact with Sanskrit in its various facets and expressions, and for that purpose we have shown no hesitation in drawing and quoting extensively from writers who have provided many interesting insights.

Sanskrit is rich in every way – rich in vocabulary, rich in literature, rich in thoughts and ideas, rich in meaning and values. The greatness, magnificence and beauty of Sanskrit has perhaps not been described better than by Sri Aurobindo, the great Rishi and Yogi of modern India:

"The ancient and classical creations of the Sanskrit tongue, both in quality and in body and abundance of excellence, in their potent originality and force and beauty, in their substance and art and structure, in grandeur and justice and charm of speech, and in the height and width of the reach of their spirit stand very evidently in the front rank among the world's great literatures. The language itself, as has been universally recognised by those competent to form a judgement, is one of the most magnificent, the most perfect and wonderfully sufficient literary instruments developed by the human mind; at once majestic and sweet and flexible, strong and clearly-formed and full and vibrant and subtle…"[5]

In this book, we begin by looking at the perfection of Sanskrit as a language through its grammar, structure and alphabet. In a related chapter are presented interesting, even unbelievable, examples of some amazing creations of the Sanskrit language, which perhaps may not be possible in any other language of the world. We then look at the use of Sanskrit as a vehicle of expression for every aspect of life, including the arts and the sciences. From here we move on to some examples of its charm and beauty and music through its literary writings, and then to Sanskrit as a language of upliftment and enlightenment, a repository of wisdom and values. Finally, we look at Sanskrit as a sacred medium for expressing the highest spiritual truths and experiences. In the end we try to understand the importance of Sanskrit for India and the world, why it is called the language of India's soul and why we believe that, in spite of the many obvious difficulties, it can and should become the national language of India.

The Rediscovery of Sanskrit

Sanskrit is one of the most ancient languages. In the words of Dr. David Frawley, "Sanskrit is the oldest most continually used language in the world… By the most conservative accounts it has been used continuously since 1500 B.C.; by more liberal accounts it was in use before 6000 B.C. Classical Sanskrit follows the same basic patterns since the time of Panini, who probably lived around the time of the Buddha. It has the largest literature of any language, along with the sacred literature of two of the world's greatest religions – Hinduism and Buddhism. It possesses a larger group of works on spirituality, metaphysics and mythology than any other language. It has an extensive literature of poetry, drama and philosophy though much of it has been lost in time."[6]

Much like the sacred river Ganga, Sanskrit has flowed across India for thousands of years, embracing and nourishing, but also uplifting and purifying an entire country and its people and creating a unique civilisation and culture. It has been the most perfect instrument for expressing the thoughts, feelings, aspirations, knowledge and experiences of this ancient culture.

It is thus a paradox that Sanskrit is known so very little in the world. And even in India, the land of its birth, it is today understood and spoken by a very small minority. We must therefore try to understand why Sanskrit has receded into the background and realise the important role it has to play in India's resurgence and future development. Sanskrit has to be rediscovered.

As mentioned earlier, this presentation is neither complete nor scholarly. It is more in the nature of a sharing of a personal journey and experience. It is meant merely to open some windows, to provide some fleeting glimpses, to give some joy as one moves through its beautiful landscape. It is an attempt to come into contact with the heart of Sanskrit and through it, the soul of India.

Kalidasa, the great Sanskrit poet, begins his famous work *Raghuvaṁśa* 'The Line of Raghu', by invoking the mighty God Shiva and his consort Parvati. He says,

वागर्थाविव सम्पृक्तौ वागर्थप्रतिपत्तये ।
जगतः पितरौ वन्दे पार्वतीपरमेश्वरौ ॥ [7]

For the mastery of word and sense I bow to the Pair close-wedded as word and sense, the parents of the world, the Mountain's child and the Mighty Lord.

May this be also the beginning of our journey into the wonder that is Sanskrit.

Vijay

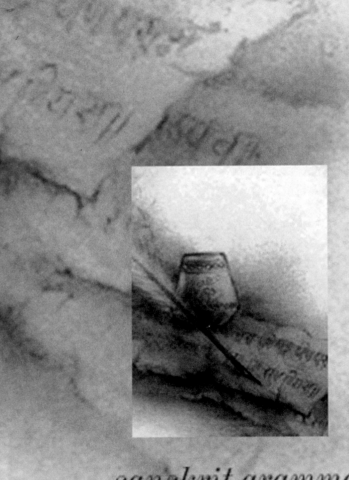

sanskrit grammar

Sanskrit Grammar

It is incredible how one tends to take the very basic things of life for granted. Have you ever wondered what it is that we call a language? How do words come about? What leads to the formulation of a sentence? A single word is rarely sufficient to form a sentence, and yet every collection of words does not make a sentence. What gives meaning to a sentence? What makes a language a fit vehicle for communication between the speaker and the listener? These questions have been asked in every language and in every country. But, according to some scholars, nowhere in the world have they been taken to such great depths and analysed in such minute details as in India. And perhaps nowhere is such an amount of technical literature available on grammar and related topics as in Sanskrit.

The Trimuni

The three Sanskrit grammarians who stand out in this field are Panini, Katyayana and Patanjali. Panini wrote the *Aṣṭādhyāyī*, 'The Work in Eight Chapters', as early as the 5th century B.C. Katyayana expanded the work of Panini in his *Vārtikas* in the 4th century B.C. Patanjali wrote his famous commentary on the works of Panini and Katyayana, known as the *Mahābhāṣya*, in the 2nd century B.C.

Panini's *Aṣṭādhyāyī* is the most ancient systematic grammar in the world. "In brevity of form coupled with comprehensiveness of content, Panini's work has certainly no parallel."[1] Through the ages, the *Aṣṭādhyāyī* and the *Mahābhāṣya* have evoked great admiration and profound reverence in India and abroad. Leonard Bloomfield, Professor of Germanic Philology in the University of Chicago, in his famous book *The Language*, speaks of Panini's grammar as "one of the greatest monuments of human intelligence."[2] He adds, "It describes with the minutest detail every inflection, derivation and composition, and every syntactic usage of Sanskrit...no other language to this day has been so perfectly described." Boehtlingk states that Panini's grammar is a masterpiece of the first rank and the more thoroughly one studies it, the more one is struck by the acuteness and the successful mastery of the vast matter shown in it.[3] Whitney asserts that even the form of presentation in Panini's work is a miracle of ingenuity.[4]

Together, Panini, Katyayana and Patanjali are known as the *Trimuni* – the 'three sages'. Even geographically, they encompassed the whole of India. Panini hailed from the West, while Katyayana was from the South and Patanjali was from the East.

The Sanskrit Alphabet

Like most things in ancient India, Sanskrit grammar too traces its mythological roots to a divine origin. It is believed that the seven great seers, the *Saptarṣi*, went to Lord Shiva and asked him to give them the essence of language. Shiva played his tiny drum, the *ḍamaru*, and the sounds that emerged from it are known as the *Māheśvarasūtrāṇi*. These 14 *sūtras* given by Shiva became the basis of the grammar created by Panini.

Even the very alphabet of Sanskrit is unique. An alphabet is meant to provide the basic sounds which the vocal chords can produce, or which will be used in a particular language. This itself is not an easy task. How does one first become aware of and decide which are the basic sounds? And then there is the question of how to arrange these sounds to form the alphabet. What shall be the organisation and the logical structure so that we can be sure that all the basic sounds have been covered and nothing has been left out? It is an interesting exercise to try and find the answers to these questions by oneself, before seeing how Sanskrit has tackled them.

According to Sanskrit grammar, the nature of the sound produced by a human voice depends on the place from where it originates in the vocal system (*sthāna*), on the nature of the effort required to produce it (*prayatna*), the duration of the sound (*kāla*) and whether it is reflected, amplified or attenuated (*karaṇa*). The Sanskrit alphabet consists of 48 letters known as *varṇas*, which are the hues that constitute the language. Out of these, 13 are vowels, 33 are consonants and in addition there is one *anusvāra,* a nasal sound like '*aṁ*', and one *visarga,* a sort of hard breathing out like '*aḥ*'.

अ आ इ ई उ ऊ ऋ ॠ ऌ ए ऐ ओ औ
a ā i ī u ū ṛ ṝ ḷ e ai o au
क ख ग घ ङ
ka kha ga gha ṅa
च छ ज झ ञ
ca cha ja jha ña
ट ठ ड ढ ण
ṭa ṭha ḍa ḍha ṇa
त थ द ध न
ta tha da dha na
प फ ब भ म
pa pha ba bha ma
य र ल व
ya ra la va
श ष स ह
śa ṣa sa ha
अं अः
aṁ aḥ

The Sanskrit word for a vowel is significant – *svara*, that which exists or shines by itself. Patanjali says that a *svara* is self-luminous and does not depend on anything else for its existence स्वयं राजते इति स्वरः (*svayaṁ rājate iti svaraḥ*). The consonants on the other hand are known as *vyañjana*, which means that which is pronounced after it has been joined with a *svara* अनु व्यज्यते इति व्यञ्जनः (*anu vyajyate iti vyañjanaḥ*), and which needs the help of *svara* to be known or heard. Among the vowels there are 5 short vowels (*hrasva*) and 8 long vowels (*dīrgha*). Of the 33 consonants, the first 25 are known as '*sparśa*', or touch. To pronounce these either the tongue has to touch a particular place in the mouth – for example in the letter त (*ta*) the tongue touches the teeth or the mouth has to be completely closed as in the letter प (*pa*).

The Consonants

The 25 '*sparśa*' consonants are divided into 5 groups of 5 letters each. All the letters in a group have the same *sthāna*; that is, they originate from the same place. The first group is formed of the gutturals. The क (*ka*) being the first letter, this group is called *ka-varga*. The letters here are क (*ka*), ख (*kha*), ग (*ga*), घ (*gha*) and ङ (*ṅa*). When we pronounce them we will notice that the vibration is created at the lower end of the vocal system, the throat.

For the next group the vibrations are created in the palate to form the palatals, the *ca-varga*, or the group of च (*ca*). The letters in this group are च (*ca*), छ (*cha*), ज (*ja*), झ (*jha*), ञ (*ña*). In the third group the sound again moves forward and the tongue touches the top of the mouth to produce the cerebrals, the *ṭa-varga*, or the group of ट (*ṭa*). The letters here are ट (*ṭa*), ठ (*ṭha*), ड (*ḍa*), ढ (*ḍha*), ण (*ṇa*). For the fourth group the sound is produced with the tongue touching the teeth, the dentals; this group is the *ta-varga* or the group of त (*ta*). The letters are त (*ta*), थ (*tha*), द (*da*), ध (*dha*), न (*na*). Finally we have the sound produced with the lips, the labials, in the *pa-varga*, or the group of प (*pa*) containing the letters प (*pa*), फ (*pha*), ब (*ba*), भ (*bha*), म (*ma*).

This is an interesting arrangement based on the anatomy of the vocal system, starting with the lowest point and moving forward at each step to end with the lips. Furthermore, even the arrangement of the letters within each group is far from random – the order of the letters is based on a deep study and logic. It depends on whether the consonant is hard (*kaṭhora*) or soft (*mṛdu*), non-aspirate (*alpaprāṇa*) or aspirate (*mahāprāṇa*) – that is, whether the breath is held back or thrown out – and whether it is heavy (*ghoṣa*) or light (*aghoṣa*) in its resonance.

The first letter of each group is hard, the breath is held back and the sound is light in its resonance. For example in त (*ta*), which is the first letter of the dentals. The second letter in each group is also hard and light in its resonance, but now the breath is thrown out. As for example in थ (*tha*), the second letter of the dentals. The third letter is soft in sound, heavier in resonance and the breath is held back – like द (*da*). The fourth letter is again soft and resonant but the breath is thrown out, as in ध (*dha*). Finally, the fifth letter in each group is soft and resonant and it is nasal; that is, to pronounce it the breath must flow both through the nose and the mouth. As for example न (*na*) in the dentals. The same categories are found in each group.

The next group of consonants consists of four letters – य (*ya*), र (*ra*), ल (*la*) and व (*va*). These are the semi-vowels, known as *īṣatsparśa*, because here the tongue touches very lightly the place of contact, and not fully as in the *sparśa*, the first 25 consonants. These are also known as *antaḥsparśa* because they are situated in between the vowels and the consonants.

The fourth group of consonants is formed of the sibilants, श (*śa*), ष (*ṣa*), स (*sa*) the name depending on the place of origin of the sound. These are also known as *uṣman* because they generate heat when one pronounces them.

Finally, the last consonant is ह (*ha*), the pure aspirate.

This makes a total of 48 letters in the alphabet, giving 48 basic sounds, by the combination of which all other sounds can be produced. No one who looks at this alphabetical structure can help being amazed at the depth of the insights, the clarity of vision and the systematic and logical presentation.

The Sandhi

Beginning with a very well structured alphabet, Sanskrit has gone further into a highly developed science of phonetics. One example of this is the *sandhi* or 'euphonic combination'. *Sandhis* exist in some form or the other in all languages. But in Sanskrit they have been refined and elaborated to such an extent that the science has been transformed into an art.

The word *sandhi* is formed by combining the prefix *sam*, which means 'together' to the root *dhā*, which means 'to hold'. Therefore *sandhi* means 'to hold together'. When syllables come together they undergo some phonological modifications to create one single sound that is a natural combination of both and which is also easier to pronounce. In fact the word *sandhi* itself is an example. When we join *sam* and *dhā* with the suffix '*i*' we have *sandhi*, where *ma* is a nasal labial while *dhā* is a dental. By *sandhi,* the *ma* changes into the nasal dental *na* and the word becomes *sandhi*, which is much easier to pronounce because *na* and *dhā* are both soft dentals. Similarly, *bhagavat gītā* becomes *bhagavadgītā* . Here the *t* at the end of the first word is a hard sound and *g* in the beginning of the second word is a soft sound. So when we pronounce these two words a choppy interruption takes place and we do not feel at ease with the pronunciation. But with *sandhi* the *t* sound at the end of the word *bhagavat* is changed into the soft *d* of the same *ta* group because of the force of the next soft sound *g*, and we get *bhagavadgītā* which is more natural. In the same way *namaḥ nārāyaṇāya* becomes *namo nārāyaṇāya*.

Let us read a *śloka* from the *Bhagavadgītā* given here without the *sandhis*.

आश्चर्यवत् पश्यति कः चित् एनम्
आश्चर्यवत् वदति तथा एव च अन्यः।
आश्चर्यवत् च एनम् अन्यः शृणोति
श्रुत्वा अपि एनं वेद न च एव कः चित् ॥

Now let us see how the beauty gets enhanced and the voice follows a more natural movement when the *sandhis* are incorporated.

आश्चर्यवत्पश्यति कश्चिदेनमाश्चर्यवद्वदति तथैव चान्यः ।
आश्चर्यवच्चैनमन्यः शृणोति श्रुत्वाप्येनं वेद न चैव कश्चित् ॥ [5]

> One sees it as a mystery, another speaks of it as a mystery, still another hears of it as a mystery, and yet, even having heard, none knows it.

The *sandhi* has been studied in great detail in Sanskrit, in all its possible permutations and combinations, involving vowels short and long, consonants hard and soft, compound syllables and the *visarga*. It is undoubtedly an integral part of the spoken and written language. It has given to Sanskrit a great fluidity and an aesthetically pleasing and melodious sound. Seeing its beauty, Professor Whitney was led to affirm that "this phonetic science is of extraordinary merit, which has called forth the highest admiration of modern scholars. Nothing at all approaching it has been produced by any ancient people; it has served as the foundation, in no small degree, of our own phonetics, even as our science of grammar and of language has borrowed much from India." [6]

Our amazement is without bounds when we realise that this was done in India in the 5th century B.C.

Amarakoṣa and Aṣṭādhyāyī

What we have seen as yet is only the alphabet and the science of phonetics. How do the letters form words, how do the words form meaningful sentences, how many types of words and sentences are there? Panini deals with these questions and many more. It is beyond our purpose and scope to enter into the intricacies of these questions, though it is this alone that would enable us to appreciate the true beauty of Sanskrit grammar. Here we will see, very briefly, some of the salient yet simpler aspects of Panini's grammar.

The traditional methods of teaching Sanskrit have some interesting and revealing features. The teaching is done through two tools – a dictionary of nouns called *Amarakoṣa* or 'Immortal Wealth' and a set of grammatical rules contained in the *Aṣṭādhyāyī*. *Amarakoṣa* and some other Sanskrit dictionaries are perhaps the only dictionaries in the world that are entirely in verse and learnt by heart in their totality. The *Aṣṭādhyāyī* contains about 4000 rules and is also committed to memory. For centuries, a large number of children in India have memorised both the *Amarakoṣa* and the *Aṣṭādhyāyī*, beginning at the age of four and completing the process by the age of eight or ten. It is believed that if one can thoroughly know these two works, one can be a master of the Sanskrit language.

The *Amarakoṣa* was created by the great scholar Amarasimha, who preceded Panini. It has three *kāṇḍas* or sections, with each section having subsections and sub-subsections, groupings and divisions according to common features and qualities. The terms in the dictionary are therefore not arranged alphabetically but are instead placed in a hierarchy based on properties and relationships. The *Amarakoṣa* was originally named *nāmaliṅgānuśāsanam* by the author because it provides the names for all possible objects, the initial vocabulary for the language, and for each object it gives simultaneously its synonyms and its gender. The objects are divided into two broad groups. The first category consists of objects that have a shape or form, a *rūpa*, which can be thus shown with the finger, '*aṅgulyā nirdeśaḥ*'. This is how the children first learn the names of the objects – an object is pointed out and its name is given. This section is further divided into two subdivisions – the living and the inanimate. The second category consists of objects that do not have a physical shape, which cannot be shown by pointing with the finger, which are abstract or transcendental – like truth, space, *dharma*, heaven. The *Amarakoṣa* observes that while the number of objects may be infinite and innumerable and therefore cannot be encompassed in a dictionary, the number of categories on the other hand are finite and through them it is possible that all objects can be grasped.

The Nouns and the Kāraka Theory

A fundamental question that Panini asks himself is regarding the possible functional roles and the relationships that a noun can have in a sentence. These are normally known as 'case relationships'. A fruit can be offered 'to Rama', an ornament can be 'on Rama' and we can receive blessings 'from Rama'. Cases exist in all languages but the beauty of Panini's work is that he declares boldly that all possible relationships can be finally grouped under just seven main heads. A noun can have only seven functional roles or relationships in a sentence and no other. These are:

1. Nominative – subject
2. Accusative – direct object
3. Instrumental – by/with
4. Dative – to/for (indirect object)
5. Ablative – from/than/out of
6. Genitive – of/belonging to
7. Locative – in/on/at/among

Addressing someone is called *sambodhanam* in Sanskrit. This has been considered in Sanskrit grammar as the eighth case, the 'Vocative' or direct address. But its functional role is like the nominative, except in the singular number.

There is an interesting verse in Sanskrit that uses all the eight cases of Rama in their proper order in a single *śloka*.

रामो राजमणिः सदा विजयते रामं रमेशं भजे
रामेणाभिहता निशाचरचमू रामाय तस्मै नमः ।
रामान्नास्ति परायणं परतरं रामस्य दासोऽस्म्यहं
रामे चित्तलयः सदा भवतु मे हे राम मामुद्धर ॥

> May *Rāma* (Nominative), the jewel among the kings, always be victorious. I worship *Rāma* (Accusative), the lord of *Lakṣmī*. The armies of the demon Ravana were killed *by Rāma* (Instrumental). *To that Rāma* (Dative) I bow down. There is no better way *than Rāma* (Ablative). I am the servant *of Rāma* (Genitive). May my mind dwell *in that Rāma* (Locative). *O Rāma*! (Vocative) Do save me (from this worldly ocean).

Panini points out that though he has tried to create a structure as complete as possible, language cannot be completely tied down in a formula. Therefore he says that the sixth case or the genitive is the *śeṣa*, the remaining, which will include all that may be left out from the others.

Patanjali, in his commentary on Panini's grammar, discusses how various possibilities and situations can all be brought under one of these cases. Take, for example, the ablative case using 'from'. Patanjali says that the simplest case is when we say that the Ganges flows from the Himalayas हिमालयात् गङ्गा प्रवहति (*himālayāt gaṅgā pravahati*). One physical object is removed 'from' another. But this separation need not be physical. One can look 'from' a balcony प्रासादात् प्रेक्षते (*prāsādāt prekṣate*), where the separation happens only in the sight. Or a *śiṣya* can learn from the teacher शिष्यः आचार्यद् अधीते (*śiṣyaḥ ācāryād adhīte*). Patanjali thus gives many possible situations where the ablative case can be suitably applied.

This is Panini's *kāraka* theory of *vibhaktis*. Once all the relationships have been categorised under the seven broad heads, Panini affirms that a noun cannot be in a sentence independent of its relationship. The relationship is integral to it. Therefore the word structure should also reflect this. This is done by taking the stem of the noun and adding to it the appropriate suffix, which signifies the functional role of that noun. In all words the stem and the suffix are joined together and both move together in the sentence. Thus when one says '*Rāmāt*' it means necessarily 'from Rāma' and when we say '*Rāmeṇa*' it means 'by Rāma'.

The analysis goes further and says that when we have a pronoun, it replaces the noun. The pronoun's functional role in a sentence is the same as that of the noun it replaces, and it must therefore have the same case ending or *vibhakti*. Next we come to the adjectives, called *viśeṣaṇa* or attributes. They cannot exist independently of the noun they qualify. Hence they too must take the colouring and the form of the noun and must have the same gender and *vibhakti*.

This is one of the ways in which the Sanskrit language combines precision and elimination of all ambiguity with a great flexibility. One can rearrange the words of a sentence in any order and the meaning does not change. Let us take as an example a very simple sentence in English:

'The small boy hit the red ball with his bat.'
If the words are rearranged as:
'The small ball hit the red boy with his bat.'
or as: 'The red bat hit the small ball with the boy.'

– the meaning changes entirely. It can even become the opposite of what was meant.

But in Sanskrit, whether one writes the sentence as:
लघुः बालकः दण्डेन रक्तं कन्दुकं प्रहृतवान्
laghuḥ bālakaḥ daṇḍena raktaṁ kandukaṁ prahṛtavān

or as: लघुः कन्दुकं दण्डेन रक्तं बालकः प्रहृतवान्
laghuḥ kandukaṁ daṇḍena raktaṁ bālakaḥ prahṛtavān

or as: रक्तं दण्डेन लघुः कन्दुकं प्रहृतवान् बालकः
raktaṁ daṇḍena laghuḥ kandukaṁ prahṛtavān bālakaḥ

– they all mean the same thing.

The Verbs

We have looked at some of the special features of the treatment of nouns in Sanskrit. The treatment of verbs too is rich and complex.

There are in Sanskrit six tenses, four moods, three numbers and three persons.

These are again found in all languages though the forms and the numbers vary. But Sanskrit brings two interesting insights into these: In most languages 'I' is denoted as the 'first person singular number', also considered in a way as the most important person, 'You' as the 'second' and 'He' or 'She' as the 'third person'. But in Sanskrit 'He', 'She'or 'it' is known as the first person, *prathamapuruṣa* and 'I' comes only afterwards. It may appear to be a very minor difference but perhaps it gives some insight into the psychology of the culture that gave birth to this language.

The second insight is that Sanskrit divides all verbs into two categories – *parasmaipada* and *ātmanepada* – those actions that are done for others and those that are done for oneself. The form of the verb itself tells us the category to which the verb or the activity belongs. There are certain activities that can be done only for the benefit of others, like 'to give' दा (ददाति) *dā* (*dadāti*). These verbs can be conjugated only as *parasmaipada*. There are verbs like 'to sleep' शी (शेते) *śī* (*śete*), which one can do only for oneself and which are therefore conjugated only as *ātmanepada*. Then there are some activities that can be done for both, like cooking. If one is cooking for others it is पचति (*pacati*) and if one is cooking for oneself it is पचते (*pacate*). These are known as *ubhayapada*. Grammatically these may appear to be trivial distinctions and are perhaps not very important, or again they may reveal something about the mind and clarity of perception behind the language.

The Verb-Roots and their Derivatives

Panini has listed about 700 activities and about 2000 verb-roots related to different aspects of these activities. In many languages several nouns are derived from verb-roots, and often the dictionaries in English give the Latin root from which the word is derived. But in Sanskrit nearly all the nouns are derived from verbs, by adding some prefixes and some suffixes, with the result that if one can learn the 700 basic roots and the rules that govern their appendages, one has at one's command a good part of the language.

Dr. V. Raghavan has written beautifully on 'the romance of a verb-root'.[7] He says that words, no doubt, "have to be known in their context. Without the context the meaning would not be complete. But on the other hand when nouns are not connected with any root, the difficulty increases manifold. The noun tells you nothing about itself. It has to be learnt and memorised with greater effort, because it is not possible to associate it with other words in the language.

As compared to other European languages English has a larger number of roots. But the interconnections between them are generally not known and hence they are learnt as distinct from one another. They do not form a beautiful long chain as the German verbs do.

In this and similar respects Sanskrit goes a longer way or rather the longest way in the realm of the world of languages. As an example let us take just one common Sanskrit root, गम् (*gam*), meaning 'to go'. Life centres around movement and it is but natural that our ancients, who named the world '*saṁsāra, jagat*', which means the 'the ever-moving', should have utilised the idea of movement to include a large number of aspects of life. But here we are not so much interested in the thought values that are associated with these words, as the numerical strength and variety of the derivatives. They cover such a wide range that we would need an entire book to exhaust their study. The direct derivatives of गम् (*gam*) are: गत (*gata*) – gone, departed, situated in, contained in, relating to, frequented; गतक (*gataka*), गति (*gati*) – movement, gait, passage, course, resource, condition; गतिक (*gatika*), गतिका (*gatikā*), अगतिक (*agatika*), गत्वन् (*gatvan*), गत्वर (*gatvara*) – transient, perishable; गन्तव्य (*gantavya*) – to be attained, to be undergone, to be approached; गन्तृ (*gantṛ*) – way, wayfarer; गन्त्रिका (*gantrikā*) – a small cart; गम (*gama*) – march, decampment, (in mathematics) removal of fractions; गमक (*gamaka*) – indicative, explanatory; गमथ (*gamatha*) – a road; गमन (*gamana*) – departure; गमनिका (*gamanikā*) –

explanatory paraphrase; गमनीय (*gamanīya*) – accessible, approachable; गमयितृ (*gamayitṛ*) – leading to; गमित (*gamita*) – sent, brought; गमिन् (*gamin*) – intending to go; गमिष्ठ (*gamiṣṭha*) – most ready to go; गमिष्णु (*gamiṣṇu*) – intending to depart; गम्य (*gamya*) – passable, attainable, dissolute; गम्यमान (*gamyamāna*), गामिक (*gāmika*), गामुक (*gāmuka*), गामिन् (*gāmin*) – reaching or extending to, directed towards etc.

Many of these forms are used with prefixes that often modify the meaning. We shall take a few here. अतिगम् (*atigam*) – to surpass, to overcome, to escape, to neglect; अतिग (*atiga*) – exceeding, transgressing, violating; अधिगम् (*adhigam*) – to find, to obtain, to accomplish, to study; अधिगत (*adhigata*) – acquired, learnt; अधिगन्तव्य (*adhigantavya*), अधिगन्तृ (*adhigantṛ*), अधिगम (*adhigama*) – mastery, study, knowledge, profit; अधिगमन (*adhigamana*), अधिगमनीय (*adhigamanīya*), अधिगम्य (*adhigamya*), अनुगम् (*anugam*), – to follow, to seek, to observe, to imitate; अनुग (*anuga*) – a follower, a servant; अनुगत (*anugata*) – tallying with; अनुगति (*anugati*) – imitation; अनुगतिक (*anugatika*), अनुगन्तव्य (*anugantavya*), अनुगम (*anugama*), अनुगमन (*anugamana*) – post-cremation; अनुगम्य (*anugamya*), अनुगामिन् (*anugāmin*), अनुगामुक (*anugāmuka*), अपगम् (*apagam*) – to depart, to vanish; अपग (*apaga*) – turning away; अपगत (*apagata*) – gone away, remote, dead; अपगम (*apagama*), अपगमन (*apagamana*), अपिगम् (*apigam*) – to enter, to join; अभिगम् (*abhigam*) – undertake, to approach, to obtain; अभिगत (*abhigata*), अभिगन्तृ (*abhigantṛ*), अभिगम (*abhigama*) – visiting; अभिगमन (*abhigamana*), अभिगम्य (*abhigamya*), अभिगामिन् (*abhigāmin*), अवगम् (*avagam*) – to descend, to obtain, to understand, to conceive; अवगत (*avagata*), अवगति (*avagati*) – anticipating; अवगन्तव्य (*avagantavya*), अवगम (*avagama*), अवगमक (*avagamaka*) – expressive of; अवगमन (*avagamana*), अवगमयितृ (*avagamayitṛ*), अवगम्य (*avagamya*), आगम् (*āgam*) – to come, to meet with, to arrive; आगत (*āgata*), आगति (*āgati*) – arrival, origin; आगन्तव्य (*āgantavya*), आगन्तु (*āgantu*) – adventitious, incidental; आगन्तुक (*āgantuka*) – a stranger, a guest; आगम (*āgama*) – arrival, appearance, income, science; आगमन (*āgamana*), आगामिन् (*āgāmin*), आगमिष्ठ (*āgamiṣṭha*) – approaching with rapidity; आगमिक (*āgamika*) – relating to the future; आगमिन् (*āgamin*) – impending; आगमुक (*āgamuka*), आजिगमिषु (*ājigamiṣu*) – intending to come; उद्गम् (*udgam*) – to come forth, to rise, to ascend; उद्गा (*udgā*), उद्गति (*udgati*), उद्गम (*udgama*) – origin, shooting forth; उपगम् (*upagam*) – to go near, to visit, to attend, to admit; उपग (*upaga*), उपगत (*upagata*) – approximate; उपगति (*upagati*), दुर्गम (*durgama*) – difficult to be traversed, impassable, inaccessible; निगम (*nigama*) – to enter, to undergo, to insert; निगम (*nigama*) – doctrine, a market-place, a caravan; निगमन (*nigamana*), निर्गम (*nirgama*) – to go out, to disappear; निर्गत (*nirgata*) – disappeared, extinct; निर्गम् (*nirgam*) – vanishing, exit, outlet, export-place; निर्गमन (*nirgamana*) – outlet, issue; परागम् (*parāgam*) – to go away; परागत (*parāgata*), परागन्तृ (*parāgantṛ*), परागम (*parāgama*), परिगम् (*parigam*) – to go round or about or through, to surround; परिग (*pariga*), परिगत (*parigata*) – encompassed, experienced; परिगन्तव्य (*parigantavya*), परिगम (*parigama*), परिगमन (*parigamana*), परिगमिन (*parigamina*), परिगम्य (*parigamya*), प्रगम् (*pragam*) – to go forward, to proceed, to advance; प्रगत (*pragata*), प्रगम (*pragama*) – first advance in courtship; प्रगमन (*pragamana*) – progress; प्रगमनीय (*pragamanīya*), प्रगामन (*pragāmana*), प्रगामिन् (*pragāmin*), प्रगे (*prage*) – early in the morning; प्रतिगम् (*pratigam*), प्रतिगत (*pratigata*), प्रतिगति (*pratigati*), प्रतिगमन (*pratigamana*) – to go towards, to go back; विगम् (*vigam*), विगत (*vigata*), विगम् (*vigam*) – to cut asunder, to separate; सङ्गम् (*saṅgam*) – to go together, to join, to harmonise, to correspond, to assemble; सङ्ग (*saṅga*) – coming together; सङ्गत (*saṅgata*) – in conjunction, alliance; सङ्गति (*saṅgati*) – association, company, appropriateness, relation; सङ्गथ (*saṅgatha*) – meeting-place; सङ्गम (*saṅgama*) – confluence, harmony, point of intersection; सङ्गमक (*saṅgamaka*), सङ्गमन (*saṅgamana*), सङ्गमनीय (*saṅgamanīya*), सङ्गमिन् (*saṅgamin*), सङ्गिन् (*saṅgin*), सुगम (*sugama*) – easy of access, easily understood…" The list goes on, all these words being derived from one single root गम् (*gam*) meaning 'to go'.

The Creation of New Words

There is, no doubt, a romance in the roots in the Sanskrit language. And it is so appealing that we may dwell on it a little longer to see some more interesting examples of how words are created from the roots. Suppose we start with the root कृ *kṛ*, meaning 'to do'. Then by adding suffixes we can have:

कृ (*kṛ*) + तृच् (*tṛc*) = कर्ता (*kartā*), the doer
कृ (*kṛ*) + ल्युट् (*lyuṭ*) = करणम् (*karaṇam*), doing
कृ (*kṛ*) + ण्यत् (*ṇyat*) = कार्य (*kārya*), the work to be done
कृ (*kṛ*) + तव्यत् (*tavyat*) = कर्तव्य (*kartavya*), that which should be done

The above are just a few stray examples of the way the words are created in Sanskrit but they have far reaching implications. The first implication is that from a single root, by adding various suffixes, we can create a large number of nouns with various shades of meanings. These are known as *kṛdantas*. If instead of adding only suffixes to a single root, we successively add a number of prefixes and suffixes to the verb-roots or nouns, we can have an even greater number of nouns and verbs, with just the precise nuances and meanings we wish to convey. We have therefore not only a very large vocabulary but also the possibility of creating new words in a very natural manner for all possible situations, actions and objects. And, what is more important, it is possible for any one with a basic knowledge of Sanskrit to follow and understand these new words.

Most languages use the process of adding prefixes and suffixes to create new words. But often it is not a conscious process, not sufficiently natural and sometimes even a bit arbitrary. Nor is it a normal part of the use of the language. On the other hand, in Sanskrit it is a very conscious and powerful tool in the hands of the speaker or the writer. To make this idea clear let us see a few more examples: हृ (*hṛ*) means 'to take away'. By adding the prefix वि (*vi*) and the suffix घञ् (*ghañ*), through some grammatical rules we have विहृ (*vihṛ*)+ घञ् (*ghañ*) = विहार (*vihāra*) which means roaming, pleasure, a park, a monastery. Similarly पठ् (*paṭh*) means 'to read'. By adding the desiderative suffix सन् (*san*) to the root पठ् (*paṭh*) we get another root पिपठिष् (*pipaṭhiṣ*) which means 'desire to learn or read' and the noun formed out of it is पिपठिषा (*pipaṭhiṣā*), by adding the feminine suffix टाप् (*ṭāp*). Says Dr.Raghavan: "Every prefix or *upasarga* conveys two or three primary meanings. Hence it is simple to comprehend how they will modify the meaning of the original verb. The twenty prefixes that are generally used in Sanskrit can be combined in almost arithmetical groups of twos and threes. Theoretically we could have as many as six to eight thousand combinations, every combination with a distinct connotation. Every one of these combinations, when joined on to the various derivatives, which may be taken as about eighty, the number goes up to about five hundred thousand. This is a big figure, too big to be ever required by any language, but this gives an idea of the great possibility which lies before us in this richness of the Sanskrit language where the meaning of every prefix and suffix is clear within certain limits and where the grammarians have laid down the smooth path to traverse."[8]

Significance of Synonyms

This brings us naturally to the idea of synonyms. Those who begin to learn Sanskrit often wonder about the large number of synonyms a word has in Sanskrit. Each language contains synonyms, but many words have few, or none. On the other hand, in Sanskrit every word seems to have not just a few synonyms, but often even ten, twenty or thirty. This appears to be a mystery and a wastage unless one understands their origin and their true *raison d'être*.

In most languages, synonyms are different names for the same object. They are words that grow out of a convention and do not often have any inherent significance. One could have used the same word to denote a completely different object and, if the convention was sufficiently strong, the word would become a synonym for that object. But this is not so in Sanskrit. Firstly, the name is not just a convention but grows out of a root with the addition of specific suffixes. Therefore, its meaning too is not a convention but is very specific and determined. The synonyms of a word are not just alternate names, where one can replace one by another. Each synonym grows out of and reveals a special quality or attribute of that object. One has to choose from the many possibilities the one that conveys best the exact property in mind.

For example, the *Amarakoṣa* gives the following 34 synonyms for 'fire':

अग्निः (*agniḥ*), वैश्वानरः (*vaiśvānaraḥ*), वह्निः (*vahniḥ*), वीतहोत्रः (*vītahotraḥ*), धनञ्जयः (*dhanañjayaḥ*), कृपीटयोनिः (*kṛpīṭayoniḥ*), ज्वलनः (*jvalanaḥ*), जातवेदाः (*jātavedāḥ*), तनूनपात् (*tanūnapāt*), बर्हिः (*barhiḥ*), शुष्मा (*śuṣmā*), कृष्णवर्त्मा (*kṛṣṇavartmā*), शोचिष्केशः (*śociṣkeśaḥ*), उषर्बुधः (*uṣarbudhaḥ*), आश्रयाशः (*āśrayāśaḥ*), बृहद्भानुः (*bṛhadbhānuḥ*), कृशानुः (*kṛśānuḥ*), पावकः (*pāvakaḥ*), अनलः (*analaḥ*), रोहिताश्वः (*rohitāśvaḥ*), वायुसखः (*vāyusakhaḥ*), शिखावान् (*śikhāvān*), आशुशुक्षणिः (*āśuśukṣaṇiḥ*), हिरण्यरेताः (*hiraṇyaretāḥ*), हुतभुक् (*hutabhuk*), दहनः (*dahanaḥ*), हव्यवाहनः (*havyavāhanaḥ*), सप्तर्चिः (*saptarciḥ*), सृमुनाः (*sṛmunāḥ*), शुक्रः (*śukraḥ*), चित्रभानुः (*citrabhānuḥ*), विभावसुः (*vibhāvasuḥ*), शुचिः (*śuciḥ*), अप्पित्तम् (*appittam*).

But each word has a specific and different connotation. For example: वह्निः (*vahniḥ*) comes from the root वह् (*vah*), to carry, and means that which carries (the offerings to the gods); while ज्वलनः (*jvalanaḥ*) comes from the root ज्वल् (*jval*), to burn, and means that which is burning; similarly पावकः (*pāvakaḥ*) comes from the root पू (*pū*) to purify, and means that which purifies; and शुष्मा (*śuṣmā*), comes from the root शुष् (*śuṣ*), to dry, and means that which dries (the water). It is for the writer to decide which is the most appropriate word for 'fire' in a given context.

The Purpose of Language

Life is infinite and rich in its possibilities. All language is an attempt to formulate and communicate the variety and richness of experiences covering the entire gamut of human sensitivity and potentiality. These experiences can be of all ranges and types – the seeing of a physical object through the senses, a feeling, an emotion, a thought, or a vision leading to the highest spiritual realisation. The language must also have the capacity to grow, to meet the demands of completely new experiences. And the language must be able to provide various alternatives and possibilities from which the speaker can choose just the right word and the right structure. He should be able to create a new word to suit his needs and at the same time the listener should be able to understand him.

Usually, the link between a word and its meaning is primarily denominative and conventional. But in Sanskrit, as we have seen, each word has its own connotation, its definite shade of meaning, its special nuance. The word and the meaning are inseparable. They fuse into one another and give life to one another.

Sound and Language

This is not all. There is one more dimension of the spoken word, the dimension of sound. Again, in most languages, the sound of a particular syllable or word is a historical convention. Sanskrit, on the other hand, starts from a deeper base. It believes that the Sound and the Word are at the origin of creation. It believes that they are aspects of the Brahman, the supreme Reality and they have light, consciousness and power. The sound has potency; any sound cannot be used to denote any meaning. Therefore the meaning of the fundamental Sanskrit roots is also not arbitrary but based on a deeper truth. Through a process of deep contemplation and intuition, it is possible for one to enter into the heart of a sound vibration and discover its meaning. This was the way of the Rishis when they gave meaning to the roots. Thus the root sound *a* has 'absolute existence' for its meaning. And the root sound *ka* means 'possession', 'mastery', 'creation'. And the root sound *la* means 'love', 'sweetness'.[9]

We come to the amazing conclusion that in Sanskrit all three, the sound, the word and the meaning, become one. They arise out of the deeper truths of life and the Reality and not only reveal but lead us in turn to realise these truths. The language then becomes universal. It has its own inherent strength and existence and it is no more just a convention or a convenience. It becomes a fit vehicle not only for communication but for transformation as well. It is not just a language. It is a self-existent truth and power.

The Samāsa

We have pointed out the clear and precise nature of the Sanskrit language. But a language also needs to be compact and rich in suggestiveness. For this a very useful and significant tool in Sanskrit is the *samāsa*. The word *samāsa* is formed by combining '*sam*' with '*as*' which is the root 'to be'. *Samāsa* therefore means 'to be together'. *Samāsas* are compound words formed out of simple words. Compounds are a powerful tool in Sanskrit which are found at every step. Sanskrit grammar has identified various types of *samāsas* and studied them in great detail.

For example, in *bahuvrīhisamāsa*, the final word denotes something very different from what is expressed by each member of the compound. Thus पीत (*pīta*) meaning yellow joins with अम्बर (*ambara*) meaning cloth to give पीताम्बर (*pītāmbara*). But the compound does not mean a yellow cloth. It means Vishnu, the one who wears the yellow cloth. Similarly किरीट (*kirīta*) is crown and चन्द्र (*candra*) is the moon. But किरीटचन्द्र (*kirīṭacandra*) means Shiva, who has the moon as his crown.

As a compound can be interpreted in several ways, many shades of meanings and implications can be packed in just a few words.

The Sūtras

The grammar that has to give a structure to such a language must itself have the same qualities. This was the admirable achievement of Panini. He presented his grammar through a set of *sūtras* or aphorisms, which are short, pithy and versatile sentences and which present the concepts in the most efficient, compact and thorough manner.

A *sūtra* must have the following qualities:

अल्पाक्षरमसन्दिग्धं सारवद्विश्वतो मुखम् ।
अस्तोभमनवद्यं च सूत्रं सूत्रविदो विदुः ॥ [10]

1. *Alpākṣaram* – It must have the minimum number of syllables. Not even one syllable should be extra or superfluous.
2. *Asandigdham* – There should be no scope for doubts or ambiguities.
3. *Sāravat* – The *sūtra* should have something worthwhile and of value to express.
4. *Viśvatomukham* – It should have a wide applicability in diverse situations and should not be confined to a few particular instances.
5. *Astobham* – It should be free from errors, inadequacies and fillers. It should stand on its own strength.
6. *Anavadyam* – It should present a truth that is irrefutable.

The Greatness of a Language

The *Aṣṭādhyāyī* of Panini is a masterpiece among the grammars of the world. Containing 4000 *sūtras*, created nearly 2500 years ago, it has not only stood the test of time but has been a source of inspiration for centuries, up to the present day. About Panini's grammar, W.W. Hunter, the grammarian, says: "It stands supreme among the grammars of the world alike for its precision of statement and for its thorough analysis of the roots of the language and the formative principle of words." [11] A popular saying in India even declares the study of the *Mahābhāṣya* of Patanjali, a commentary on Panini's *Aṣṭādhyāyī,* as equal to the ruling of a kingdom.

The Indian spiritual tradition believes that such profound works cannot be created by mere mental reasoning and logic. These can only be produced or created by a Rishi, a seer, through the process of *yoga* and *sādhanā*. For such persons all desires of wealth, fame and power fall away, because one cannot be a seer or approach the Truth if one is burdened with such attachments. To create such masterpieces one has to be able to look at the bright light of Truth without blinking, to affirm it boldly with no considerations of gain or fear, to communicate it to others out of love and compassion, and to have the humility to realise that one does not create the Truth, one can only be a fit and pure channel for it to express itself. This has been the inspiring tradition established by the *Trimuni* of Sanskrit grammar, Panini, Katyayana and Patanjali.

To conclude, language is born when the need is felt to express oneself. It is the fire that is lit by the coming together of *anubhava*, or experience, and *vivakṣā*, a desire to express. Therefore the first statement of Panini is आत्मा बुद्ध्या समेत्यर्थान् मनो युङ्क्ते विवक्षया (*ātmā buddhyā sametyarthān mano yuṅkte vivakṣayā*) "Out of desire to speak, the soul gathers all the meaning with the help of *buddhi* and impels the mind."[12]

The greatness of a language depends on how perfectly it can communicate and arouse in the listener the exact experience of the speaker. It has to encompass the infinite variety and richness of life, its moods, its depths and its heights and reflect them like a perfect mirror, without any distortions. This is a difficult and challenging task. It demands the capacity to harmonise contradictory qualities. The language must be supple and flexible, capable of subtle shades and nuances, and yet efficient and efficacious, clear, precise and unambiguous. It must be compact and pithy and also rich and opulent; concise yet suggestive, strong and powerful yet sweet and charming, capable of growth and expansion to meet new challenges of the future, and at the same time an inspiring repository of all the great achievements of the past. An impossible demand, one would say. But Sanskrit has met this challenge so beautifully that it is even known as 'Sanskrit' – that which has been well structured and refined to the utmost.

interesting and amazing creations in sanskrit

Interesting and Amazing Creations in Sanskrit

There is in Sanskrit a whole body of literature that is based on a play with the language. This is not great literature or inspired poetry, but more in the nature of linguistic acrobatics. These writings are often obtuse and not very easy to understand because they require a great mastery over all the complex grammatical structures. Therefore, they are known as *adhamakāvyas*, meaning 'poems of a lower quality'. However, far from being worthless, they demonstrate the amazing possibilities inherent in the language, along with the originality and creativity of the writers.

Several great poets, including Kalidasa, Bhartrihari, Magha and Sriharsha have made use of the *adhamakāvyas*, sometimes even in their major works, in a spirit of playful indulgence. There are instances where entire epics have been written in this style. These are known as *citrakāvyas* and are part of the *alaṅkāraśāstra* or Sanskrit rhetorics. Some of the creations border on the unbelievable and would perhaps be impossible in any other language. Here we will look briefly at a few examples to enjoy their flavour and taste.

Varṇacitras

The *varṇacitras* are *ślokas* written with certain constraints on the use of consonants. For example, here is a *śloka* where all the 33 consonants in Sanskrit come in their natural order.

कः खगौघाङचिच्छौजा झाञ्ज्ञोऽटौठीडडण्ढणः ।
तथोदधीन् पफर्बाभीर्मयोऽरिल्वाशिषां सहः ॥[1]

> Who is he, the lover of birds, pure in intelligence, expert in stealing the strength of others, leader among the destroyers of the enemies, the steadfast, the fearless, the one who filled the ocean? He is the king Maya, the repository of the blessings that can destroy the foes.

And here is a *śloka* which uses only three consonants out of the 33 – द (*da*), व (*va*) and न (*na*).

देवानां नन्दनो देवो नोदनो वेदनिन्दिनाम् ।
दिवं दुदाव नादेन दाने दानवनन्दिनः ॥[2]

> The God (Vishnu) who causes pleasure to the other gods and pain to the opponents of the *Vedas*, filled the heavens with a loud sound as he killed Hiranyakashipu [a demon who forbade his son to take the name of Vishnu.]

This is a *śloka* which uses only two consonants, भ (*bha*) and र (*ra*).

भूरिभिर्भारिभिर्भीराभूभारैरभिरेभिरे ।
भेरीरेभिभिरभ्राभैरभीरुभिरिभैरिभाः ॥[3]

> The fearless elephant, who was like a burden to the earth because of its heavy weight, whose sound was like a kettle-drum, and who was like a dark cloud, attacked the enemy elephant.

Most amazingly, entire *ślokas* have been written using a single consonant. Here are two examples – one using न (*na*) and the other using द (*da*) :

न नोननुन्नो नुन्नेनो नाना नानानना ननु ।
नुन्नोऽनुन्नो ननुन्नेनो नानेना नुन्ननुन्ननुत् ॥[4]

A man is not a man who is wounded by a low man. Similarly, he is also not a man who wounds a low man. The wounded one is not considered to be wounded if his master is unwounded. And he who wounds a man who is already wounded, is not a man.

दाददो दुद्ददुद्दादी दाददो दूददीददोः ।
दुद्दादं ददे दुद्दे दादाददददोऽददः ॥[5]

Sri Krishna, the giver of every boon, the scourge of the evil-minded, the purifier, the one whose arms can annihilate the wicked who cause sufferings to others, shot his pain-causing arrow at the enemy.

And here is a *śloka*, where each quarter is written using only one consonant. The first quarter is formed of ज (*ja*), the second of त (*ta*), the third of भ (*bha*) and the fourth of र (*ra*).

जजौजोजाजिजिज्जाजी
तं ततोऽतितताततुत् ।
भाभोऽभीभाभिभूभाभू-
रारारिररिरीररः ॥[6]

Balarama, the great warrior and winner of great wars, resplendent like Shukra and Brihaspati, the destroyer of wandering enemies, went to the battle like a lion stopping the movement of his foes, who were endowed with a four-fold army.

Sthānacitras and Svaracitras

The *sthānacitras* are formed either by using the consonants of only one group or avoiding certain groups. This is a *śloka* using only the gutturals:

अगा गाङ्गाङ्गकाकाकगाहकाघककाकहा ।
अहाहाङ्क खगाङ्कागकङ्कागखगकाकक ॥[7]

O you (the traveller of many countries), who bathes in the tortuous current of the rippling Ganga; you have no acquaintance with the sorrowful sound of the suffering world; you have the ability to go till the Meru mountain; you are not under the control of the crooked senses. You, being the dispeller of sins, have come on this land.

In the *svaracitras* the restrictions are on the use of vowels. This *śloka* uses only the vowel इ (*i**) in the first line and the vowel अ (*a*) in the second line.

क्षितिस्थितिमितिक्षिप्तिविधिविन्निधिसिद्धिलिट् ।
मम त्र्यक्ष नमद्दक्ष हर स्मरहर स्मर ॥[8]

O Lord Shiva, the possessor of three eyes, the knower of existence, measurer and destroyer of the earth, enjoyer of the eight-fold superhuman power and nine treasures of Kubera, you who killed Daksha and Kamadeva. O Lord, do remember me.

Next is a *śloka* formed entirely with the vowel उ (*u*).

उरुगुं द्युगुरुं युत्सु चुक्रुशुस्तुष्टुवुः पुरु ।
लुलुभुः पुपुषुर्मुत्सु मुमुहुर्नु मुहुर्मुहुः ॥[9]

---

*Sanskrit vowels retain their full forms only in the beginning of a word; in the middle or at the end they are used in their respective symbolic forms, e.g. ा for आ (*ā*), ि for इ (*i*), ी for ई (*ī*), ु for उ (*u*), ू for ऊ (*ū*), ृ for ऋ (*ṛ*), ॄ for ॠ (*ṝ*), े for ए (*e*), ै for ऐ (*ai*), ो for ओ (*o*), ौ for औ (*au*); *anusvāra* is marked as a dot above a letter; *visarga* is marked as two vertically aligned dots on the right side of a letter.

> The gods took refuge in Brihaspati, the lord of speech, the preceptor of the gods in heaven, when they went for the battle. They prayed so that he would remain happy and strong, and not withdraw into unconsciousness, again and again.

And this unbelievable *śloka* of 32 syllables uses only one consonant and one vowel in the entire verse – य (*ya*) and आ (*ā*).

> यायायायायायायायायायायायायायायाया ।
> यायायायायायायायायायायायायायायाया ॥ [10]

To enable the reader to understand this difficult verse, we give the *anvaya* or the arrangement of the words of the verse in their proper prose order.

यायाया (*yāyāyā*), आय (*āya*), आयाय (*āyāya*), अयाय (*ayāya*), अयाय (*ayāya*), अयाय (*ayāya*), अयाय (*ayāya*), अयाया (*ayāyā*), यायाय (*yāyāya*), आयायाय (*āyāyāya*), आयाया (*āyāyā*), या (*yā*), या (*yā*), या (*yā*), या (*yā*), या (*yā*), या (*yā*), या (*yā*), या (*yā*).

The meaning of the verse is as follows:

> The sandals (*pādukā*) which adorn the Lord, which help in attainment of all that is good and auspicious, which give knowledge, which cause the desire (of having the Lord as one's own), which remove all that is hostile, which have attained the Lord, which are used for going and coming from one place to another, by which all places of the world can be reached, these sandals are for Lord Vishnu.

Amitā Compositions

There are many other possibilities in the interplay of consonants, vowels and syllables or the words resulting from them. This *śloka* has an interesting sound effect through the use of क (*ka*) and

ल (*la*). This type of composition is called *amitā*, where the same letters are used frequently.

बकुलकलिकाललामनि कलकण्ठीकलकलाकुले काले ।
कलया कलावतोऽपि हि कलयति कलितास्त्रतां मदनः ॥[11]

> Madana, the god of love, uses even the spots of the moon as his beautiful weapon at the time when the *bakula* plant shines with new buds and when the cuckoos and women with melodious voices fill the air with their enchanting sounds.

Here is another interesting example. The *śloka* is formed of four *pādas* or parts. The letters and their sequence in each quarter are exactly the same. But because they are broken and combined in various ways, different words and meanings emerge.

सभासमानासहसापरागात् सभासमाना सहसा परागात् ।*
सभासमाना सहसापरागात् सभासमाना सहसापरागात् ॥[12]

---

*1. सभा मान-आसः - हस (एतैः सह वर्तत इति) सभा समानासहसा, (यतः) अपरागम् अत्ति *sabhā māna-āsaḥ-hasa (etaiḥ saha vartata iti) samānāsahasā*, (*yataḥ*) *aparāgam atti*

2. सभासमाना (भासमानैः सह वर्तत इति) सहसा (मार्गशीर्षेण हेतुना) परागात् (रजः कणान्) अतति (प्राप्नोति - परागात्) *sabhāsamānā (bhāsamānaiḥ saha vartata iti) sahasā (mārgaśīrṣeṇa hetunā) parāgāt (rajaḥ kaṇān) atati (prāpnoti-parāgāt)*

3. भा (कान्तिः) समाना (सरूपाः , तैः सह वर्तते) सभासमाना । (स्यन्ति परान् इति साः , तैः सह वर्तत इति) सहसा । अपरागात् (अपरस्मात् पर्वतात्) *bhā (kāntiḥ) samānā (sarūpāḥ, taiḥ saha vartate) sabhāsamānā. (syanti parān iti sāḥ, taiḥ saha vartata iti) sahasā. aparāgāt (aparasmāt parvatāt)*

4. एवं भूता असमाना - सभा - सहसा - परागात् (परागता) *evaṁ bhūtā asamānā - sabhā-sahasā- parāgāt (parāgatā)*

> The beautiful assembly of the people inseparably connected with each other went away quickly from that mountain. This assembly was bright with lustre, pride, jubilation and a will to annihilate the enemies. It was also shining with brilliant people. Because of the month *Mārgaśīrṣa* the atmosphere was filled with dust caused by the rushing assembly which was adorned by the people of the same lustre who were annihilators of the enemies.

Gaticitras

The next category of *citrakāvyas* are the *gaticitras*. These are variations of what are known as palindromes in English – words or sentences that remain the same even in their mirror images. For example, 'noon' and 'eve' are examples of palindromic words and 'able was I ere I saw Elba' is an example of a palindromic sentence.

Here we have a verse in Sanskrit where each line is a palindrome; that is, it does not change when read forward or backward. The *śloka* therefore has an axis of symmetry at the centre.

वारणागगभीरा सा साराभीगगणारवा ।
कारितारिवधा सेना नासेधावरितारिका ॥[13]

> It is very difficult to face this army which is endowed with elephants as big as mountains. This is a very great army and the shouting of frightened people is heard. It has slain its enemies.

In the following *śloka* the entire verse forms a palindrome. Therefore the second line is the same as the first line but in reverse.

निशितासिरतोऽभीको न्येजतेऽमरणा रुचा ।
चारुणा रमते जन्ये को भीतो रसिताशिनि ॥[14]

> O immortals, indeed, the lover of sharp swords, the fearless man does not tremble like a frightened man in this battle full of beautiful chariots and demons who are devourers of men.

This is a *śloka*, which if written in reverse creates another *śloka* with a different meaning. Both the *śloka*s are given below with their respective meanings.

वाहनाजनि मानासे साराजावनमा ततः ।
मत्तसारगराजेभे भारीहावज्जनध्वनि ॥[15]

> And after this, that great army, which is capable of destroying the pride of the enemies and which has never experienced defeat, marched towards the enemy with strong and maddened elephants and people roaring in enthusiasm and jubilation.

निध्वनज्जवहारीभा भेजे रागरसात्तमः ।
ततमानवजारासा सेना मानिजनाहवा ॥[16]

> That great army, with majestic and trumpeting elephants of high speed, and people filling the battlefield with their jubilant roar, suddenly became ferocious in anger in that battle of proud heroes.

There are many interesting examples of this variety. Here is an example from a poem where in each *śloka* the first line describes Rama and the second line Krishna. The striking feature is that the second line is always the reverse of the first line.

तं भूसुतामुक्तिमुदारहासं वन्दे यतो भव्यभवं दयाश्रीः ।
श्रीयादवं भव्यभतोयदेवं संहारदामुक्तिमुतासुभूतम् ॥[17]

The first line addressed to Rama in prose order is:

भूसुतामुक्तिम् उदारहासं भव्यभवं यतो दयाश्रीः तं वन्दे ।

I pay my homage to him who released Sita, whose laughter is deep, whose embodiment is grand and from whom mercy and splendour arise everywhere.

The second line addressed to Krishna in prose order is:

भव्यभतोयदेवं संहारदामुक्तिम् उत असुभूतं श्रीयादवं वन्दे ।

I bow down before Krishna, the descendant of Yadava family, who is the lord of the sun as well as the moon, who liberated even her (Pootana) who wanted to bring an end to his life, and who is the soul of this entire universe.

Citrabandhas

In the *citrabandhas*, when the *śloka* is written out, the letters form interesting geometric patterns. In our first example the alternate letters of the first and the second *pāda*s and of the third and the fourth *pāda*s are the same. This design is known as *gomūtrikā* or the crisscross pattern formed by the urine of a moving cow.

काङ्क्षन्पुलोमतनयास्तनपीडितानि
वक्षःस्थलोत्थितरयाञ्चनपीडितानि ।
पायादपायभयतो नमुचिप्रहारी
मायामपास्य भवतोऽम्बुमुचां प्रसारी ॥[18]

May Indra, who uses the thunder-bolt as his weapon, who disperses the clouds in the sky, who desires to embrace and enjoy the pleasures of the bosoms of his consort Sachi, the daughter of the demon Puloma – may that Indra, having removed all illusions, protect you from the fear of all dangers and misfortunes.

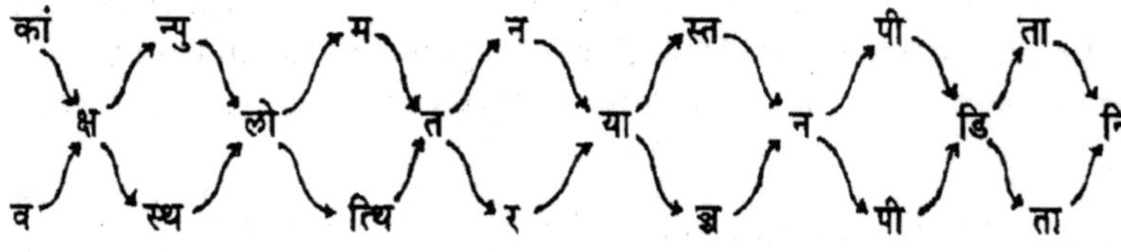

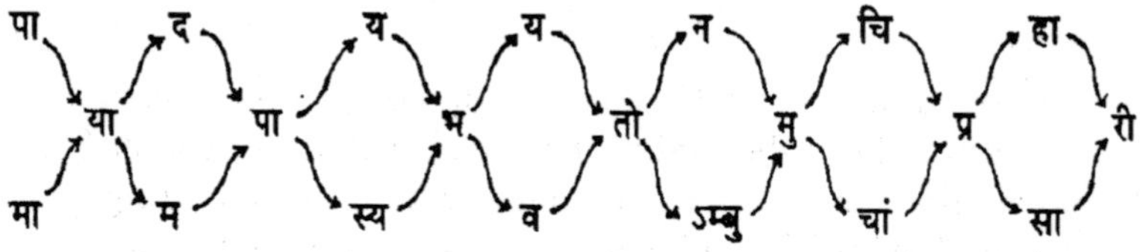

This *śloka* creates an interesting design of a *mūraja* or drum.

> सा सेना गमनारम्भे रसेनासीदनारता ।
> तारनादजना मत्तधीरनागमनामया ॥[19]

> That army was very efficient and as it moved, the warrior heroes were very alert and did their duties with great concentration. The soldiers in that army made a loud sound. The army was adorned with intoxicated and restive elephants. No one was there with any thought of pain.

Let us now see how the drum is formed. First the four *pādas* are written in their normal order. Now the first of the two major strings of the drum (ABC in the following figure) are created by starting from the left-hand corner and then moving to the centre of the opposite side and then back to the right-hand upper corner. Then the second major string (DEF) is created by following a similar movement starting from the lower left-hand corner. It is interesting to observe that the syllables lying on these two strings form the first and fourth lines of the *śloka*. Then there are the two minor strings of the drum forming two squares (GHIJ) and (KLMN) which form the second and third lines of the *śloka*.

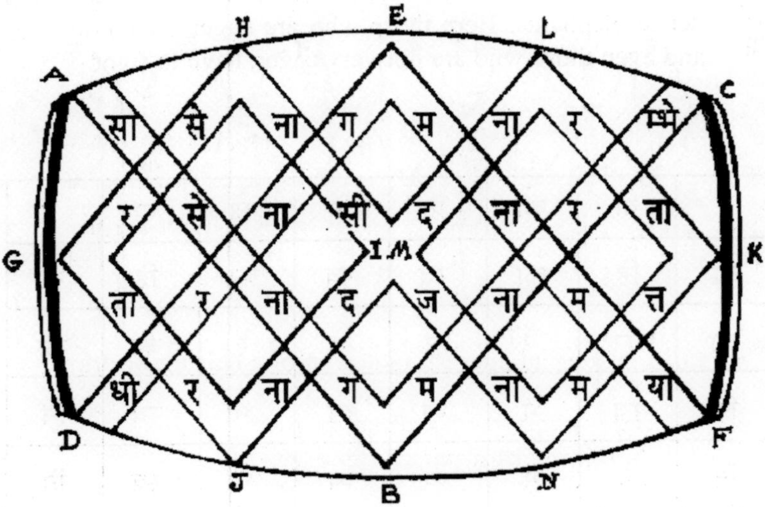

Here is an amazing verse that creates a type of magic square. When each syllable is written in one box of the square, one can read the *pāda*s horizontally, vertically, and in many other ways, even in reverse order, and always get the same verse. This type of verse is called *sarvatobhadra* (valid in all ways), and is a complicated mixture of syllabic palindromes and acrostics. Each quarter-stanza is a palindrome; the first four syllables of the first quarter are formed by taking the first syllables of each quarter in the same order; the first four syllables of the second quarter are similarly the same as the second syllables of each quarter, and so on.

देवाकानिनि कावादे वाहिकास्वस्वकाहि वा ।
काकारेभभरेऽकाका निस्वभव्यव्यभस्वनि ॥ [20]

O man who desires war! This is that battlefield which excites even the gods, where the battle is not of words. Here people fight and stake their lives not for themselves but for others. This field is full of herds of maddened elephants. Here those who are eager for battle and even those who are not very eager, have to fight.

दे	वा	का	नि	नि	का	वा	दे
वा	हि	का	स्व	स्व	का	हि	वा
का	का	रे	भ	भ	रे	का	का
नि	स्व	भ	व्य	व्य	भ	स्व	नि
नि	स्व	भ	व्य	व्य	भ	स्व	नि
का	का	रे	भ	भ	रे	का	का
वा	हि	का	स्व	स्व	का	हि	वा
दे	वा	का	नि	नि	का	वा	दे

Our last example in this category is exceptionally beautiful. It is based on a well-known problem in mathematics. The challenge is to place a knight in one corner of the chessboard and to cover all 64 squares with the knight, without landing on any square twice. The French mathematician Euler found the answer to this problem in the 17th century. This is why this is known as Euler's chess and knight problem.

In India a manuscript called *Pādukāsahasram* has been found, written by a Tamil saint Shri Desikan, in which there are a thousand verses written in praise of the wooden sandals of Lord Rama. In one of the chapters the saint has written the verses in various *citrakāvyas*. In the example given here, there are two *ślokas*, one after the other. The syllables of the first *śloka* are written out in the squares on a chessboard. Then, beginning with the first syllable, if the second *śloka* is read among the letters of the first *śloka*, one finds that the letters follow the movement of the knight on the chessboard, giving simultaneously a solution to the chess knight problem. In fact the writing of the verses in this fashion is far more difficult than the original chess-knight problem. One is even more amazed when one realises that the manuscript is of the 10th century and the saint lived 700 years before Euler.

स्थिरागसां सदाराध्या विहताकततामता ।
सत्पादुके सरासा मा रङ्गराजपदं नय ॥[21]

O sacred sandals (*pādukā*) of the *Brahman*, you are always adored by those who have committed unpardonable sins; you remove all that is sorrowful and unwanted; you create a musical sound; (be pleased) and lead me to the feet of Lord Rangaraja (Rama).

When this verse is read as per the movement of a knight on the chessboard, it creates the following *śloka*.

स्थिता समयराजत्पागतरा मादके गवि ।
दुरंहसां सन्नतादा साध्यातापकरासरा ॥

The sandals (*pādukā*) which protect those who shine by their right attitude, whose place is in the centre of the blissful rays, which destroy the melancholy of the distressed, whose radiance brings peace to those who take refuge in them, which move everywhere, – may those golden and radiating sandals of the Brahman lead me to the feet of Lord Rangaraja.

स्थि 1	रा 30	ग 9	सां 20	स 3	दा 24	रा 11	ध्या 26
वि 16	ह 19	ता 2	क 29	त 10	ता 27	म 4	ता 23
स 31	त्पा 8	दु 17	के 14	स 21	रा 6	सा 25	मा 12
रं 18	ग 15	रा 32	ज 7	प 28	द 13	न्न 22	य 5

Samasyā

We now come to some other varieties of *citrakāvyas*. There is a variety known as *samasyā*. Here the last *pāda* or the fourth quarter of a *śloka* is given to a poet, but this *pāda* does not seem to make sense or appears to be absurd. The challenge for the poet is to create the remaining three quarters in a matching metre, giving meaning to the last quarter. For example, the last quarter given to a poet was मृगात् सिंहः पलायते (*mṛgāt siṁhaḥ palāyate*),meaning 'the lion runs away from the deer'. The verse created by the poet in *anuṣṭup-chanda* was:

तिष्ठार्जुनाद्य सङ्ग्रामे त्वां हनिष्याम्यहं शरैः ।
तिष्ठामि कर्ण किं मूढ मृगात् सिंहः पलायते ॥ 22

> Karna says: O Arjuna, stand (there)! I will kill you today in the battle by my arrows. Arjuna replies: O foolish Karna! Look, I am standing here. Does the lion run away from the deer?

The next example is from Kalidasa. He was given as the last *pāda* just the sounds ठंठंठंठंठंठंठंठं (*ṭhaṭhaṇ ṭhaṭhaṇ ṭhaṇ ṭhaṭhaṭhaṇ ṭhaṭhaṇ ṭha*). Kalidasa came out with the *śloka* in *Indravajrā* metre, which describes a scene in the palace as Ayodhya was getting ready for the coronation of Rama. The verse is:

रामाभिषेके मदविह्वलाया हस्ताच्च्युतो हेमघटस्तरुण्याः ।
सोपानमासाद्य करोति शब्दं ठंठंठंठंठंठंठंठं ॥[23]

> During the coronation ceremony of Rama a golden pot fell on the staircase from the hands of a young maiden, excited and happy. While rolling down the steps the golden pot made the sound ठंठंठंठंठंठंठंठं (*ṭhaṭhaṇ ṭhaṭhaṇ ṭhaṇ ṭhaṭhaṭhaṇ ṭhaṭhaṇ ṭha*).

There are some *ślokas* that appear to be absurd or strange in their meaning. But a more careful study reveals another hidden meaning. Here is an example of one such *śloka*:

हनूमति हतारामे वानरा हर्षनिर्भराः ।
रुदन्ति राक्षसाः सर्वे हा हारामो हतो हतः ॥[24]

At the first reading it gives the meaning that when Hanuman killed Rama, the monkeys started dancing with joy and the demons cried. But the real meaning of this verse is:

> When the garden (of Ravana) was destroyed by Hanuman, the monkeys started dancing with joy and the demons cried saying that 'the garden is destroyed, the garden is destroyed'.

There are also verses in the form of riddles. For example, the following verse asks one to name an object such that:

> "It is black-faced but it is not a cat. It has two tongues but it is not a snake. It has five husbands but it is not Draupadi. What is it? He who knows it is a great scholar."

कृष्णमुखी न मार्जारी द्विजिह्वा न च सर्पिणी ।
पञ्चभर्त्री न द्रौपदी यः जानाति स पण्डितः ॥[25]

The answer to this riddle is 'a pen'.

Some Interesting Verses

The devotional movement in India gave rise to different types of poetic expressions. Here are two interesting dialogues. The first is a charming episode between the little Krishna and a gopi, the milk maid. Once, a Gopi caught Krishna stealing butter from her house. Here is the little Krishna replying to the Gopi's questions:

कस्त्वं बाल बलानुजः त्वमिह किं मन्मन्दिराशङ्कया
बुद्धं तन्नवनीतकुम्भविवरे हस्तं कथं न्यस्यसि ।
कर्तुं तत्र पिपीलिकापनयनं सुप्ताः किमुद्बोधिता-
बाला वत्सगतिं विवेक्तुमिति सञ्जल्पन् हरिः पातु वः ॥[26]

Gopi:	Who are you little boy?
Krishna:	I am the younger brother of Balarama. (The allusion is that Balarama had a good reputation, just the opposite of Krishna)
Gopi:	Why are you here?
Krishna:	I thought this is my house.
Gopi:	But why have you put your hand in that butter-pot?
Krishna:	To remove the ants from there.
Gopi:	Then why did you wake the sleeping calf?

Krishna: To know how it moves.
The Poet: May this babbling Krishna protect you all.

The second dialogue is between Krishna and Satyabhama. Once Krishna went to Satyabhama's room when she was displeased with him. Finding the door closed he knocked. Satyabhama pretended that she did not recognise him and asked her companion Vishikha to see who it was. Krishna, hearing the voice of Satyabhama told his name. But Satyabhama gave a different meaning to the word. Krishna gave another of his names but each time Satyabhama teased him in the same manner pretending not to know him.

अङ्गुल्या कः कपाटं प्रहरति विशिखे माधवः किं वसन्तो
नो चक्री किं कुलालो न हि धरणिधरः किं द्विजिह्वः फणीन्द्रः ।
नाहं घोराहिमर्दी किमुत खगपतिर्नो हरिः किं कपीन्द्रः
इत्येवं सत्यभामा प्रतिवचनजितः पातु वश्चक्रपाणिः ॥[27]

Satyabhama:	O Vishikha, just see who knocks on the door.
Krishna:	I am Madhava (a name of Krishna).
Satyabhama:	Is it spring season? (Madhava also means Spring).
Krishna:	No I am Chakri, the holder of the disk.
Satyabhama:	Is it a potter? (Chakri also means a potter).
Krishna:	No I am Dharanidhara, the one who holds the earth.
Satyabhama:	O, then you are the serpent king. (Dharanidhara also means Sheshanaga, the serpent king who carries the earth on its head.)
Krishna:	No, I am not the serpent king. I am the one who killed the poisonous snake (Kaliya).

Satyabhama:	O, then are you Garuda, the king of the birds? (It is Garuda who kills snakes).
Krishna:	No I am Hari.
Satyabhama:	O, then you are a monkey. (Hari also means monkey).
The Poet:	May Lord Krishna, thus defeated by the words of Satyabhama, protect you.

Then we have two verses in praise of Lord Shiva and goddess Parvati. The first verse is very typical of a certain type of devotional movement which, in its adoration for Parvati, does not hesitate to speak in a disparaging tone about Shiva himself. The two verses run:

स्वयं पञ्चमुखः पुत्रौ गजाननषडाननौ ।
दिगम्बरः कथं जीवेद् अन्नपूर्णा न चेत् गृहे ॥[28]

He himself has five faces; of his two sons, Ganesha has an elephant face and Kartikeya is of six faces. How then would Lord Shiva live, if Annapurna [another name for Parvati as the giver of food] was not there in the house?

स्वयं महेशः श्वशुरो नगेशः सखा धनेशः तनयो गणेशः ।
तथापि भिक्षाटनमेव शम्भोः बलीयसी केवलमीश्वरेच्छा ॥[29]

He is himself the lord of the gods, his father-in-law, Himalaya, is the lord of the mountains, his friend Kubera is the lord of wealth, his son Ganesha is the lord of the *gaṇas*, and yet Lord Shiva begs and lives on alms. Indeed, the will of the Supreme is more mighty than all else.

We end this chapter with two interesting anecdotes regarding king Bhoja, whose court-poet was Kalidasa. Bhoja was a great patron of Sanskrit and himself a poet.

It was a common saying that in the kingdom of Bhoja, everyone was a poet. An ambassador from another kingdom happened to be there but said this was an exaggeration and was not possible. So he went out into the kingdom and far away found a poor weaver, working from morning to night to earn his living. He brought the weaver to the court and in front of the king asked him whether he could compose poetry. The weaver replied in all humility:

काव्यं करोमि न हि चारुतरं करोमि
यत्नात् करोमि यदि चारुतरं करोमि ।
भूपालमौलिमणिमण्डितपादपीठ
हे भोजराज कवयामि वयामि यामि ॥[30]

> I compose poetry but not very well. If I make an effort I may be able to improve. O Bhoja, whose footrest is encrusted with jewels from the crowns of kings, I compose poetry, I weave and with your permission I am going.

The *śloka* of the weaver is charming in its beauty and its humility, and its final play with the three words *Kavayāmi, vayāmi, yāmi* where each subsequent verb is obtained from the previous one by deleting the first syllable.

On another occasion there was a serious discussion in the court. Kalidasa was absent that day and the thought came to Bhoja that what would be the verse that Kalidasa would compose if the king passed away suddenly. Bhoja was so taken up by the idea that he went with his minister to the residence of Kalidasa where he stayed hidden behind the door. The minister went in and very sorrowfully informed Kalidasa that king Bhoja had suddenly passed away. Kalidasa was overcome by grief and the sorrow burst forth in verse:

अद्य धारा निराधारा निरालम्बा सरस्वती ।
पण्डिताः खण्डिताः सर्वे भोजराजे दिवं गते ॥[31]

> Today Dhara [the kingdom of Bhoja], is without a support, even Goddess Sarasvati has no support, the poets, the scholars are all overcome with grief with the passing away of king Bhoja.

The king was so moved that he walked in. Everybody was taken aback and wondered what would Kalidasa do now. Kalidasa realised what had happened and immediately came out with a new verse, echoing the first and yet with a completely new meaning.

> अद्य धारा सदाधारा सदालम्बा सरस्वती ।
> पण्डिताः मण्डिताः सर्वे भोजराजे भुवं गते ॥ [32]

> Today Dhara [the kingdom of Bhoja], has gained its support, and also the Goddess Sarasvati. The poets and the scholars are now all adorned with joy with the coming of king Bhoja on this earth.

The literature of *citrakāvyas* is a veritable ocean. What have been given here are just a few examples, which give merely a fleeting glimpse of the extent, the variety and the richness of its contents. These types of creations demand a great ingenuity and creativity from the writers and reveal the versatility and immense possibilities of this language, which can become a perfect tool and vehicle in the hands of a master.

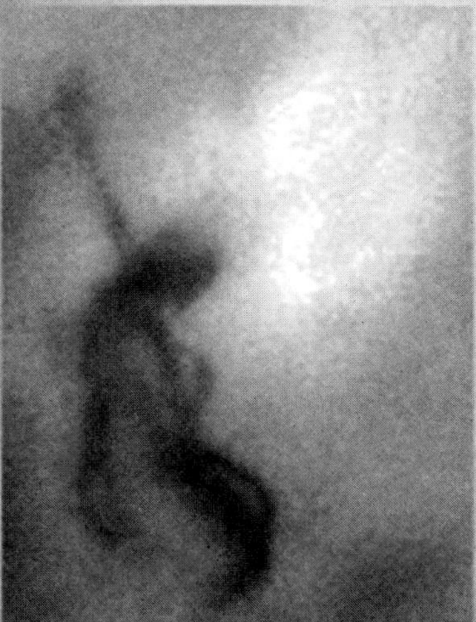

sanskrit in arts,
sciences and daily life

Sanskrit in Arts, Sciences and Daily Life

Today Sanskrit has come to be identified very closely with Indian spirituality, religion and philosophy. So much so that not many are aware of the vast amount of literature available in Sanskrit on practically every field – *yoga*, philosophy, psychology, music, dance, drama, poetry, grammar, mathematics, astronomy, chemistry, architecture, sculpture, painting, education, polity, warfare – in fact on every aspect of work and daily life. What little is known is primarily through a few translations. But there are several books that are available only in Sanskrit and the majority of the literature is in the form of unpublished manuscripts. Some scholars estimate that there are about 100,000 such manuscripts and feel that there may be even more.

Prolific Creativity of India

Regarding this prolific creativity of India, Sri Aurobindo says: "In what field indeed has not India attempted, achieved, created, and in all on a large scale and yet with much attention to completeness of detail? Of her spiritual and philosophic achievements there can be no real question. They stand there as the Himalayas stand upon the earth, in the phrase of Kalidasa, '*pṛthivyā iva mānadaṇḍaḥ*' ('as if earth's measuring rod') mediating still between earth and heaven, measuring the finite, casting their plummet far into the infinite, plunging their extremities into the upper and lower seas of the superconscient and the subliminal, the spiritual and the natural being. But if her philosophies, her religious disciplines, her long list of great spiritual personalities, thinkers, founders, saints are her greatest glory, as was natural to her temperament and governing idea, they are by no means her sole glories, nor are the others dwarfed by their eminence. It is now proved that in science she went farther than any country before the modern era, and even Europe owes the beginning of her physical science to India as much as to Greece, although not directly but through the medium of the Arabs...

"Especially in mathematics, astronomy and chemistry, the chief elements of ancient science, she discovered and formulated much and well and anticipated by force of reasoning or experiment some of the scientific ideas and discoveries which Europe first arrived at much later, but was able to base more firmly by her completer method. She was well-equipped in surgery and her system of medicine survives to this day and has still its value, though it declined intermediately in knowledge and is only now recovering its vitality. For three thousand years at least – it is indeed much longer – she has been creating abundantly and incessantly, lavishly, with an inexhaustible many-sidedness, republics and kingdoms and empires, philosophies and cosmogonies and sciences and creeds and arts and poems and all kinds of monuments, palaces and temples and public works, communities and societies and religious orders, laws and codes and rituals, physical sciences, systems of yoga, systems of politics and administration, arts spiritual, arts worldly, trades, industries, fine crafts – the list is endless and in each item there is almost a plethora of activity."[1]

However, a proper assessment of these achievements remains to be done and a proper history remains to be written. We will be satisfied with casting a brief glance at some interesting discoveries and results in the sciences, and some highlights in life and culture, which will give an indication of the great treasures in Sanskrit that still lie hidden, awaiting discovery.

Sanskrit and Artificial Intelligence

We may perhaps begin with a little-known yet important and striking finding of the recent times. The modern exploding science of computers and artificial intelligence, in their search for an ideal computer language, have found the ancient language Sanskrit to be the most suited for this purpose. We may quote here the words of Rick Briggs of the NASA Ames Research Center. He says, in an introduction to an article in the *AI* magazine, "In the past twenty years, much time, effort, and money has been expended on designing an unambiguous representation of natural languages to make them accessible to computer processing. These efforts have centered around creating schemata designed to parallel logical relations with relations expressed by the syntax and semantics of natural languages, which are clearly cumbersome and ambiguous in their function as vehicles for the transmission of logical data. Understandably, there is widespread belief that natural languages are unsuitable for the transmission of many ideas that artificial languages can render with great precision and mathematical rigour.

But this dichotomy, which has served as a premise underlying much work in the areas of linguistics and artificial intelligence, is a false one. There is at least one language, Sanskrit, which for the duration of almost 1000 years was a living spoken language with a considerable literature of its own. Besides works of literary value, there was a long philosophical and grammatical tradition that has continued to exist with undiminished vigour until the present century. Among the accomplishments of the grammarians can be reckoned a method for paraphrasing Sanskrit in a manner that is identical not only in essence but in form with current works in Artificial Intelligence. This article demonstrates that a natural language can serve as an artificial language also, and that much work in Artificial Intelligence has been reinventing a wheel millennia old."[2]

Some Interesting Discoveries

Next let us take a look at some ancient discoveries in Mathematics and Astronomy. Ask any child the famous Pythagoras theorem and pat comes the reply '$a^2 = b^2 + c^2$'. Ask him if the name Baudhayana sounds familiar and even if one is fortunate to receive an answer in the affirmative, it is highly unlikely that the child will know why it is a familiar name. And yet it was Baudhayana who discovered the theorem around 600 B.C. And in order to make the unbelievable more believable we have here a *śloka* penned by Baudhayana himself.

दीर्घचतुरस्रस्याक्ष्णया रज्जुः पार्श्वमानी तिर्यङ्मानी च
यत्पृथग्भूते कुरुतस्तदुभयं करोति ॥[3]

The diagonal of a rectangle produces by itself both (the areas) produced separately by its two sides.

This is not just a stray example. Take another instance of a mathematical discovery by Baudhayana. It is a calculation of the approximate value of the irrational number $\sqrt{2}$. He says

करणीं तृतीयेन वर्धयेत्तच्च
स्वचतुर्थेनात्मचतुस्त्रिंशोनेन सविशेष इति विशेषः ॥[4]

Increase the measure by its third and this third by its own fourth less the thirty-fourth part of that fourth. The name of this increased measure is *saviśeṣa*.

If we take unity as the basic measure and write Baudhyana's *śloka* in an algebraic language, we get

$$\sqrt{2} = 1 + \frac{1}{3} + \frac{1}{3 \times 4} + \frac{1}{3 \times 4 \times 34} = 1.4142156$$

which is a very close approximation of $\sqrt{2}$ for someone writing around 600 B.C.

Then we have the case of the more familiar, Aryabhatta I. He gave a value for π which is correct to four decimal places in this *śloka* :

चतुरधिकं शतमष्टगुणं द्वाषष्टिस्तथा सहस्राणाम् ।
अयुतद्वयविष्कम्भस्यासन्नो वृत्तपरिणाहः ॥[5]

100 plus 4, multiplied by 8, and added to 62,000: this is the approximate measure of the circumference of a circle whose diameter is 20,000.

This gives π = circumference/diameter = 62,832/20,000 = 3.1416. It is interesting to note that Aryabhatta I lived around 1st century B.C. and has called the above value approximate. In *Sadratnamālā,* a nineteenth century treatise on astronomy by Sankara Varman, the value of π is given correct to 17 decimal places. He says: In this way, if the diameter of a circle measures one *parārdha* (10^{17}), its circumference will be 314159265358979324. Therefore, π = 3.14159265358979324.

Aryabhatta also gave, for the sidereal period of earth's rotation about its axis, a value that is astonishingly close to the modern one. This is obtained from the number of eastward rotations of the Earth in a *yuga*, as stated in part of a *śloka*:

युग ... ङिशिबुण्लृष्खृ प्राक् ।[6]

In a *yuga*, the eastward rotations of the Earth are 1,58,22,37,500. Sidereal period of earth's rotation = 1577917500/1582237500 days = $23^h\ 56^m\ 4.1^s$ The corresponding modern value is $23^h\ 56^m\ 4.091^s$. The numerical values borne by the letter chronograms of the preceding verse have been deciphered using Aryabhatta I's rule on the alphabetical system of expressing numbers:

वर्गाक्षराणि वर्गेऽवर्गेऽवर्गाक्षराणि कात् ङमौ यः ।
खद्विनके स्वरा नव वर्गेऽवर्गे नवान्त्यवर्गे वा ॥[7]

A point of interest is that the dates of most of these writings and discoveries are much earlier than the dates ascribed to them by modern science.

The True Learning

All learning in ancient India was divided into two categories: द्वे विद्ये

वेदितव्ये...परा चैव अपरा च (*dve vidye veditavye...parā caiva aparā ca*), *parāvidyā* and *aparāvidyā*. While the former (also known as *Brahmavidyā*) was considered as the greater learning, that which yields the knowledge and realisation of godhead – leading ultimately to *Sat* (Truth), *Cit* (Knowledge) and *Ānanda* (Beatitude), and after learning which nothing else remains यस्मिन् दृष्टे न कश्चिदिह अस्ति (*yasmin dṛṣṭe na kaścidiha asti*) – the latter, *aparāvidyā,* encompasses all other learning including the *Vedas*, the *Vedāṅga*, *Śilpa*, *Tarka*, *Āyurveda* and so on. These too are necessary and worth being cultivated, but the greater value of the former is undeniable.

A living spirituality that permeated all life was the foundation of all learning. A philosopher was no philosopher if he did not practise what he preached and made instead a division between his teaching and living. He would then be a वेदवादरत (*vedavādarata*) one merely engaged in argumentation on the *Vedas*. A clear distinction existed among the *brahmavid* (one who has knowledge of *Brahman*), *brahmaniṣṭha* (one who is living in *Brahman*) and *brāhmībhūta* (one who has become *Brahman*). It is due to this aspect of holism and the supreme value given to *dharma* that, for instance, even the medical science of *Āyurveda* was believed to have been created because of its ethical need, and the *dhārmic* values were never forgotten even in Vatsyayana's *Kāmasūtra*, so that the secular and the spiritual became harmoniously combined in India's ancient literature. *Dharma* was not religion but the right law of life, that which sustains – धारणात् धर्म इत्याहुः (*dhāraṇāt dharma ityāhuḥ*). You protect *dharma* and *dharma* will protect you – धर्मो रक्षति रक्षितः (*dharmo rakṣati rakṣitaḥ*) .

These are not mere poetic musings but statements of scientific law. What constitutes the ethos of India is this recognition of the supremacy of *dharma*, under which alone everything has to flourish and nothing need be neglected, neither the mundane nor the ethereal, *iha* and *para*. The distinction between humanities and sciences disappears in this view. Science needs philosophy as much as philosophy needs science.

The Vedas and the Vedāṅgas

The *Vedas* have been the great sources of inspiration and shapers of life in India. While the *Ṛgveda* and *Yajurveda* provide the material for spiritual and philosophical thought, the *Atharvaveda* presents the more popular, as well as active aspects of the life of ancient India, of wars, agriculture, domestic life, medicine, magic. The six *vedāṅgas* or disciplines ancillary to the mastery, preservation, understanding and use of the *Vedas*, together with the four *upavedas*, provide some insights into the beginnings of scientific and technological knowledge, as also into artistic developments. Phonetics and linguistic analysis, semantics and etymology, geometry and astronomy, mathematics, metre, music, medicine, archery and military science all developed to a high degree. Linguistics, including semantics, was the exemplar of scientific analysis and it dominated all schools of philosophy and logic, besides the allied field of rhetoric. By *saṁskāra* (refinement) and *vyutpatti* (etymology) a grammatically correct and well structured word, analysable into its component parts, its base, affixes and terminations, became the very symbol of a synthesis, of a unity in diversity, which is the most prominent, significant and persisting character of the very culture and civilization of which Sanskrit was the vehicle and repository. Numbers, up to more than thirteen digits, with names for each (*daśa* to *parārdha*) already appear in the *Yajurveda saṁhitās*. The zero and the place value and decimal system are credited generally to ancient India. The construction of Vedic altars and the *śulba sūtras* dealing with them give us an insight into the development of geometrical and astronomical knowledge.

The extensive later literature on *Jyotiṣa* or astrology places at our disposal, materials for a connected history of ancient Indian mathematics and geometry. The *Brāhmaṇas* deal with *yajñas* of long durations, their correlations to the days and *muhūrtas* of the year (*samvatsara*), the new moon and the full moon, the northern and southern courses of the sun (*ayanas*) and the seasons. The opening section of the *Taittirīya Āraṇyaka,* referred to popularly as *sūrya-namaskāra,* provides a record of observations of the various atmospheric phenomena, the sun and its course, and the resultant atmospheric and terrestrial changes. A section of the *Brāhmaṇa* of the same *Veda*, describing the 27 constellations and their characteristics, the *vedāṅga jyotiṣa* and some of the *kalpas* and *pariśiṣṭas* of the *Atharvaveda* provide data for tracing the growth of astronomical knowledge.

In the *śatarudrīya* section of the *Kṛṣṇa Yajurveda*, the well-known hymns describe Shiva as taking the form of all kinds of persons, high and low, thereby allowing many avocations and occupational workers to figure; the epics also refer to different classes of workers and include information on implements and tools of agriculture, water-lifting, weaving, building, pottery, iron-foundry and so on. Implements of war are mentioned – bridges, stone-throwing machines (*yantras)*, arrows with metal heads, metal clubs, spears and so on.

The Itihāsas and the Purāṇas

The two great epics, the *Rāmāyaṇa* and *Mahābhārata*, form an encyclopaedia of information on all aspects of the history, life and culture of the peoples of the ages they describe; of the tribes and ruling families and dynasties, the geography of the country and its neighbourhood as also of distant parts of the world, the commercial organisations, the polity, its limbs and forms of government, life at home, in the palace, countryside and forest, the role of the forests, deforestation and founding of cities and state-capitals and settlement of people, the condition of learning, arts, occupations, ethics and philosophy. All this is in addition to their primary significance as epic poems, sources of Indian poetry and other forms of literature. As guides to the people and as moulders of human character and the norms of righteous conduct, the *Rāmāyaṇa* and the *Mahābhārata* have played a spiritual role and continue to inspire the hearts and minds of the masses to the present day, a role which has few parallels among the poems of ancient nations.

A subject common to the two epics and the prodigious *Puranic* literature is geography, not only of India and its immediate neighbourhood but also of the entire world as known then, of the continents (*khaṇḍas* and *varṣas*) and the seas, their inhabitants, *Bhuvanakoṣa*, the larger universe or cosmos, and the cyclic creations and dissolutions. The *Itihāsa-Purāṇas* evidently preserve the race memory of a people who had been residents and travellers of a great part of the world and the data incorporated in the *Bhuvanakoṣa* includes information on several nations of antiquity and their geographical habitat.

The *Purāṇa*s developed pilgrimage on a pan-Indian scale and this institution of *tīrtha-yātrā* acted as one of the most potent forces in fostering the territorial and cultural unity of the country, which was further strengthened by the network of holy spots and temples, hallowed by saints, incarnations and forms of divinity. Pilgrimage (*tīrtha-yātrā* and *kṣetrāṭana*) became one of the objectives of one's life and by traversing the length and breadth of the country, whether it was to Dwaraka in the west or to pour a pot of *gaṅgājala* (the Ganga's water) on the Rameshwaram *Śiva-liṅgam* in the South, each individual participated in and gave expression to this unity.

The codification of the virtues, norms and ideals of life and the occupations and activities of the different social groups that had been articulated in the *Vedas* and presented concretely through the heroes, heroines and other characters of the great epics was the work of the *Dharmasūtras* and *Dharmaśāstras*, of Manu, Gautama, Apastamba, Yajnavalkya and others. For the concepts lying at the very base of life and animating it, this branch of Sanskrit literature is of direct importance, as it supplies the readymade frames or patterns which identify the Indian life and personality. This codification of the *Dharmaśāstra* is not a rigid frame; from Vedic times, flexible factors existed and internal mobility, as well as external accession, were not ruled out.

The *Purāṇa*s, encyclopaedias that they are, embody a line of integration in respect of the diverse forms of worship, to manifold forms of divinities. All these were synthesised or arranged according to the twin doctrines of *iṣṭadevatā*, the tutelary deity, and *adhikārabheda*, the doctrine of worthiness. When we remember that the *Ṛgveda* had proclaimed at so early a stage in the history of Indian culture that Truth was one but the sages called it by many names, we shall be able to appreciate how from the most ancient Vamadeva to the modern Ramakrishna Paramahamsa, this belief has been the tonic note of the symphony of this culture.

The Śāstras and the Philosophies

Kautalya is the epitome of thoroughness in his *Arthaśāstra*, another encyclopaedia of Indian civilisation. Its primary subject is polity and government, but as everything comes under government there is hardly any aspect of life and activity that the *Arthaśāstra* does not mirror. Kautalya gives the concept of *cakravartin* and *cakravartikṣetra*, the idea of one country united under one sovereign. His *maṇḍala* theory and the disposition of friendly and inimical powers is a contribution to the problems of war and peace and external relations. In internal administration, in gathering intelligence and the rooting out of the thorns (*kaṇṭakaśodhana*) of internal enemies, traitors, spies, corrupt officials etc., Kautalya's genius leaves no stone unturned. Simultaneously exploiting natural resources on land or sea, production, trade and commerce, inland and overseas, on city laying and fortification, on occupations, revenue, taxation – Kautalya deals with these and many other subjects, so as to give a total picture of a welfare state under a benevolent monarchy, but also expounds on the Republican State.

Side by side with *Arthaśāstras* is another encyclopaedic work sharing many literary features with Kautalya's treatise, namely, the *Kāmasūtra* of Vatsyayana. The two together give an answer to the criticism that the Indian is other-worldly, world-negating, abstemious and self-denying. If Kautalya enunciated at the very outset the idea that man should not deprive himself of happiness, Vatsyayana augments it further. Social life, education and cultivation of artistic pursuits and accomplishments, social festivities and celebrations, conditions relating to love at all levels, dress and decoration are all reflected here.

A third encyclopaedic work, having closer affinity with Vatsyayana's, is Bharata's *Nāṭyaśāstra*. Here again, besides music, dance, drama and poetry, different parts of the country and their peoples and languages, regional dress, manners, complexions, colours and their mixing, ornaments and their varieties are described.

Intellectual development, academic pursuits and the cultivation of arts and crafts and useful skills, recreational activities, literary and otherwise, sports and pastime – all these were part and parcel of ancient Indian education which did not stop with the scriptures and the philosophies.

We now come to a branch of Sanskrit literature that constitutes an important peak of its intellectual attainment in the *śāstra*s. Among these, *vyākaraṇa* or grammar and linguistics have a great importance. Second in the place is the *vākya* or *pūrvamīmāṁsā*, which deals with the interpretation of sentences or statements and the principles involved therein. The third is *pramāṇa*, that is logic or correct thinking. These three go together as the *sine qua non* of scholarship.

Which brings us to the next question – who is a sound scholar? The Sanskrit literary tradition replies – a पदवाक्यप्रमाणज्ञ (*padavākya-pramāṇajña*), a master of the grammar of thought, word and expression and interpretation.

In *pramāṇa* are included logic and the atomic theory of the universe of the *Nyāya* and *Vaiśeṣika* schools. The *Sāṅkhya* was the first philosophy of reaction to ritual and declared knowledge as the means of salvation. Its doctrine of the three *guṇa*s, *sattva*, *raja*s, *tama*s provided a universal tool of analysis for classifying things. This doctrine and the separation of *puruṣa* and *prakṛti* and the theory of causation *satkāryavāda*, were assimilated in *Vedānta*, which in turn is the philosophy of India par excellence.

Literature and History

Apart from being a source for history and culture, classical Sanskrit literature holds its own place as one of the high peaks of the achievements of the Indian aesthetic genius.

Indian drama, in its variety and intrinsic artistic worth, holds much that adds to the inspiration of the experimentalist today who is looking out for lines of fresh developments. As a historian of drama says, after all, in the long gap between Greek drama and the Renaissance drama, it is Sanskrit drama that fills the pages of the history of world drama.

The *mahākāvya*, which is an extension of the *itihāsa* and the *nāṭaka*, held up the ideal of the *mahāpuruṣa* or *dhīrodātta*, the sublime type of hero. It is in the *prakaraṇa*, social play, that the picture of society is given; and the foremost specimen of this class, the *Mṛcchakaṭika* is indeed full of interesting data, including the actual judicial conduct of a criminal case. In both classes – the *mahākāvya* and *nāṭaka* as well as the *prakaraṇa* and the *nāṭikā* – there are historical works. The *Mālavikāgnimitra*, the *Mṛcchakaṭika*, the *Mudrārākṣasa*, the *Devīcandragupta*, fill a large gap in Gupta history and contain important historical material. Prologues and epilogues of several plays refer to ruling kings who patronised the poets.

Historical writings begin with the *Purāṇa*s, one of whose five topics is *vaṁśānucarita* or the history of royal dynasties. In some of the major *Purāṇa*s we have dynastic lists that have been specially studied and used by historians. In classical literature, the leading historical work is Bana's life of Harshavardhana of Kanauj. But the most important work of historical value – which throws considerable light on administration, society, life and learning is Kalhana's *Rājataraṅgiṇī* (A.D. 1148–1150) on the history of Kashmir; which although written earlier by Kshemendra, Helaraja, Chavilakara and Shankuka, was later incorporated by Kalhana. It is often regretted that Indian writers lacked the historical sense. If this is true then how can one explain the huge mass of epigraphs, only part of which has been copied and studied.

The 64 Kalās

The *Veda*s, the six *vedāṅga*s, the four *upaveda*s, the *itihāsa–purāṇa*s, *dharmaśāstras* and *kāvyas* – this successive expansion of the range of knowledge and intellectual activity is completed in the body of practical knowledge and accomplishments, put together as the 64 arts, *catuṣṣaṣṭi-kalā*s. In this context it is revealing to read about the education and training of princes in the ashram of the sage Sandipani, as it is described in the *Bhāgavatapurāṇa*, which provided an all round growth and training.

The 64 *kalā*s or arts included items like singing, playing of various musical instruments, dancing, dramatics, painting, arranging flowers, making perfumes, making ornaments, cooking, weaving, working puppets, writing poetry, story-telling, architecture, carpentry, knowledge of precious stones, fluency in different dialects, and even nursing and treating plants, magic, playing at dice and making a bed.

Aesthetics, Arts and Medicine

The materials in Sanskrit form the sole basis for building up Indian aesthetics. The major contribution to this is the theory of *rasa,* the nine moods of poetics and dramaturgy, as set forth by Bharata and a succession of critics, who developed several theories culminating in that of the *rasa-dhvani* doctrine of Anandavardhana and Abhinavagupta. The *Śilpaśāstra* consists of a considerable number of texts dealing with architecture and iconography and this subject also forms a substantial part of the branch of knowledge called *āgama*, which in its divisions of *śaiva, vaiṣṇava* and *śākta*, forms another prolific class of Sanskrit writings. These are closely related to worship in temples, as also to personal worship.

In music, the Indian system is rich in respect of melodic modes, rhythmic varieties, number and variety of instruments, and compositions. Starting with the *Sāmaveda* and its *lakṣaṇa* texts including the *Nāradīya-śikṣā*, the art has been described and codified in numerous works, the earliest of which is Bharata's *Nāṭyaśāstra*.

During their development, Indian music and dance took in a lot of regional and folk material and, in their concepts of *mārga* and *deśī*, offered a pattern of integration of the classical tradition and the folk or local modes and practices.

The same large body of Sanskrit texts that deal with music deal with Indian dance as well. In addition, there are also many texts dealing exclusively with dance; here again, the rich variety of classical forms leading up to dance-dramas, and the elaborate language of gestures and their use in the minute interpretation of the theme is the specialty of Indian dance. As in music, there is a codification of a large number of local dance-forms, brought under the sophisticated *nṛtta* and *nṛtya* of the classical tradition. All the various elements of *nāṭya*, *nṛtta* and *nṛtya*, *gīta* and *vādya* were applied to the presentation of the plays of Kalidasa and Shudraka and gave Sanskrit drama its special identity. It is in this form that the art went over to South East Asia, where, in the *Rāmāyaṇa* and *Mahābhārata* plays of Indonesia and Thailand, the form still lives, preserving aspects of the art and techniques which, ironically have been lost in India.

Spices, ivory, peacock, Vedantic and Buddhistic ideas, fables, chess, numbers and the sciences of *Jyotiṣa* (mathematics and astronomy) and *Āyurveda* (medicine) figured as the chief exports during ancient times. Of the book of animal fables, the *Pañcatantra*, Edgerton says: 'No other Hindu work has played so important a part in world literature.' It was first rendered into Pahlavi, and from this no less than 200 versions in no less than 50 languages, of which three-fourths are non-Indian, arose. During the Caliphate, the Middle East and India, particularly Sind, were in close intellectual collaboration and Sanskrit treatises in *Jyotiṣa* and medicine were translated into Arabic.

Medicine or the *Veda* of life had, as already pointed out, its origin in the *Veda* and the *upaveda*. The literature of *Āyurveda* in Sanskrit is not only large but covers all departments of treatment including that of horses and elephants. Indian medicine was known to the Greeks and ancient Indian surgery and surgical instruments spread to Europe through the Middle East.

Sanskrit and the Spread of Buddhism

As more and more of the Buddhist texts from the ruins of Central Asian monasteries come to light, it is becoming increasingly clear that Buddhism had a parallel canon in the Sanskrit medium. Later, when its teachers had to wrestle hard with the canons of the Indian orthodox schools, they wrote their dialectical works in Sanskrit. A galaxy of Buddhist metaphysicians and logicians like Nagarjuna, Diṇnaga, Dharmakirti, illumined the history of Indian philosophy with their brilliant contributions. The *mādhyamika* metaphysic developed as one of the high points of the Indian mind. Crossing over the period of Kumarila and Shankara, the succession of Buddhist logicians continued to the time of Udayana (6th century A.D.), after which at about the time of the Muslim invasions, Buddhism disappeared. The story of the spread of Buddhism to Central Asia, China, Japan and also to Korea, and nearer home over Tibet, is in itself an interesting study. The growth of the so-called Buddhist-hybrid Sanskrit may, in part, be the result of the adoption of Sanskrit as a medium of expression by Buddhist teachers and writers in areas outside India. Chinese pilgrims visited India as their holy land, carried loads of Buddhist works and with the help of a host of Indian monks who visited and stayed there, translated the Sanskrit Buddhist works into Chinese. According to some scholars over 2000 Sanskrit works, as listed in old catalogues, were translated with the help of about 100 Sanskrit scholars from India and this corpus of translations is of use not only in editing the Sanskrit originals covered by them, but also include works whose originals have astrology etc. Buddhism went to Japan in 552 A.D. Some of the been lost in India. This activity led to the cultivation of Sanskrit in China for a long time, which had a wide influence on development of literature, the arts of painting, music and dance, and of medicine, astrology etc. Buddhism went to Japan in 552 A.D. Some of the Sanskrit manuscripts there are in archaic *Brāhmī* giving rise to a large number of students of Sanskrit, Indian religion and philosophy, Pali and Buddhism.

The spread of Buddhism was more complete and enduring in the next-door neighbour, Tibet. Here also one finds a library of translations specially from Tantric and Buddhist texts. It further spread in its Pali form to Burma and Sri Lanka. In Sri Lanka, the influence of Sanskrit was not insignificant and one of the major *mahākāvya*s in Sanskrit, the *Jānakīharaṇa* of Kumaradasa comes from the island, along with some Sanskrit works on technical subjects like medicine. As part of the continuous influence and contact with the Tamil language, Shaivism, dance and drama and Tamil music established themselves in Sri Lanka.

Perhaps the most fascinating aspects of the history and role of Sanskrit and of the literature, religions and arts imbedded in it, in countries outside India, is its abiding influence which has continued to this day, in the South East Asian countries, Indonesia, Malaysia, Thailand, Cambodia and Vietnam.

The mere examination of the various texts in Sanskrit covering the meaningful arts and sciences and all aspects of dailylifewould cover an entire encyclopaedia. This becomes even more striking when one realises that there are still thousands of manuscripts lying undiscovered in all parts of India, which in itself is a small fraction of the huge number of manuscripts that have been lost over the centuries.

the beauty and charm of sanskrit poetry

The Beauty and Charm of Sanskrit Poetry

"*Devabhāṣā* – the language of the gods. Sanskrit, as the word denotes, is a sculpted language. A language sculpted to perfection. There is a grandeur in the accented syllables of this language, a rare plasticity of utterance, a tranquillity too that goes beyond our understanding," says Dr. Prema Nandakumar.[1]

"Some believe that India is a land where the gods must have walked on its earth in flesh and blood, speaking Sanskrit. Did they? But what have we to do with history and sociology, we in India who count time in terms of centuries and do not care to hurry about with targets. Who knows how many centuries had been spent before the advent of the *Vedic Ṛṣis* in polishing this divine language! The Indian aim has always been perfection, and all the world be well lost if we can achieve that perfection…

"Truly, when we deal with this language of the gods, we deal with God's plenty. You do not pick and choose here. This is an ocean of gems, a *ratna-garbhā*. Whenever you come to gaze at it, you just pick up a handful. No, not empty, dead shells. These are gleaming, pulsating, life-giving, soul-enriching gems of priceless value, companions who accompany us in our life's journey, teaching us self-mastery and self-perfection, drawing us upwards, teaching us how to live nobly and how to die nobly as well."[2]

If we look at the great poets of Sanskrit, peak after peak rises up, forming a veritable Himalayan range. But to get a brief glimpse, a feel of the beauty, charm and sublimity of Sanskrit poetry, perhaps it will be sufficient to look at a few verses from the three great towering peaks of outstanding splendour – Valmiki, Vyasa and Kalidasa.

The two great works of Valmiki and Vyasa are the famous epics of India, the *Rāmāyaṇa* and the *Mahābhārata*. The master poets have written these epics, says Sri Aurobindo, with a sense of their "function as architects and sculptors of life, creative exponents, fashioners of significant forms of the national thought and religion and ethics and culture. A profound stress of thought on life, a large and vital view of religion and society, a certain strain of philosophic idea runs through these poems and the whole ancient culture of India is embodied in them with a great force of intellectual conception and living presentation."[3]

"The poetical manner of these epics is not inferior to the greatness of their substance. The style and the verse in which they are written have always a noble epic quality, a lucid classical simplicity and directness rich in expression but stripped of superfluous ornament, a swift, vigorous, flexible and fluid verse constantly sure of the epic cadence."[4]

Valmiki and the Rāmāyaṇa

"The *Rāmāyaṇa* embodied for the Indian imagination its highest and tenderest human ideals of character; made strength and courage and gentleness and purity and fidelity and self-sacrifice familiar to it in the suavest and most harmonious form, coloured so as to attract the emotion and the aesthetic sense; stripped morals of all repellent austerity on one side or on the other of mere commonness; and lent a certain high divineness to the ordinary things of life, conjugal and filial and maternal and fraternal feeling, the duty of the prince and leader and the loyalty of follower and subject, the greatness of the great and the truth and worth of the simple, toning things ethical to the beauty of a more psychical meaning by the glow of its ideal hues. The work of Valmiki has been an agent of almost incalculable power in the moulding of the cultural mind of India: it has presented to it to be loved and imitated in figures like Rama and Sita, made so divinely and with such a revelation of reality as to become objects of enduring cult and worship, or like Hanuman, Lakshmana, Bharata the living human image of its ethical ideals…"[5]

When we read a verse in the epic, we become participants of the action, the drama. Yet it is done "so unobtrusively that we come upon a great truth face-to-face in an unexpected manner. Rishi Valmiki asks Narada to tell him whether there can be an ideal man in this world of human affairs, and receives a rather lengthy reply detailing the life of Rama. After Narada's withdrawal from the scene, Valmiki walks towards the Tamasa river along with his young disciple Bharadhwaja, carrying the bark to perform his midday prayers. It is an everyday occurrence, nor are we strangers to such a scene in our own lives at some time or other. The elderly sage stops at the edge of the river, gazes at the beautiful scenery around and looks at the flowing waters of Tamasa. Then very quietly the words come, an unconsciously sculpted poetic image, a perfect simile, a great teaching for the earnest disciple:

> अकर्दममिदं तीर्थं भरद्वाज निशामय ।
> रमणीयं प्रसन्नाम्बु सन्मनुष्यमनो यथा ॥

> Look at these waters, O Bharadhwaja. It is crystal clear and is pleasant to look at. The water is as transparent as the mind of a righteous man.

A great calm descends upon us as the scene grows upon our consciousness and the words, *akardamam, ramaṇīyam, prasannāmbu* and *sanmanuṣya manaḥ* echo in our inner spaces. This is life divine, where the good people with crystalline hearts are our companions. The young disciple imbibes the teaching with unconscious reverence." [6]

Or let us turn to the *Laṅkā-kāṇḍa.* "The scene has been etched in our hearts through centuries. For one whole year Sita has been held captive in the *Aśoka* grove. The first ten months have been unrelieved horror as she has had no news of Rama. Ravana has been increasingly belligerent. It has been a living hell amidst all these perversions of humanity that surround her in the grove. Then comes Hanuman with the message and Rama's signet ring. Once again the play of light and darkness, hope and hopelessness in her life. Then she hears that Rama and his army have landed in Lanka. The terrible war is over at last. Hanuman comes to her again bringing the message of Rama's victory. He now requests her permission to destroy the demonesses who had been torturing her all these months. Listen to the reply of Sita:

पापानां वाशुभानां वा वधार्हाणां प्लवङ्गम ।
कार्यं करुणमार्येण न कश्चिन्नापराध्यति ॥

Sita says it would be meaningless to wreak vengeance on such small fry, who were but doing the bidding of their ruler. Compassion should be the universal rule for all human beings. Be they good or evil or even worthy of being killed for performing heinous deeds, how can a human being dare judge another? Sita, who has received nothing but harsh treatment throughout the year and is going to be put to a very cruel test very soon, is standing as it were on the knife-edge of *dharma:* Who is there who has not sinned?"[7]

Or we can be enraptured by the description of nature. "There are some poets who are the children of Nature, whose imagination is made of her dews, whose blood thrills to her with the perfect impulse of spiritual kinship; one of these is Valmiki. Their voices in speaking of her unconsciously become rich and liquid and their words are touched with a subtle significance of thought or emotion."[8]

Look at the wonderful silhouette of night in Valmiki's 'Book of the Child':

निष्पन्दास्तरवः सर्वे निलीना मृगपक्षिणः ।
नैशेन तमसा व्याप्ता दिशश्च रघुनन्दन ॥
शनैर्वियुज्यते सन्ध्या नभो नेत्रैरिवावृतम् ।
नक्षत्रतारागहनं ज्योतिभिरवभासते ॥
उत्तिष्ठति च शीतांशुः शशी लोकतमोनुदः ।
ह्लादयन् प्राणिनां लोके मनांसि प्रभया स्वया ॥
नैशानि सर्वभूतानि विचरन्ति ततस्ततः ।
यक्षराक्षससंघाश्च रौद्राश्च पिशिताशनाः ॥[9]

> Motionless are all trees and shrouded the beasts and birds and the quarters filled, O joy of Raghu, with the glooms of night; slowly the sky parts with evening and grows full of eyes; dense with stars and constellations it glitters with points of light; and now yonder with cold beams rises up the moon and thrusts away the shadows from the world, gladdening the hearts of living things on earth with its luminousness. All creatures of the night are walking to and fro and spirit-bands and troops of giants and the carrion-feeding jackals begin to roam.

"Here every detail is carefully selected to produce a certain effect, the charm and weirdness of falling night in the forest; not a word is wasted; every epithet, every verb, every image is sought out and chosen so as to aid this effect, while the vowelisation is subtly managed and assonance and the composition of sounds skillfully yet unobtrusively woven so as to create a delicate, wary and listening movement, as of one walking in the forests by moonlight and afraid that the leaves may break under his footing or his breath grow loud enough to be heard by himself or by beings whose presence he does not see but fears."[10]

Vyasa and the Mahābhārata

Vyasa is of a different mould. "In his austere self-restraint and economy of power he is indifferent to ornament for its own sake, to the pleasures of poetry as distinguished from its ardours, to little graces and indulgences of style… Even his most romantic pieces have a virgin coldness and loftiness in their beauty… But to those who have bathed even a little in the fountainhead of poetry, and can bear the keenness and purity of these mountain sources, the naked and unadorned poetry of Vyasa is as delightful as to bathe in a chill fountain in the heats of summer. They find that one has an unfailing source of tonic and refreshment to the soul; one comes into relation with a mind whose bare strong contact has the power of infusing strength, courage and endurance."[11]

"There was never a style and verse of such bare, direct and resistless strength as this of Vyasa's or one that went so straight to the heart of all that is heroic in a man. Listen to the cry of insulted Draupadi to her husband:

उत्तिष्ठोत्तिष्ठ किं शेषे भीमसेन यथा मृतः ।
नामृतस्य हि पापीयान् भार्यामालभ्य जीवति ॥

> Arise, arise, O Bhimasena; wherefore liest thou like one that is dead? For nought but dead is he whose wife a sinful hand has touched and lives."[12]

"Strong, simpler and perfect is the grief of the queen Damayanti when she is abandoned by king Nala and wakes to find herself alone in that desolate cabin. The restraint of phrase is perfect, the verse is clear, equable and unadorned, yet what can be a truer utterance of emotion than this:

हा नाथ हा महाराज हा स्वामिन् किं जहासि माम् ।
हा हतास्मि विनष्टास्मि भीतास्मि विजने वने ॥
ननु नाम महाराज धर्मज्ञः सत्यवागसि ।
कथमुक्त्वा तथा सत्यं सुप्तामुत्सृज्य मां गतः ॥
पर्याप्तः परिहासोऽयमेतावान्पुरुषर्षभ ।
भीताहमतिदुर्धर्ष दर्शयात्मानमीश्वर ॥
दृश्यसे दृश्यसे राजन्नेष दृष्टाऽसि नैषध ।
आवार्य गुल्मैरात्मानं किं मां न प्रतिभाषसे ॥
नृशंस बत राजेन्द्र यन्मामेवङ्गतामिह ।
विलपन्तीं समागम्य नाश्वासयसि पार्थिव ॥
न शोचाम्यहमात्मानं न चान्यदपि किञ्चन ।

कथं नु भवितास्येक इति त्वां नृप रोदिमि ॥
कथं नु राजंस्तृषितः क्षुधितः श्रमकर्षितः ।
सायाह्ने वृक्षमूलेषु मामपश्यन्भविष्यसि ॥[13]

> Ah my lord! Ah my king! Ah my husband! Why hast thou forsaken me? Alas, I am slain, I am undone, I am afraid in the lonely forest. Surely, O king, thou wert good and truthful; how then, having sworn to me so, hast thou abandoned me in my sleep and fled? Long enough hast thou carried this jest of thine, O lion of men; I am frightened, O unconquerable; show thyself, my lord and prince. I see thee! I see thee! Thou art seen, O lord of Nishadas, covering thyself there with the bushes; why dost thou not speak to me? Cruel king! That thou dost not come to me thus terrified here and wailing and comfort me! It is not for myself I grieve, nor foe aught else; it is for thee I weep thinking what will become of thee left all alone. How wilt thou fare under some tree at evening, hungry and thirsty and weary, not beholding me, O my king?

"The whole of this passage with its first pang of terror and the exquisite anticlimax, 'I am slain, I am undone, I am afraid in the desert wood', passing quietly into sorrowful reproach, the despairing and pathetic attempt to delude herself by thinking the whole a practical jest, and the final outburst of that deep maternal love which is a part of every true woman's passion, is great in its truth and simplicity. Steep and unadorned is Vyasa's style, but at times it has far more power to move and to reach the heart than mere elaborate and ambitious poetry."[14]

Here is one more example of this style, strong, hard and bare as granite and yet which reaches straight to the heart of the reader. It is from the *Sāvitrī-upākhyāna* in the *Mahābhārata*; "a short *upākhyāna*, but every word lined with whorls of significances. The tale has been a living legend, for though Savitri's story is referred to as a very old one by Rishi Markandeya in the *Mahābhārata*, the legend continues to live as Indian women perform the *Sāvitrī-*

vrata even today. The epithets used for Savitri – *kanyā tejasvinī, devakanyā, jvalantīmiva tejasā, pativratā, dhyāna-yoga-parāyaṇā* – are carefully imbedded so as to create the vision of a saviour incarnation. However, though the married *yogeśvarī* Savitri who pleases Yama by her *tapasyā* and meaningful speech to regain Satyavan's life is the holy icon for everyone, the young girl Savitri's clear-minded sense of assurance in the face of Narada's shocking revelation holds our imagination in thrall. The dear and only daughter of king Aswapati and Malavi, Savitri had chosen Satyavan in the woods. Rishi Narada says the youth has only one more year to live. The parents feel she should change her mind and Aswapati urges her to do so. But her brief, firm statement silences the royal couple and the divine sage. These are immortal lines in Sanskrit.

दीर्घायुरथवाल्पायुः सगुणो निर्गुणोऽपि वा ।
सकृद्वृतो मया भर्ता न द्वितीयं वृणोऽम्यहम् ॥ [15]

> Whether he is going to be short-lived or will be blessed with a long life, a man of good qualities or evil, once having chosen him as husband, I shall not choose another.

Nothing could be simpler or more direct and yet so full of beauty and passion and calm strength.

Kalidasa: The Poet of Sensuous Beauty and Emotion

Kalidasa, the third among our trinity, is again of a very different nature from Vyasa and Valmiki. "He is the great, the supreme poet of the senses, of aesthetic beauty, of sensuous emotion. His main achievement is to have taken every poetic element, all great poetical form and subdued them to a harmony of artistic perfection set in the key of sensuous beauty… He is, besides a consummate artist, profound in conception and suave in execution, a master of sound and language... The characteristic features of his style are a compact but never abrupt brevity, a soft gravity and smooth majesty, a noble harmony of verse, a strong and lucid beauty of chiselled prose, above all, an epic precision of phrase, weighty, sparing and yet full of colour and sweetness."[16]

Look at his poem *Kumārasambhava*, 'The Birth of the War-God'. From the very first line, or rather from the very first word, one can feel the hand of the master, as he describes the beauty and the grandeur of the mighty Himalayas.

अस्त्युत्तरस्यां दिशि देवतात्मा हिमालयो नाम नगाधिराजः ।
पूर्वापरौ तोयनिधी वगाह्य स्थितः पृथिव्या इव मानदण्डः ॥ [17]

A God mid hills northern Himaloy rears
His snow-piled summit's dizzy majesties,
And in the eastern and western seas
He bathes his giant sides; lain down appears
Measures the dreaming earth in an enormous ease.

"*Kumārasambhava* is a triumph of the sound movements and image plays in Sanskrit. The main characters of the story are all *Devas*. Shiva, the *yogi* is the hero; Goddess Parvati is the heroine, exhibiting all the controlled passion of a girl in love who is prepared to undergo terrible austerities to gain her Lord. The epic speeds towards the *yogic* union of these lovers. The *tapasyā* of Parvati is *yoga* in action. Verse after verse describing Parvati's askesis enriches Sanskrit poetics. Sanskrit rhetoricians have lavished high praise on Kalidasa's poetics and they have reserved the highest praise for this verse that is the image of *yoga* as well.

स्थिताः क्षणं पक्ष्मसु ताडिताधराः पयोधरोत्सेधनिपातचूर्णिताः ।
बलीषु तस्याः स्खलिताः प्रपेदिरे चिरेण नाभिं प्रथमोदबिन्दवः ॥

The first drops of the rain first fall on the eyelids of Parvati. Soon they move down and lash her lips, then fall on her breasts where they break into tiny droplets and land on the folds of her stomach, then after a tremble reach her navel.

Kalidasa does not directly speak about the loveliness of Parvati but conveys it in a subtle manner, through his description of the movement of a raindrop on her body. The drop trembles for just a moment on the eyelids; hence the eyes are half-open and the eyelashes are long and thick. By referring to the 'lashing' of the lips and the breaking of the drop on the bosom the poet hints that Parvati's lips are very soft and her breasts firm. The motion of the raindrop also indicates that Parvati is sitting motionless in the right meditative mood, spine and body erect. Otherwise this would not have been possible. The passage is often compared to the verses in the *Gita* that describe the manner in which a *yogi* has to sit for his meditation. It is indeed a superb feat to have dealt with the idiom of carnal romance and yet heightened the telling to a *yogic* recordation."[18]

Let us now move to an entirely different scene. The son of Shiva and Parvati is named Kumara or Skanda, the War-God. He is appointed general of the gods and leads them forth to battle with the terrible demon Taraka, who has long been afflicting the whole universe. As Taraka marshals his army of demons, bad and terrible omens meet them. Kalidasa's description is remarkable for its atmosphere of frightening and terrifying darkness, which reveals the beauty even in a macabre scene, the *rasa* in the *vibhatsa*.

आगामिदैत्याशनकेलिकाङ्क्षिणी कुपक्षिणां घोरतरा परम्परा ।
दधौ पदं व्योम्नि सुरारिवाहिनीरुपर्युपर्येत्य निवारितातपाः ॥

A fearful flock of evil birds,
Ready for the joy of eating the army of demons,
Flew over the host of the gods,
And clouded the sun.

मुहुर्विभग्नातपवारणध्वजश्चलद्धराधूलिकलाकुलेक्षणः ।
धूताश्वमातङ्गमहारथाकरानवेक्षेणोऽभूत्प्रसभं प्रभञ्जनः ॥

A wind continually fluttered their umbrellas and banners,
And troubled their eyes with clouds of whirling dust,

So that the trembling horses and elephants
And the great chariots could not be seen.

सद्यो विभिन्नाञ्जनपुञ्जतेजसो मुखैर्विषाग्निं विकिरन्त उच्चकैः।
पुरः पथोऽतीत्य महाभुजङ्गमा भयङ्कराकारभृतो भृशं ययुः ॥

Monstrous serpents, as black as powdered soot,
Scattering poison from their upraised heads,
Frightful in form,
Appeared in the army's path.

त्विषामधीशस्य पुरोऽधिमण्डलं शिवाः समेताः पुरुषं ववाशिरे ।
सुराररिराजस्य रणान्तशोणितं प्रसह्य पातुं द्रुतमुत्सुका इव ॥ [19]

And before the very disc of the sun
Jackals bayed harshly together,
As though eager fiercely to lap the blood
Of the king of the foes of the gods fallen in the battle.

Meghadūtam and Śākuntalam

Two of the most well known works of Kalidasa are *Meghadūtam*, 'The Cloud-Messenger', and *Abhijñānaśākuntalam*.

Just by reading a translation of these two, the German poet Goethe was led to exclaim:

"What more pleasant, shall we know,
Than Sakuntala, Nala, that we must kiss;
And Megha-Duta, the cloud-messenger.
Who is there who will not like to send him to his soul!"[20]

The *Meghadūtam* describes a *Yakṣa* who has been exiled from his abode in the Himalayas and therefore separated from his young and beautiful wife. At the beginning of the rainy season he sees a large dark cloud passing northward to the mountains. Pouring out his pining heart, he requests the cloud to be his messenger and take a message to his beloved.

Says Sri Aurobindo, "The *Meghadūtam* is the most marvellously perfect, descriptive and elegiac poem in the world's literature. Every possible beauty of phrase, every possible beauty of sound, every grace of literary association, every source of imaginative and sensuous beauty has been woven together into a harmony which is without rival and without fault; for amidst all its wealth of colour, delicacy and sweetness, there is not a word too much or too little, no false note, no excessive or defective touch; the colouring is just and subdued in its richness, the verse movement regular in its variety, the diction simple in its suggestiveness, the emotion convincing and fervent behind a certain high restraint, the imagery precise, right and full of beauty and power. The *Śakuntalām* and the *Cloud-Messenger* are the *ne plus ultra* of Hindu poetic art."[21]

मन्दं मन्दं नुदति पवनश्चानुकूलो यथा त्वां
वामश्चायं नदति मधुरं चातकस्ते सगन्धः ।
गर्भाधानक्षणपरिचयान्नूनमाबद्धमालाः
सेविष्यन्ते नयनसुभगं खे भवन्तं बलाकाः ॥[22]

As gentle breezes on their steady stream
Waft thee to her: close on thy left will cry
The faithful rain-lark, seized with joy extreme
At sight of thee; and forming in the sky –
For through thy union do their wombs conceive –
Into bright garlands, the hen-cranes will fly
Charmingly near thee…

शब्दायन्ते मधुरमनिलैः कीचकाः पूर्यमाणाः
संरक्ताभिस्त्रिपुरविजयो गीयते किन्नरीभिः ।
निर्ह्रादस्ते मुरज इव चेत्कन्दरेषु ध्वनिः स्यात्
सङ्गीतार्थो ननु पशुपतेस्तत्र भावी समग्रः ॥[23]

Of Tripur slain in lovely dances joined
And linked troops the Oreads of the hill
Are singing and inspired with rushing wind

Sweet is the noise of bamboos fluting shrill;
Thou thundering in the mountain-glens with cry
Of drums shouldst the sublime orchestra fill.

त्वामालिख्य प्रणयकुपितां धातुरागैः शिलाया-
मात्मानं ते चरणपतितं यावदिच्छामि कर्तुम् ।
अस्रैस्तावन्मुहुरुपचितैर्दृष्टिरालुप्यते मे
क्रूरस्तस्मिन्नपि न सहते सङ्गमं नौ कृतान्तः ॥[24]

When thee with rustic chalk on stone I trace
Feigning some jealous rage, then would proceed
My prostrate figure at thy feet to place,
Resistless wellings-up of tears impede
At once my plundered sight: not even such
A union will fate's cruelty concede.

As for the poetical drama *Śākuntalam*, this again is the enthused response of Goethe,

"In case you desire to rejoice in the blossoms of early years,
The fruits of the age advanced,
In case you want to have something that charms,
Something that is enchanting,
In case you want to call both the heaven and earth
By a common name,
I refer you to Shakuntala,
And with this I describe these all."[25]

In India too, *Śākuntalam* is considered to be a masterpiece of dramatic poetry. In fact a popular adage says,

काव्येषु नाटकं रम्यं तत्र रम्या शकुन्तला ।
तत्र रम्यश्चतुर्थोऽङ्कस्तत्र श्लोकचतुष्टयम् ॥

Among the different types of poetry the drama is the most beautiful; among the dramas, *Śākuntalam*; in it, Act IV, and there too the four stanzas (namely those in which the sage Kanva bids farewell to his foster-daughter.)

Shakuntala, the daughter of sage Vishvamitra and the Apsara Menaka, grows up in the forest in the hermitage of Rishi Kanva. It is here that the King Dushyanta sees her, like a drop of fresh dew. Even though dressed in bark and flowers, this is the image of beauty. So the king exclaims, and Kalidasa's similes come down crowding:

सरसिजमनुविद्धं शैवलेनापि रम्यं
मलिनमपि हिमांशोर्लक्ष्मलक्ष्मीं तनोति ।
इयमधिकमनोज्ञा वल्कलेनापि तन्वी
किमिव हि मधुराणां मण्डनं नाकृतीनाम् ॥[26]

The lotus, though moss may overlay it, is nevertheless beautiful; the spot on the moon, for all its darkness, heightens the charm of the moon; this slender (maiden) is more lovely even in her dress of bark: for what indeed is not an embellishment of sweet forms?

When Shakuntala takes leave of Rishi Kanva, who has brought her up like his own daughter, of the beloved hermitage where she has grown up from her childhood, we have one of the most poignant and beautiful descriptions in poetry.

उद्गलितदर्भकवला मृग्यः परित्यक्तनर्तना मयूराः ।
अपसृतपाण्डुपत्रा मुञ्चन्त्यश्रूणीव लताः ॥[27]

(Knowing that Shakuntala is departing):

The female deer have dropped their cud of *darbha* grass; the peacocks have given up their dancing; and the creepers, with their yellow leaves falling off, seem as if shedding tears.

यस्य त्वया व्रणविरोपणमिङ्गुदीनां
तैलं न्यषिच्यत मुखे कुशसूचिविद्धे ।

श्यामाकमुष्टिपरिवर्द्धितको जहाति
सोऽयं न पुत्रकृतकः पदवीं मृगस्ते ॥[28]

This fawn here, regarded by you as your son, whom you affectionately reared with a handful of rice, and to whose mouth, when wounded with the sharp points of *kuśa* grass, you applied the healing oil of *iṅgudī*, does not leave (but follows you).

पातुं न प्रथमं व्यवस्यति जलं युष्मास्वपीतेषु या
नादत्ते प्रियमण्डनापि भवतां स्नेहेन या पल्लवम् ।
आद्ये वः कुसुमप्रसूतिसमये यस्या भवत्युत्सवः
सेयं याति शकुन्तला पतिगृहं सर्वैरनुज्ञायताम् ॥[29]

She who never attempts to drink water first when you (plants and creepers) have not drunk it, she who, though fond of ornaments, never plucks your leaves through affection for you, she to whom it is a festivity when you first put forth your blossoms, that same Shakuntala now departs to her husband's house; let her be permitted by you all.

यास्यत्यद्य शकुन्तलेति हृदयं संस्पृष्टमुत्कण्ठया
कण्ठः स्तम्भितबाष्पवृत्तिकलुषश्चिन्ताजडं दर्शनम् ।
वैक्लव्यं मम तावदीदृशमिदं स्नेहादरण्यौकसः
पीड्यन्ते गृहिणः कथं नु तनयाविश्लेषदुःखैर्नवैः ॥[30]

At the thought that Shakuntala will go away now, my heart is smitten with melancholy, my throat is choked owing to the flow of tears being suppressed; and my eyes are heavy with anxiety. If such be the grief of a forest dweller like me, how much more should householders be tormented by the fresh pangs of separation from their daughters.

Kalidasa is no doubt a poet of love and a poet of nature par excellence. Nothing can exceed the beauty, pathos and power of the cry of Pururavas as he seeks for his lost Urvasie, in the drama *Vikramorvaśīyam.*

सरसि नलिनीपत्रेणापि त्वमावृतविग्रहां
ननु सहचरीं दूरे मत्वा विरौषि समुत्सुकः ।
इति च भवतो जायास्नेहात् पृथक् स्थितिभीरुता
मयि च विधुरे भावः कान्ताप्रवृत्तिपराङ्मुखः ॥[31]

Thou wild-drake, when thy love,
Her body hidden by a lotus-leaf,
Lurks near thee in the pool, deemest her far
And wailest musically to the flowers
A wild deep dirge. Such is thy conjugal
Yearning, thy terror such of even a little
Division from her nearness. Me thus afflicted,
Me so forlorn thou art averse to bless
With just a little tidings of my love.

And see the beauty of the similes of Kalidasa when in the 'Seasons', "he speaks of the Moon towards dawn, growing pale with shame at the lovelier brightness of a woman's face,"

सितेषु हर्म्येषु निशासु योषितां सुखं प्रसुप्तानि मुखानि चन्द्रमाः ।
विलोक्य नूनं भृशमुत्सुकश्चिरं निशाक्षये याति ह्रियेव पाण्डुताम् ॥

"of the rains coming like the pomp of some great king all blazing with lights, huge clouds moving along like elephants, the lightning like a streaming banner and the thunder like a peal of drums,"

ससीकराम्भोधरमत्तकुञ्जरस्तडित्पताकोऽशनिशब्दमर्दलः ।
समागतो राजवदुद्धतद्युतिर्घनागमः कामिजनप्रियः प्रिये ॥

"of the clouds like archers shooting their rain-drops at the lover from the rainbow stringed with lightning."

बलाहकाश्चाशनिशब्दमर्दलाः सुरेन्द्रचापं दधतस्तडिद्गुणम् ।
सुतीक्ष्णधारापतनोग्रसायकैस्तुदन्ति चेतः प्रसभं प्रवासिनाम् ॥

"Most decisive of all are the strokes of vivid description that give the poem its main greatness and fulfil its purpose. The seasons live before our eyes as we read. Summer is here with its sweltering heat, the sunbeams burning like fires of sacrifice and the earth swept with whirling gyres of dust driven by intolerable gusts."[32]

ज्वलति पवनवृद्धः पर्वतानां दरीषु
स्फुरति पटुनिनादैः शुष्कवंशस्थलीषु ।
प्रसरति तृणमध्ये लब्धवृद्धिः क्षणेन
ग्लपयति गृहवर्गं प्रान्तलग्नो दवाग्निः ॥[33]

Clinging to the woodland edges, the forest fire increases with the wind and burns in the glens of the mountains; it crackles with shrill shouting in the dry bamboo reaches, it spreads in the grasses gathering hugeness in a moment and harasses the beasts of the wilderness.

Some other Poets

One can dwell eternally on Vyasa, Valmiki and Kalidasa and not be satisfied. However it would be good to end this chapter with just a few stray examples from some other poets. Here is a beautiful passage from Bana's *Harṣacaritam* 'The Deeds of Harsha', painting so graphically, almost anatomically, the picture of a great stallion waking up from sleep, with subtle alliterative effects, conveying also his own deep delight in the horse.

पश्चादङ्घ्रिं प्रसार्य त्रिकनतिविततं द्राघयित्वाङ्गमुच्चै-
रासज्या भुग्नकण्ठो मुखमुरसि सटा धूलिधूम्रा विधूय ।
घासग्रासाभिलाषादनवरतचलत् प्रोथतुण्डस्तुरङ्गो
मन्दं शब्दायमानो विलिखति शयनादुत्थितैः क्ष्मां क्षुरेण ॥
कुर्वन्नाभुग्नपृष्ठो मुखनिकटकटिः कन्धरामातिरश्चीं
लोलेनाहन्यमानं तुहिनकणमुचा चञ्चला केशरेण ।
निद्राकण्डूकषायं कषति निविडित श्रोत्रशुक्तिस्तरङ्गा-
स्त्वङ्गत्पक्ष्माग्रलग्नप्रतनुबुसकणं कोणमक्ष्णः क्षुरेण ॥[34]

He stretches his hind leg and, bending his spine,
extends his body upwards.

Curving his neck, he rests his muzzle on his chest,
    and tosses his dust-grey mane.
The steed, his nostrils ceaselessly quivering
    with desire of fodder,
Rises from his bed, gently whinnies, and paws the
    earth with his hoof.
He bends his back and turns his neck sideways,
    till his face touches his rear,
And then the horse, the curls matted about his ears,
Rubs with his hoof the red corner of his eye,
    itching from sleep;
His eye, struck by his dewdrop-scattering mane,
    waving and tossing;
His eye, to the point of whose quivering eyelash
    there clings a tiny fragment of chaff.

As for the sweetness and beauty of sound, what can be more musical and charming than these verses from the famous *Gītagovindam* of Jayadeva when he describes the amorous play of Radha and Krishna:

ललितलवङ्गलतापरिशीलनकोमलमलयसमीरे ।
मधुकरनिकरकरम्बितकोकिलकूजितकुञ्जकुटीरे ॥[35]

Soft sandal mountain winds caress
    quivering vines of clove.
Forest huts hum with droning bees
    and crying cuckoos.

चन्दनचर्चितनीलकलेवरपीतवसनवनमाली ।
केलिचलन्मणिकुण्डलमण्डितगण्डयुगस्मितशाली ॥[36]

Yellow silk and wildflower garlands lie on
    dark sandal-oiled skin.
Jewel earrings dangling in play ornament
    his (Krishna's) smiling cheeks.

Now see the contrast in the power and the strength of the description when Ravana worships Mahadeva in the *Śivatāṇḍava-stotra*. It is the veritable sound of the Dance of Shiva.

जटाकटाहसम्भ्रमभ्रमन्निलिम्पनिर्झरी
विलोलवीचिवल्लरीविराजमानमूर्धनि ।
धगद् धगद् धगज्ज्वलल्ललाटपट्टपावके
किशोरचन्द्रशेखरे रतिः प्रतिक्षणं मम ॥[37]

Let my devotion be eternal in Lord Shiva, on whose head shines the crescent moon, who breaks the surging torrent of Ganga swirling in the cauldron of his matted locks and whose forehead is bright with the fiery glow of his third eye.

कदा निलिम्पनिर्झरीनिकुञ्जकोटरे वसन्
विमुक्तदुर्मतिः सदा शिरःस्थमञ्जलिं वहन् ।
विलोललोललोचनो ललामभाललग्नकः
शिवेति मन्त्रमुच्चरन् कदा सुखी भवाम्यहम् ॥[38]

By sitting in the arbour near the bank of the River Ganga and fixing my mind on the beautiful forehead of Lord Shiva [which is adorned with the crescent moon] and keeping my folded hands on my forehead with eyes anxious [to get the vision of Lord Shiva] and being freed from bad thoughts when shall I become happy by chanting the *mantra* 'Shiva'.

We end this chapter with the beautiful and charming description in Sanskrit of the creation of woman by Tvashtri, the divine architect:

स्निग्धत्वं पल्लवेभ्यो मृगिनयनमिनस्याङ्घ्रितः सद्विलास-
मस्त्रं तावत्तुषारादतिचपलयुतं साध्वसं शाशमेवम् ।
मायूरं गर्वभावं मधुरमथ मधुभ्यस्तथा व्याघ्रतोऽपि
क्रौर्यं काठिन्यमेवं कुलिशगतमथौष्ण्यञ्च वह्नेस्ततश्च ॥
स्वीकृत्यैतच्च सर्वं मिलितमथ च संपीड्य पारावतानां
कूङ्कारञ्चैवमल्पेतरमपि विहिता सा विधात्रा च नारी ।

विश्वस्योत्पत्तिसम्यक्स्थितिगतिविलयप्राप्तये सादरेण
तस्मै मर्त्याय दत्तं वरमतिमहितं सुन्दरञ्चोपहारम् ॥ [39]

He took the lightness of the leaf and the glance of the fawn; the gaiety of the sun's rays and the tears of the mist; the inconstancy of the wind and the timidity of the hare; the vanity of the peacock and the softness of the down on the throat of the swallow. He added the harshness of the diamond, the sweet flavour of honey, the cruelty of the tiger, the warmth of fire and the chill of snow. He added the chatter of the jay and the cooing of the turtle-dove. He melted all this and formed a woman.Then he made a present of her to man.

a language of upliftment and enlightenment

A Language of Upliftment and Enlightenment

It is but natural that a language will reflect the nature of the people who use it – mirror their culture, their outlook, their goals in life. While speaking about Sanskrit, Swami Parmarthananda says: "Its richness, beauty, subtlety, clarity and rigour reveals a culture which is rich in its interests, beautiful in its variety, subtle in its depth, clear in its understanding and rigorous in its penetrating analysis."[1]

In Sanskrit there are a very large number of verses that express the highest and noblest thoughts, enlighten and uplift the emotions and reveal a deep insight into human psychology and nature. One such treasure-trove is the *Mahābhārata*, where "the sayings of profoundest wisdom are scattered with a lavish hand. Some are worldly-wise, others show how highly Truth was valued, others again are tender and sweet or extol the spirit of forgiveness."[2] Here are just a few of these selected at random:

अन्तो नास्ति पिपासायास्तुष्टिस्तु परमं सुखम् ।[3]

Desire is endless; contentment is the best happiness.

यत् पृथिव्यां ब्रीहि यवं हिरण्यं पशवः स्त्रियः ।
नालमेकस्य तत् सर्वं ...... ॥[4]

If one man were to possess all the grain, all the gold, all the cattle and all the women in the world, yet he would not be content.

गतासूनगतासूंश्च नानुशोचन्ति पण्डिताः ।[5]

The wise mourn neither the living nor the dead.

य ईर्षुः परवित्तेषु रूपे वीर्ये कुलान्वये ।
सुखसौभाग्यसत्कारे तस्य व्याधिरनन्तकः ॥[6]

When the wealth, beauty, heroism, birth, happiness, good fortune, and hospitality of one man excites the envy of another, the pain and the trouble of the envious man are endless.

सुखार्थी वा त्यजेद् विद्यां विद्यार्थी वा त्यजेत् सुखम् ।[7]

The seeker after pleasure must abandon knowledge and the seeker after knowledge must abandon pleasure.

अहन्यहनि भूतानि गच्छन्तीह यमालयम् ।
शेषाः स्थावरमिच्छन्ति किमाश्चर्यमतः परम् ॥[8]

What can be more wonderful than the fact that in spite of deaths occurring daily before their eyes, the survivors think that for them there is no death!

And here is a beautiful verse from the *Rāmāyaṇamañjarī* of Kshemendra:

यथा चतुर्भिः कनकः परीक्ष्यते
निघर्षणच्छेदनतापताडनैः ।
तथा चतुर्भिः पुरुषः परीक्ष्यते
कुलेन शीलेन गुणेन कर्मणा ॥[9]

Gold is tested in four ways – by rubbing, by cutting, by

heating and by hammering. So a person is tested in four ways – by the family, by character, by quality and by deed.

And this oft-quoted verse is from the *Hitopadeśa* of Narayana:

अयं निजः परो वेति गणना लघुचेतसाम् ।
उदारचरितानां तु वसुधैव कुटुम्बकम् ॥[10]

This is mine, this is a stranger's – such is the thinking of the narrow-minded, while to the large minded the whole world is their family.

Subhāṣitas

न चौरहार्यं न च राज्यहार्यं
न भ्रातृभाज्यं न च भारकारि ।
व्यये कृते वर्धत एव नित्यं
विद्याधनं सर्वधनप्रधानम् ॥[11]

The wealth of wisdom is the greatest of all wealth – for it cannot be stolen by thieves, it cannot be confiscated by the king, it cannot be appropriated by brothers, nor can it become a burden to preserve. When shared, it rather increases continuously.

Such compact verses are known as *subhāṣitas* or 'things well-said'. Some of the most beautiful and well-known *subhāṣitas* are from the king-turned sage, Bhartrihari. When Bhartrihari speaks about the futility of man running after pleasures and the satisfaction of desires, we can observe not only the loftiness of the thought but can also feel the sound rhythms and their vibrations:

भोगा न भुक्ता वयमेव भुक्ताः
तपो न तप्तं वयमेव तप्ताः ।
कालो न यातो वयमेव याताः
तृष्णा न जीर्णा वयमेव जीर्णाः ॥[12]

Pleasures have not been enjoyed; it is we who are consumed. *Tapas*, the fire of askesis, has not been kindled, it is we who are burnt up. Time is not passed; it is we who are spent. Desires have not waned; it is we who have grown old.

Here is Bhartrihari speaking of the wealth of wisdom and the ornament of speech:

केयूराणि न भूषयन्ति पुरुषं हारा न चन्द्रोज्ज्वला
न स्नानं न विलेपनं न कुसुमं नालङ्कृता मूर्धजाः ।
वाण्येका समलङ्करोति पुरुषं या संस्कृता धार्यते
क्षीयन्ते खलु भूषणानि सततं वाग्भूषणं भूषणम् ॥ [13]

It is not armlets that adorn a man,
Nor necklaces all crammed with moonbright pearls,
Nor baths, nor ointments, nor arranged curls.
'Tis the art of excellent speech that alone can
Adorn him: jewels perish, garlands fade;
This only abides and glitters undecayed.

What is the difference between ordinary men and the great and the best?

प्रारभ्यते न खलु विघ्नभयेन नीचैः
प्रारभ्य विघ्नविहता विरमन्ति मध्याः।
विघ्नैः पुनः पुनरपि प्रतिहन्यमानाः
प्रारभ्य चोत्तमगुणा न परित्यजन्ति ॥ [14]

Some from high action through base fear refrain;
The path is difficult, the way not plain.
Others more noble to begin, are stayed
By a few failures. Great spirits undismayed
Abandon never what once to do they swore.
Baffled and beaten back, they spring once more,
Buffeted and borne down, rise up again,
And, full of wounds, come on like iron men.

Finally, in an amusing and humorous verse, Bhartrihari describes a fool who is firmly set in his opinions:

प्रसह्य मणिमुद्धरेन्मकरवक्त्रदंष्ट्रान्तरात्
समुद्रमपि सन्तरेत् प्रचलदूर्मिमालाकुलम् ।
भुजङ्गमपि कोपितं शिरसि पुष्पवद्धारयेत्
न तु प्रतिनिविष्टमूर्खजनचित्तमाराधयेत् ॥ [15]

Go, with strong violence thy jewel tear
From the fierce alligator's yawning jaws;
Swim the wild surges when they lash the air
Billow on billow thundering without pause;
Or set an angry serpent in thy hair
For a garland! Sooner shalt thou gain their ruth
Than conquer the fool's obstinate heart with truth.

Ancient Sayings and Modern Times

But do the ancient sayings of Sanskrit have any relevance to our life today? This question has been dealt with beautifully in a talk by Professor H.N. Mukherjee.[16] He says: "To Sanskrit we look for inspiration even in this regard, because its message has many elements which are, as far as we can see, of perennial value. There are doubtless in our past, and therefore also in the wide corpus of Sanskrit literature, things that require to be discarded, but there is much also that we should cherish and apply in our tasks of today." As Professor Radhakrishnan, President of the Republic of India, once said: 'From the past let us collect the fire and the glow and not the ashes.'

There is so much talk today of dynamism as the feature of life if it is to be worthwhile. While Indian thought, enshrined in Sanskrit, often glorified the idea of what might be called static tranquillity, there is no lack also in the treasury of Sanskrit of exhortations to dynamism. Who can ever forget the sublimity of the injunction:

चरन् वै मधु विन्दति चरन् स्वादुमुदुम्बरम् ।
सूर्यस्य पश्य श्रोमाणं यो न तन्द्रयते चरन् ॥ चरैवेति चरैवेति ॥ [17]

Marching forward one gets all that is sweet;
marching forward one gets the sweet *udumbara* fruit;
look at the labour of the Sun,
who moves and moves, and is never tired.
Let us march ahead, let us march ahead.

The Search for Truth

Let it be stressed that the genius of India has not been one of conformity, of mere obedience to the regulations of society, of the entire subordination of the individual to the body social. There is no doubt, of course, of the stress in India on social cohesion, the setting up of a social order where different elements can fit in, aware of their station and their duties – which degenerated later most unhappily into the caste system and the conservative ideology it connotes. But at the same time there has been, as Sanskrit literature indicates, a continuous tradition of non-conformity, a habit of asking questions and never resting till the truth is comprehended. The effort was to go from level to level never remaining satisfied till the ultimate truth was found – नेति नेति (*neti neti*), 'not this, not this'.

It is this tradition which explains the sublime philosophy of the Sanskrit epics, where there is comprehensive, fearless and sometimes surprisingly uninhibited depiction of psychological processes, of the sorrow and happiness that comprises life, and the stress is on a kind of non-attachment which one achieves only after having sampled life in its glory as well as in its lower depths. If this concept is not relevant to modern life, what is? A modern mind in every continent will indeed find, in the treasury of Sanskrit, gems that glitter like stars in the night.

The motto of the Republic of India is सत्यमेव जयते (*satyameva jayate*) – 'Truth alone triumphs'. The wonderful exhortation in the *Taittirīya Upaniṣad* – सत्यं वद धर्मं चर (*satyaṁ vada dharmaṁ cara*) – 'Speak the Truth; follow the *dharma*' – is nearly without parallel in the sublimity and compact strength of the formulation. The same passage includes such statements as सत्यान्न प्रमदितव्यं कुशलान्न प्रमदितव्यं । भूत्या न प्रमदितव्यम् ॥ (*satyānna pramaditavyaṁ kuśalānna pramaditavyaṁ. bhūtyā na pramaditavyam.*) –'Do not deviate from the truth; do not deviate from the pursuit of welfare; do not deviate from the ways of prosperity'. In the *Upaniṣads* one finds the beautiful injunction कुर्वन्नेवेह कर्माणि जिजीविषेच्छतं समाः (*kurvanneveha karmāṇi jijīviṣecchataṁ samāḥ*), 'Always performing good deeds, one should live to work a hundred years'. The hundred years, however, should be spent in a worthwhile manner and not in the pursuit of trivial things. The Sanskrit injunction is that knowledge is to be acquired, प्रणिपातेन परिप्रश्नेन सेवया (*praṇipātena paripraśnena sevayā*), 'by devotion, by questioning, by humility'.

Max Mueller has spoken of Sanskrit displaying in its wonderful literature an "extreme sensitivity of conscience" in regard to Truth, which is hardly paralleled elsewhere. The law-givers like Manu tried of course to place this extreme emphasis on truth-telling in a broader perspective when, for example, they cite a primeval rule – सत्यं ब्रूयात् प्रियं ब्रूयात् मा ब्रूयात् सत्यमप्रियम् (*satyaṁ brūyāt priyaṁ brūyāt mā brūyāt satyamapriyam*) 'Tell the truth when it is pleasant, but remain silent if it is unpleasant'. But the fundamental emphasis in the thinking always remained unchanged and unshaken on truth and righteousness. When Gandhari, one of the sublimest characters in the *Mahābhārata*, was asked to confer her blessing upon her hundred sons (who, it was said, would win the battle of Kurukshetra if their virtuous mother prophesied their victory), she said in words that can never be forgotten यतो धर्मस्ततो जयः (*yato dharmastato jayaḥ*) – 'Where righteousness is, there alone is victory'. Not even maternal love could detract her from the pursuit of what is right.[18]

Democracy, Secularism and Socialism

There is a famous *Vedic* invocation that goes: सं गच्छध्वं संवदध्वं संवो मनांसि जानताम् (*saṅgacchadhvam saṁvadadhvaṁ saṁvo manāṁsi jānatām*), 'Let us move together, let us speak together, let our minds be attuned together', ending with the words यथाव सुसहासति (*yathāva susahāsati*), 'so that all may happily live together'.

Democracy is usually taken to be a distinguishing mark of progressive humanity in the present day and, in spite of the hierarchic society that the institution of caste consolidated on Indian soil, one could refer to countless instances in Sanskrit literature from the Vedic age onwards, which refer to concepts and practices that are firmly in tune with the spirit of democracy. The stress on *sabhā* and *samiti* in Vedic literature is to be remembered in this connection. The concept of a new society where peace reigned – सर्वं शान्तिमाप्नुयात् (*sarvaṁ śāntim āpnuyāt*), 'Peace all over, peace and ever peace' – beautifully portrayed the dream of a happy community which finds further and entrancing expression in the beautiful evocation of मधु वाता ऋतायते मधु क्षरन्ति सिन्धवः (*madhu vātā ṛtāyate madhu kṣaranti sindhavaḥ*), 'Let honeyed winds blow, let the waters flow with honey'. In the large corpus of political literature in Sanskrit, of which the Kautalya's *Arthaśāstra* is a representative and outstanding example, there is evidence of a vivid political life where even democracy, though of course necessarily different and somewhat remote from the modern conception of it, is the basic guiding feature. Even a rudimentary acquaintance with Sanskrit literature would make it clear that whatever the deviations, the organisation of society was on the basis of righteousness and right conduct has been the fundamental Indian conception – 'have concord and hold together' is the age old exhortation of the *Atharvaveda.*

Secularism is another ideal cherished by modern society that has always been a characteristic of Indian society particularly since ancient times. Look, for instance, at the role of *dharma* which is the modality of keeping society together, and not any exclusive and dogmatic assertion of the superiority of one set of beliefs and practices over another. Unlike in many countries of the world, where the Church and the State came into conflict, ancient India never experienced a similar kind of aberration in the powers of organised religion at the cost, among other things, of freedom of belief. Since the earliest days there has been no bar to society in India comprising the utterly devout as well as the complete atheist, the philosophical idealist and the unqualified materialist, all co-existing in a society which never wanted to rule out dissent. Throughout the centuries millions of Indian children have learnt to recite:

> यं शैवाः समुपासते शिव इति ब्रह्मेति वेदान्तिनो
> बौद्धा बुद्ध इति प्रमाणपटवः कर्तेति नैयायिकाः ।
> अर्हन्नित्यथ जैनशासनरताः कर्मेति मीमांसकाः
> सोऽयं नो विदधातु वाञ्छितफलं त्रैलोक्यनाथो हरिः ॥[19]

> May the Lord of the universe, the remover of evil – whom the devotees of Shiva worship as Shiva, the *Vedantins* as *Brahman*, the Buddhists as Buddha, the followers of *Nyāya* Philosophy who are clever in logic as the Agent, those devoted to the *Jaina* doctrines as *Arhat*, the ritualists of the *Mīmāṁsā* school as *Karma* – may he grant us all our heart's desires.

How good it is to find in the *Mahābhārata* unqualified condemnation of the person 'who trades in religion' धर्मवाणिज्यक (*dharma vāṇijyaka*). Needless to say, secularism in the deepest sense is something that was ingrained in the traditions of this country and particularly in the legacy of Sanskrit writing.

Socialism is yet another aspect of human thinking and activity that today we want to make an organic part of life. Unless one forgets all idea of change in history, one cannot expect socialism, for instance scientific socialism as expounded by Marx and Engels, to be found in the same form a millennium ago in our country. But socialism is not something that is whisked out of the clouds; it evolves out of the development of life and of the social forces operating through the centuries. We do not know much about the nature of primitive society in India, but we find in the historical period such superb *Upaniṣadic* statements beginning with ईशावास्यमिदं सर्वं (*īśāvāsyam-idaṁ sarvaṁ*) and ending with मा गृधः कस्यस्विद्धनम् (*mā gṛdhaḥ kasyasvid dhanam*) 'do not covet, for whose indeed is wealth?' This, of course, is not socialism, but it is a formulation which seeks for the community a happy life based on equity and honour among everybody; a life untainted by the vice of covetousness which is the foundation of those practices of exploitation and acquisition that socialism intends to abolish. How good it is to find a formulation to the effect that one has no right to more than what one needs for oneself यावत् भ्रियेत जठरम् ! (*yāvat bhriyeta jaṭharam*!) When Mahatma Gandhi wrote in Harijan, 'All land belongs to Gopal (God) and hence nobody has the right to exploit anybody else', he was expressing an idea that is repeated beautifully in Sanskrit literature over the ages.

The *Mahābhārata* states that 'big money', महती श्रीः (*mahatī śrīḥ*), cannot be acquired unless one tears the hearts of others, unless one does hard things, unless one is prepared to kill as the fisherman kills his prey.

नाच्छित्वा परमर्माणि नाकृत्वा कर्म दारुणम् ।
नाहत्वा मत्स्यघातीव प्राप्नोति महतीं श्रियम् ॥[20]

This striking passage can be compared with what Karl Marx wrote at the end of his celebrated historical chapter in *Das Kapital*: 'If money, as Augier says, comes into the world with a congenital stain on its cheek, Capital, when it emerges, drips with blood and dirt from every pore'.

There is, indeed, in the tradition enshrined in Sanskrit literature, more than enough to sustain whatever ideas we might have at the present point of time regarding the construction of a society built on the principles of democracy, socialism and secularism for the benefit of the people.[21]

The True Ascetic

India has always admired the individual who had the strength to renounce worldly life and pleasures and follow the path of the ascetic and the spiritual seeker. The robe of the *Sannyāsin* has been revered, but it was always a veneration of the inner renunciation and not of the outer garb. Here are some verses in Pali, a dialect derived from Sanskrit, on the real qualities to be developed by the *Sannyāsin* and the *Bhikkhu*:

न परेसं विलोमानि न परेसं कताकतम्।
अत्तनो व अवेक्खेय्य कतानि अकतानि च ॥ [22]

Let none find faults in others.
Let none see omissions and commissions in others.
But let one see one's own acts done and undone.

कायेन संवरो साधु साधु वाचया संवरो
मनसा संवरो साधु साधु सब्बत्थ संवरो
सब्बत्थ संवुतो भिक्खु सब्बदुक्खा पमुच्चति ॥ [23]

Good is restraint in action,
Good is restraint in speech,
Good is restraint in thought,
Restraint everywhere is good,
The monk restrained everywhere
Is freed from all suffering.

न नग्गचरिया न जटा न पंका
नानासका थण्डिलसायिका वा
रजोवजल्लं उक्कुटिकप्पधानं
सोधेन्ति मच्चं अवितिण्णकङ्खम् ॥ [24]

Not going about naked, not matted locks, not filth, not fasting, not smearing oneself with ashes and dust, not sitting on the heels (in penance), can purify a mortal who has not overcome cynicism.

अलंकतो चेपि समं चरेय्य सन्तो दन्ता नियतो ब्रह्मचारी ।
सब्बेसु भूतेसु निधाय दण्डं सो ब्राह्मणो सो समणो स भिक्खु ॥ [25]

Even though he be richly and gaily decked but if he is poised, calm, controlled and established in holy life, having laid aside the cudgel against all beings – he truly, is a holy man, a recluse, a *Bhikkhu* (monk).

सहस्समपि ये वाचा अनत्थपदसंहिता ।
एकम् अत्थपदं सेय्यो यं सुत्वा उपसम्मति ॥[26]

Better than a thousand useless words is one useful word, hearing which one attains peace.

यो सहस्सं सहस्सेन संगामे मानुसे जिने ।
एकं च जेय्यमत्तानं स वे संगामजुत्तमो ॥[27]

Though he may conquer a thousand times, a thousand men in battle, yet he indeed is the noblest victor who would conquer himself.

Indeed one cannot study a language without turning to its way of thinking. And the study of Sanskrit is a delightful endeavour that brings to us liberation, a great inner strength, enlightenment and an uplifting refinement.

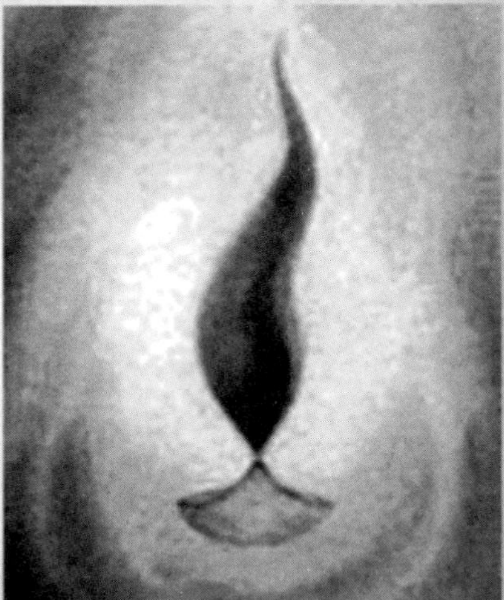

a sacred and
spiritual language

A Sacred and Spiritual Language

"Man is perhaps the greatest of living beings," says Sri Aurobindo in a striking sentence, "because he is the most discontented, because he feels most the pressure of limitations. He alone, perhaps is capable of being seized by the divine frenzy for a remote ideal."[1] He cannot refrain from asking himself, 'Who am I? Why am I here? What is the meaning of my life? Why am I born if it is only to die?' It is because man has always sought to overpass his limits, to look for his true self, to find God, light, freedom, bliss and immortality that a language like Sanskrit came into being. Ancient *Vedānta* formulated the three great truths of existence through the three declarations of the *Upaniṣads* – सोऽहम् *so'ham* "I am He"; तत्त्वमसि *tattvamasi* "Thou art That"; सर्वं खल्विदं ब्रह्म *sarvaṁ khvalvidaṁ brahma* "All this is the Brahman; this self is the Brahman."

From ancient times Sanskrit has been looked upon and even venerated in India as a sacred and a spiritual language. It was not known as 'Sanskrit', which is a relatively recent development, but rather as '*Devavāṇī*' or '*Devabhāṣā*', the language of the gods.

In India, it is believed that at the origin of creation the Supreme manifested as sound, as *nāda-brahman*, as Om, the Divine Word. It is from this sacred syllable that Sanskrit is said to have originated. However, this is only the ground formation of its sacredness.

The real source of its sanctity and spirituality lies, in fact, in the way the language has been used in India. This is a country where, for thousands of years, spiritual seekers have devoted their entire lives to determining the truth behind their existence, behind God and the world. Nowhere has this search been as all-consuming, intense and widespread. And the means of this search has been *Yoga* and the instrument of its expression has been the Sanskrit language.

In the words of Dr. Vyas Houston, "India has made two great and enduring contributions to the world – the Sanskrit language and *Yoga*. For millennia, these two have mutually enhanced and over-powered one another to elevate human consciousness to the sub-lime. Within the great spiritual traditions of India, Sanskrit could be seen as the vehicle and *Yoga* the driver, for the great inner journey."[2]

The Sanskrit language has grown and developed not only as a means of communication, but out of a search for the true and the real. Its entire literature and indeed, its vocabulary vibrate and pulsate with the many dimensions of this endeavour. In fact, it is commonly held that "Sanskrit has more words for the Divine and more precise terms for deepening consciousness and meditative experiences than any other language."[3]

Dr. Vyas Houston continues, "Ultimately, there is just one reason for our being here; to know who we are. And so long as one is engaged in the study of Sanskrit, the truth is unavoidable."[4]

The Power of Sanskrit

Sanskrit is not just a language. It is a power. "Its very alphabet is a *Mantra*, a sound or phrase of spiritual significances and power," observes Dr. Judith Tyberg.[5] "The language is constructed in har-monious relation with the very truths of existence, hence its power of illumination." She adds, "Sanskrit grammarians hold that every word or sound (*śabda*) has a power (*śakti*). This intrinsic power can always convey the sense that is inseparably related to the sound... In the sacred Sanskrit scriptures this power was not only intuitively expressed but consciously wielded. And the power was not only of the human mind but of the Spirit."

Sceptical minds may dismiss this as an offshoot of an enamoured Western mind or else view it narrowly in the light of superstitious beliefs but it is only when one separates each thread which weaves together the intricate web of Sanskrit, that one can fully comprehend the power it possesses.

Says Sri Aurobindo, "Every one of its vowels and consonants has a particular and inalienable force, which exists by the nature of things and not by development or human choice; these are the fundamental sounds which lie at the base of the Tantric *bījamantras* or constitute the efficacy of the *mantra* itself."[6]

Poetry as Mantra

Mantra is a Sanskrit word that has no English equivalent. The *mantra* is "the inspired word and the supreme inevitable utterance" where, in the words of Sri Aurobindo, the "three highest intensities of poetic speech meet and become indissolubly one, a highest intensity of rhythmic movement, a highest intensity of verbal form and thought-substance, of style, and a highest intensity of the soul's vision of truth."[7] Poetry becomes the *mantra* "when it is the voice of the inmost truth and is couched in the highest power of the very rhythm and speech of that truth."

One of the most well known *mantras* in Sanskrit is the *Gāyatrī* of Rishi Vishwamitra. It remains the prime mover in literature, religious practices, aesthetic experience and spiritual illumination.

> ॐ भूर्भुवः स्वः तत् सवितुर्वरेण्यम् ।
> भर्गो देवस्य धीमहि ।
> धियो यो नः प्रचोदयात् ॥ [8]

Om. Let our intelligence dwell on the beloved light of

> that creative Godhead, the Sun who is the Creator, so that he may endow us with right intelligence.

This is a prayer of supreme guardianship. Considered as the essence of the *Vedas*, its etymology explains its power: गायन्तं त्रायते इति गायत्री (*gāyantaṁ trāyate iti gāyatrī*) – 'It is known as *Gāyatrī* as it guards or protects those who recite it.' It is the name of the metre as well. With the Saviour Name of the Supreme that illumines not only what we see but what we are to be, life must need be an endless progression.

Another well known and beautiful *mantra* is the famous verse from the *Bṛhadāraṇyaka Upaniṣad*:

ॐ असतो मा सद्गमय।
तमसो मा ज्योतिर्गमय।
मृत्योर्माऽमृतं गमय ॥
ॐ शान्तिः शान्तिः शान्तिः [9]

From the unreal lead me to the Real,
From darkness lead me to Light,
From death lead me to Immortality.
Om Peace, Peace, Peace.

This is a prayer expressing the innermost aspiration of man, from time immemorial, in a language that could not be more direct and simple and yet expressive of the inspired word and inevitable utterance.

It is not easy to write poetry that is *mantra*, where the Truth directly takes on a body of speech and sound. But Sanskrit literature has often tried to realise this goal with a rare intensity and thus created a mass of mantric poetry. To quote from Nolini Kanta Gupta, "When the *Kaṭha Upaniṣad* (2:17) says:

एतदालम्बनं श्रेष्ठमेतदालम्बनं परम् ।
एतदालम्बनं ज्ञात्वा ब्रह्मलोके महीयते ॥

> This is the highest Refuge, the Refuge supreme. When one realises it, one shines in the status of the Brahman.

Or when the *Gītā* (2:56) says,

> दुःखेष्वनुद्विग्नमनाः सुखेषु विगतस्पृहः ।

> Unperturbed in the midst of sorrow, unelated in the midst of happiness

– we have poetry as *mantra*. But it is not that *mantra* means something solely dealing with spiritual disciplines or religious practices. Even the experiences and realisations of this terrestrial world can reveal themselves through the *mantra* provided their fundamental truth is the truth of delight."[10]

Sanskrit touches us at many levels. Says Dr. Vyas Houston: "Its great power lies in bringing body, mind and spirit into harmonic alignment. Physically, its resonating power promotes healing. Mentally it awakens the natural brightness, agility and order of the mind. Spiritually, it facilitates an expansion of awareness, tranquillity and bliss...there is no other language which models life itself so perfectly as Sanskrit. No other language in fact even begins to approach the power which Sanskrit has, to penetrate to the very heart of life."[11]

The Vedas

Sanskrit abounds in spiritual literature of a very high order but the three great creations that occupy an eminent place are the *Vedas*, the *Upaniṣads* and the *Gītā*.

The *Vedas* are mystic poetry of the highest order but because of their very mysticism, symbolism and antiquity, they are greatly misunderstood. Some scholars have taken them to be the early writings of Nature worshippers. But a deeper study and understanding reveals their true meaning and makes them the very fountain head of all that is great in Indian culture.

Sri Aurobindo, while explaining the true significance of the *Vedas*, says, "The Veda... stands out, apart from its interest as the world's first yet extant Scripture, its earliest interpretation of man and the Divine and the universe, as a remarkable, a sublime and powerful poetic creation. It is in its form and speech no barbaric production. The Vedic poets are masters of a consummate technique; their rhythms are carved like chariots of the gods and borne on divine and ample wings of sound, and are at once concentrated and wide-waved, great in movement and subtle in modulation; their speech, lyric by intensity and epic by elevation, an utterance of great power, pure and bold and grand in outline, a speech direct and brief in impact, full to overflowing in sense and suggestion so that each verse exists at once as a strong and sufficient thing in itself and takes its place as a large step between what came before and what comes after... The utterances of the greatest seers – Vishwamitra, Vamadeva, Dirghatamas and many others – touch the most extraordinary heights and amplitudes of a sublime and mystic poetry and there are poems like the Hymn of Creation that move in a powerful clarity on the summits of thought on which the Upanishads lived constantly with a more sustained breathing."[12]

Some Verses from the Vedas

Our purpose here is not to present the mysticism underlying the *Vedas* or to reveal the secret of their symbolism. Let us rather listen to the word of the *Veda* and attempt to feel the reverberation of the *mantras* within us. Here are a few verses from the 'Hymn to Dawn', by Rishi Kutsa, in the *Ṛgveda*:

इदं श्रेष्ठं ज्योतिषां ज्योतिरागाच्चित्रः प्रकेतो अजनिष्ट विभ्वा ।
यथा प्रसूता सवितुः सवायँ एवा रात्र्युषसे योनिमारैक् ॥ [13]

Lo, the supreme Light of lights is come:
A varied knowledge is born in front spreading
far and wide. She is born to give birth to the Sun.

Even so Night opens her womb for the Dawn.

रुशद्वत्सा रुशती श्वेत्यागादारैगु कृष्णा सदनान्यस्याः ।
समानबन्धू अमृते अनूची द्यावा वर्णं चरत आमिनाने ॥

With her reddening child, the white Mother comes blushing red: the dark Mother flings open her dark chambers. Both have the same Comrade, both are immortals, they follow each other, as they move measuring out earth and heaven and the hue beyond.

भास्वती नेत्री सूनृतानामचेति चित्रा वि दुरो न आवः ।
प्रार्प्या जगद्व्यु नो रायो अख्यदुषा अजीगर्भुवनानि विश्वा ॥

The Shining One, the Leader, she awakens the right movements: she opens wide for us many a variegated door. She moves the creation forward, she discloses for us felicity; Dawn manifests here all the worlds.

क्षत्राय त्वं श्रवसे त्वं महीया इष्टये त्वमर्थमिव त्वमित्यै ।
विसदृशा जीविताभिप्रचक्ष उषा अजीगर्भुवनानि विश्वा ॥

You are for the warrior strength; you are for the mighty Impulsion; you are the Purpose of our travelling: Dawn fronts all creatures of all varieties, she manifests here all the worlds.

उदीर्ध्वं जीवो असुर्न आगादप प्रागात् तम आ ज्योतिरेति ।
आरैक् पन्थां यातवे सूर्यायागन्म यत्र प्रतिरन्त आयुः ॥

Climb high, O soul; strength is come to us,
Darkness has fled; behold, the Light approaches.
She has opened the path for the passage of the Sun:
We go there where life is carried ever forward.

And here is the inspiring last hymn from the *Ṛgveda*, burning high with the flame of a unified and collective aspiration:

सं गच्छध्वं सं वदध्वं सं वो मनांसि जानताम् ।
देवा भागं यथा पूर्वे संजनाना उपासते ॥
समानो मन्त्रः समितिः समानी
समानं मनः सह चित्तमेषाम् ।
समानं मन्त्रमभि मन्त्रये वः
समानेन वो हविषा जुहोमि ॥
समानी व आकूतिः समाना हृदयानि वः ।
समानमस्तु वो मनो यथा वः सुसहासति ॥ [14]

Come together, all of you, speak in one voice, know with one mind, even like the gods who, of yore, knew with one mind and together had their share of enjoyment.

Together may they utter the *mantra*, may they unite together, may their mind be one, their consciousness mingle. I utter the same *mantra* with you all, with you all equally I make the offering.

May your yearning be one, may your hearts be one, may your mind be one, so that your union may be perfect.

The Upaniṣads

We now come to the *Upaniṣads*. The word *Upaniṣad* literally means 'to sit near' (the *Guru*). While writing about the *Upaniṣads* in his book, *The Foundations of Indian Culture*, Sri Aurobindo says: "The Upanishads are at once profound religious scriptures (for they are a record of the deepest spiritual experiences), documents of revelatory and intuitive philosophy of an inexhaustible light, power and largeness and, whether written in verse or cadenced prose, spiritual poems of an absolute, an unfailing inspiration inevitable in phrase, wonderful in rhythm and expression. It is the expression of a mind in which philosophy and religion does not end with a cult nor is limited to a religio-ethical aspiration, but rises to an infinite discovery of God, of Self, of our highest and whole reality of spirit and being…

Here the intuitive mind and intimate psychological experience of the Vedic seers pass into a supreme culmination in which the Spirit, as is said in a phrase of the *Kaṭha Upaniṣad*, discloses its own very body, reveals the very word of its self-expression and discovers to the mind the vibration of rhythms which repeating themselves within in the spiritual hearing seem to build up the soul and set it satisfied and complete on the heights of self-knowledge..."[15]

"The beauty of the Upanishadic verse is 'bare and austere, simple and sheer'. The *Upaniṣad* sees the beauty of the form but lays a greater stress upon what is beyond the form, what the eye cannot see nor the vision reflect. As the *Kaṭha Upaniṣad* (6:9) says,

न संदृशे तिष्ठति रूपमस्य न चक्षुषा पश्यति कश्चनैनम् ।

> Its figure does not lie in the field of vision, none can see
> it with the eye.

The form of a thing can be beautiful; but the formless too has its beauty. Indeed, the beauty of the formless, that is to say, the very sum and substance, the ultimate essence, the soul of beauty – that is what suffuses, with in-gathered colour and enthusiasm, the realisation and poetic creation of the Upanishadic seer.

The perception of beauty in the Upanishadic consciousness is something elemental – of concentrated essence. It silhouettes the main contour, outlines the primordial gestures. Pregnant and pulsating with the burden of beauty, the *mantra* here reduces its external expression to a minimum..."[16] What can be more bare and brief and full to the brim of a self-gathered luminous energy than, for example:

यत् प्राणेन न प्राणिति येन प्राणः प्रणीयते तदेव ब्रह्म....[17]

> That which lives not by Life, but which makes Life live:
> That is Brahman.

नाल्पे सुखमस्ति भूमैव सुखम् यो वै भूमा तदमृतम्
अथ यदल्पं तन्मर्त्यम्[18]

In the Little there lies no happiness, the Vast alone is the Happiness. The Vast is the Immortality, the Little is the mortality.

Some Verses from the Upaniṣads

There are, as usually accepted, 108 major *Upaniṣads* and countless minor ones. This literature is a veritable ocean. We will have to be satisfied here with just a few gems that carry with them the breath and the surge of this ocean of delight.

वृक्ष इव स्तब्धो दिवि तिष्ठत्येकः [19]

The One stands alone in the heaven motionless, like a tree against the sky.

शरवत् तन्मयो भवेत् [20]

Be wholly fixed on That, like an arrow on its target.

न ह्यध्रुवैः प्राप्यते हि ध्रुवं तत् [21]

Not by things unstable shall one attain That One which is stable.

आत्मानं रथिनं विद्धि शरीरं रथमेव तु।
बुद्धिं तु सारथिं विद्धि मनः प्रग्रहमेव च ॥
इन्द्रियाणि हयानाहुर्विषयांस्तेषु गोचरान् ।
आत्मेन्द्रियमनोयुक्तं भोक्तेत्याहुर्मनीषिणः ॥[22]

Know the body for a chariot and the soul for the master of the chariot; know reason for the charioteer and the mind for the reins only. The senses they speak of as the steeds and the objects of senses as the paths in which they move; and One yoked with self and the mind and the senses, as the enjoyer, say the thinkers.

कः शोक एकत्वमनुपश्यतः [23]

Whence shall he have grief, he who sees everywhere oneness?

अङ्गुष्ठमात्रः पुरुषो मध्य आत्मनि तिष्ठति ।...
...ईशानो भूतभव्यस्य स एवाद्य स उ श्वः॥ [24]

A conscious being, no larger than a man's thumb, stands in the centre of our self; he is master of the past and the future, he is today and he is tomorrow.

उत्तिष्ठत जाग्रत प्राप्य वरान्निबोधत ।
क्षुरस्य धारा निशिता दुरत्यया दुर्गं पथस्तत् कवयो वदन्ति ॥ [25]

Arise, awake, find out the great ones and learn of them; for sharp as a razor's edge, hard to traverse, difficult of going is that path, say the sages.

The Seeking after Immortality

न तस्य रोगो न जरा न मृत्युः प्राप्तस्य योगाग्निमयम् शरीरम् । [26]

For him who has obtained a body ablaze with the fire of *Yoga* there is no disease, no aging, no death.

The search of the *Upaniṣads* is for the Self's light and delight and immortality. The *Upaniṣad* declares human beings to be the children of immortality, अमृतस्य पुत्राः (*amṛtasya putrāḥ*), and these deep truths are often presented through beautiful stories which are very typical of the Indian mind. One of the most well-known stories is that of the young boy Nachiketas, who seeks out and confronts Yama, the Lord of Death, to win from him the secret of immortality, rejecting all the boons of worldly pleasures which men seek after.

Here is an excerpt from that magnificent dialogue between Yama and Nachiketas:

After having granted the first two boons Yama asks Nachiketas to choose the third boon. Nachiketas answers, " Well there rises a doubt as to the beings who depart from hence: some say they continue to exist, others say they do not. I want to know the truth of this matter, you please give me this knowledge. This is the third boon I ask."

येयं प्रेते विचिकित्सा मनुष्येऽस्तीत्येके नायमस्तीति चैके ।
एतद्विद्यामनुशिष्टस्त्वयाऽहं वराणामेष वरस्तृतीयः ॥[27]

This seems to create a little difficulty for Yama. He says, "You see, this debate has been going on even among the gods from times sempiternal. This is a very subtle point, this knowledge is not easy to get, nor easy to grasp. You had better ask for some other boon, do not press me further on this point, give up this quest."

देवैरत्रापि विचिकित्सितं पुरा न हि सुविज्ञेयमणुरेष धर्मः ।
अन्यं वरं नचिकेतो वृणीष्व मा मोपरोत्सीरति मा सृजैनम् ॥[28]

But, Nachiketas was not to be put off like that. He exclaims, "But this is strange! Even the gods find it a matter for debate, you too are saying it is not easily grasped. But I am not going to have another like you to speak to me about this matter. And I do not consider any other boon worth having, as compared to this."

देवैरत्रापि विचिकित्सितं किल त्वं च मृत्यो यन्न सुज्ञेयमात्थ ।
वक्ता चास्य त्वादृगन्यो न लभ्यो नान्यो वरस्तुल्य एतस्य कश्चित्॥[29]

Death, on his part tries to cajole the boy into forgetting about it, perhaps taking him to be a mere child. He says, "Nachiketas, choose sons and grandsons living to a hundred years, choose an abundance of cattle, horses and elephants, gold and jewels. Take as your portion vast stretches of land, live for as many years as you please. If, in addition, you consider any other boon equally worth having, ask for it; choose as much wealth as you like and life eternal. Or else, if you desire a whole kingdom, I shall fulfill your wish for all these desirable things."

शतायुषः पुत्रपौत्रान्वृणीष्व बहून्पशून्हस्तिहिरण्यमश्वान् ।
भूमेर्महदायतनं वृणीष्व स्वयं च जीव शरदो यावदिच्छसि ॥
एतत्तुल्यं यदि मन्यसे वरं वृणीष्व वित्तं चिरजीविकां च ।
महाभूमौ नचिकेतस्त्वमेधि कामानां त्वा कामभाजं करोमि ॥[30]

Yama goes on adding to the list of desirable things in the hope that perhaps in the end the boy can be won over: "All the desirable things that are hard to get on this mortal earth, you can demand exactly as you please. Charming damsels with their chariots and song and dance, than whom there is nothing more acceptable to men – all this I shall give you for your enjoyment at will. But do not ask any more about death."

ये ये कामा दुर्लभा मर्त्यलोके सर्वान्कामाँश्छन्दतः प्रार्थयस्व ।
इमाः रामाः सरथाः सतूर्या नहीदृशा लम्भनीया मनुष्यैः ।
आभिर्मत्प्रत्ताभिः परिचारयस्व नचिकेतो मरणं मानुप्राक्षीः ॥[31]

But Nachiketas is no mere boy or unripe youth. His reply is immediate, "All that you have named, O Destroyer, lasts only till the morrow. There is no organ or sense that does not get blunt in course of time. And even if it lasts a whole lifetime, that too is but little. Let yours, O Yama, be all those chariots and the damsels, yours the song and the dance. Man is not satisfied by riches, O Death. And here will be no dearth of wealth when I have looked upon you in person. I shall live as long as you like, but my choice is for that boon alone. You might yourself consider this. Once a mortal being dwelling here below in the grip of physical matter has felt the presence of unaging Immortals, gained the true knowledge, has realised the true nature of beauty and passion and pleasure, what joy can he have in this transient life? Tell me, O Death, more about this endless debate on what is or is not after the great annihilation. The deep secret of the beyond, it is this that I want to understand. Nachiketas demands no other boon of you."

श्वोभावा मर्त्यस्य यदन्तकैतत्सर्वेन्द्रियाणां जरयन्ति तेजः ।
अपि सर्वं जीवितमल्पमेव तवैव वाहास्तव नृत्यगीते ॥

न वित्तेन तर्पणीयो मनुष्यो लप्स्यामहे वित्तमद्राक्ष्म चेत्त्वा ।
जीविष्यामो यावदीशिष्यसि त्वं वरस्तु मे वरणीयः स एव ॥
अजीर्यताममृतानामुपेत्य जीर्यन्मर्त्यः क्वधःस्थः प्रजानन् ।
अभिध्यायन्वर्णरतिप्रमोदानतिदीर्घे जीविते को रमेत ॥
यस्मिन्निदं विचिकित्सन्ति मृत्यो यत्साम्पराये महति ब्रूहि नस्तत् ।
योऽयं वरो गूढमनुप्रविष्टो नान्यं तस्मान्नचिकेता वृणीते ॥[32]

Yama does not find it possible to put him off any more. He expounds this secret knowledge to Nachiketas. He begins with that secret Word which Nachiketas has already received and grasped all by himself.

Man has open before him two doors leading to two different paths: one is that of the good, the other of what is pleasant. The two lead in opposite directions. Nachiketas had renounced the pleasant and had chosen the good. On the basis of this choice depend, in the beginning and throughout at each step, the progress and the upward evolution of man. He alone who can recognise and choose the good gains the Highest, the supreme Reality. Nachiketas too had made these gains; he had become foremost among spiritual men, *brahmiṣṭha.*

अन्यच्छ्रेयोऽन्यदुतैव प्रेयस्ते उभे नानार्थे पुरुषँ सिनीतः ।
तयोः श्रेय आददानस्य साधु भवति हीयतेऽर्थाद्य उ प्रेयो वृणीते ॥
श्रेयश्च प्रेयश्च मनुष्यमेतस्तौ सम्परीत्य विविनक्ति धीरः ।
श्रेयो हि धीरोऽभि प्रेयसो वृणीते प्रेयो मन्दो योग क्षेमाद्वृणीते ॥
स त्वं प्रियान्प्रियरूपाँश्च कामानभिध्यायन्नचिकेतोऽत्यस्राक्षीः ।
नैतां सृङ्कां वित्तमयीमवाप्तो यस्यां मज्जन्ति बहवो मनुष्याः ॥
दूरमेते विपरीते विषूची अविद्या या च विद्येति ज्ञाता ।
विद्याभीप्सिनं नचिकेतसं मन्ये न त्वा कामा बहवोऽलोलुपन्त ॥
अविद्यायामन्तरे वर्तमानाः स्वयं धीराः पण्डितंमन्यमानाः ।
दन्द्रम्यमाणाः परियन्ति मूढा अन्धेनैव नीयमाना यथान्धाः ॥[33]

This unique dialogue between Yama and Nachiketas is found in the *Kaṭha Upaniṣad*, which contains one of the most magnificent verses in the *Upaniṣads*. Here, Rishi Yajnavalkya declares boldly: "All other lights, lights of the heaven, lights upon earth are evanescent. They pass away; the only light that endures and never fails is the light of the soul." Here is the original verse along with the beautiful translation of Sri Aurobindo, recreating in English the Upanishadic *mantra:*

> न तत्र सूर्यो भाति न चन्द्रतारकं नेमा विद्युतो भान्ति कुतोऽयमग्निः ।
> तमेव भान्तमनुभाति सर्वं तस्य भासा सर्वमिदं विभाति ॥ [34]

> There the sun cannot shine and the moon has no lustre; all the stars are blind; there our lightnings flash not, neither any earthly fire. For all that is bright is but the shadow of His brightness and by His shining all this shines.

The Gītā

As for the *Gītā*, the colloquy between Krishna and Arjuna on the battlefield of Kurukshetra, not only is it the most widely read scripture in the whole of India, but perhaps it is also the most well known Indian scripture all over the world.

About the *Gītā* Sri Aurobindo says, "The peculiarity of the Gita among the great religious books of the world is that it does not stand apart as a work by itself, the fruit of the spiritual life of a creative personality like Christ, Mohammed or Buddha or of an epoch of pure spiritual searching like the Vedas and Upanishads, but is given as an episode in an epic history of nations and their wars and men and their deeds and arises out of a critical moment in the soul of one of its leading personages, face to face with the crowning action of his life – a work terrible, violent and sanguinary, at the point when he must either recoil from it altogether or carry it through to its inexorable completion…

There are indeed three things in the Gita which are spiritually significant, almost symbolic, typical of the profoundest relations and problems of the spiritual life and of human existence at its roots; they are the divine personality of the Teacher, his characteristic relations with his disciple and the occasion of his teaching. The teacher is God himself descended into humanity; the disciple is the first, as we might say in modern language, the representative man of his age, closest friend and chosen instrument of the *Avatar*, his protagonist in an immense work and struggle, the secret purpose of which is unknown to the actors in it, known only to the incarnate Godhead who guides it all from behind the veil of his unfathomable mind of Knowledge; the occasion is the violent crisis of that work and struggle at the moment when the anguish and moral difficulty and blind violence of its apparent movements forces itself with the shock of a visible revelation on the mind of its representative man and raises the whole question of the meaning of God in the world and the goal and drift and sense of human life and conduct." [35]

But these questions are fundamental questions and do not admit of an easy answer. Nor is the solution provided by the *Gītā* a simple mental formula. The *Gītā* reveals how the Truth can be found and lived and the Divine manifested through *yoga*. The *Gītā* is a book of *sādhanā*, not merely to be read but to be practised.

Some Verses from the Gītā

We will not enter into the main thought and argument of the *Gītā* but confine ourselves to a few *ślokas* that have been repeated by millions of Indians through the ages, and have served as a source of light for spiritual seekers.

न जायते म्रियते वा कदाचिन्नायं भूत्वा भविता वा न भूयः ।
अजो नित्यः शाश्वतोऽयं पुराणो न हन्यते हन्यमाने शरीरे ॥ [36]

> This [the Self] is not born, nor does it die, nor is it a thing that comes into being once and passing away will never come into being again. It is unborn, ancient, and sempiternal, it is not slain with slaying of the body.

यदा यदा हि धर्मस्य ग्लानिर्भवति भारत ।
अभ्युत्थानमधर्मस्य तदात्मानं सृजाम्यहम् ॥
परित्राणाय साधूनां विनाशाय च दुष्कृताम् ।
धर्मसंस्थापनार्थाय सम्भवामि युगे युगे ॥ [37]

Whensoever there is the fading of the *Dharma* and the uprising of unrighteousness, then I loose myself forth into birth for the deliverance of the good, for the destruction of the evil-doers, for the enthroning of the Right, I am born from age to age.

विद्याविनयसम्पन्ने ब्राह्मणे गवि हस्तिनि ।
शुनि चैव श्वपाके च पण्डिताः समदर्शिनः ॥ [38]

Sages see with an equal eye the learned and cultured brahmin, the cow, the elephant, the dog and the outcaste.

यो न हृष्यति न द्वेष्टि न शोचति न काङ्क्षति ।
शुभाशुभपरित्यागी भक्तिमान्यः स मे प्रियः ॥ [39]

He who neither desires the pleasant and rejoices at its touch nor abhors the unpleasant and sorrows at its touch, who has abolished the distinction between fortunate and unfortunate happenings because his devotion receives all things equally as good from the hands of his eternal Lover and Master, he is dear to Me.

And here are a few verses from that magnificent description of the *Virāṭ Rūpa*, when Sri Krishna reveals himself to Arjuna, who overwhelmed bows his head and prays to the Lord:

त्वमक्षरं परमं वेदितव्यं त्वमस्य विश्वस्य परं निधानम् ।
त्वमव्ययः शाश्वतधर्मगोप्ता सनातनस्त्वं पुरुषो मतो मे ॥ [40]

Thou art the supreme Immutable whom we have to know. Thou art the high foundation and abode of the universe. Thou art the imperishable guardian of the eternal laws. Thou art I say, the sempiternal soul of existence.

अनादिमध्यान्तमनन्तवीर्यमनन्तबाहुं शशिसूर्यनेत्रम् ।
पश्यामि त्वां दीप्तहुताशवक्त्रं स्वतेजसा विश्वमिदं तपन्तम् ॥ [41]

I behold Thee without end or middle or beginning,
of infinite power and numberless arms,
Thy eyes are sun and moon.
Thou hast mouth of burning fire, burning up the whole universe by the flame of Thy energy.

द्यावापृथिव्योरिदमन्तरं हि व्याप्तं त्वयैकेन दिशश्च सर्वाः ।
दृष्ट्वाद्भुतं रूपमुग्रं तवेदं लोकत्रयं प्रव्यथितं महात्मन् ॥[42]

The whole space between earth and heaven and all directions are pervaded by Thee alone. Beholding this Thy fierce and astounding form, the three worlds are all in pain, O Thou great Spirit.

आख्याहि मे को भवानुग्ररूपो नमोऽस्तु ते देववर प्रसीद ।
विज्ञातुमिच्छामि भवन्तमाद्यं न हि प्रजानामि तव प्रवृत्तिम् ॥[43]

Declare to me who Thou art that wearest this form of fierceness. Salutation to Thee, O Thou great Godhead, turn Thy heart to grace. I wish to know Thee, O Thou who wast from the beginning, for I know not the will of Thy workings.

We will end this section on the *Gītā* with those well-known and beautiful verses revealing the supreme secret of *sādhanā* and *yoga* – a complete and unreserved surrender to the Divine.

Sri Krishna says:

मन्मना भव मद्भक्तो मद्याजी मां नमस्कुरु ।
मामेवैष्यसि सत्यं ते प्रतिजाने प्रियोऽसि मे ॥
सर्वधर्मान् परित्यज्य मामेकं शरणं व्रज ।
अहं त्वा सर्वपापेभ्यो मोक्षयिष्यामि मा शुचः ॥[44]

Become My-minded, My lover and adorer, a sacrificer to Me, bow thyself to Me; to Me thou shalt come, this is My pledge and promise to thee, for dear art thou to Me.

Abandon all *Dharmas* and take refuge in Me alone. I will deliver thee from all sin and evil, do not grieve.

A Hymn by Shankaracharya

The spiritual and sacred nature of Sanskrit will not be complete without the poetry of devotion, of *Bhakti*, full of a deep spiritual fervour, enriched with the contributions of devotees and sages through the centuries. Here are three stanzas from the famous hymn to the goddess Bhavani by Shankaracharya.

न तातो न माता न बन्धुर्न भ्राता
न पुत्रो न पुत्री न भृत्यो न भर्ता ।
न जाया न विद्या न वृत्तिर्ममैव
गतिस्त्वं गतिस्त्वं त्वमेका भवानि ॥

Nor father nor mother, nor friends nor brother,
Nor son nor daughter, nor servants nor master,
Nor bride nor learning nor profession have I:
Thou art the refuge, thou the sole refuge, O Bhavani!

न जानामि दानं न च ध्यानयोगं
न जानामि तन्त्रं न च स्तोत्रमन्त्रम् ।
न जानामि पूजां न च न्यासयोगं
गतिस्त्वं गतिस्त्वं त्वमेका भवानि ॥

I know neither benefaction nor meditation nor yoga,
Nor do I know secret practices nor charms nor chants occult;
I know not rites of worship, nor the process of renouncing:
Thou art the refuge, thou the sole refuge, O Bhavani!

न जानामि पुण्यं न जानामि तीर्थं
न जानामि मुक्तिं लयं वा कदाचित् ।
न जानामि भक्तिं व्रतं वाऽपि मात-
र्गतिस्त्वं गतिस्त्वं त्वमेका भवानि ॥ [45]

I know not virtue, I know not pilgrimage,
I know not liberation, nor any annihilation either,
I know not devotion nor even ascetic discipline, O Mother;
Thou art the refuge, thou the sole refuge, O Bhavani!

sanskrit as the national language of india

Sanskrit as the National Language of India

We have seen the important role Sanskrit has played in India's past. And this brings us naturally to the role it has to play in India's future. The Nobel Laureate physicist, Dr. C.V. Raman, believed that Sanskrit was the only language that could be the national language of India. He said, "Sanskrit flows through our blood. It is only Sanskrit that can establish the unity of the country." It is true that a national language is a very important element in the growth and self-actualisation of a people and a nation. It helps to develop and also to give expression to their heart, mind and soul. Says Sri Aurobindo, "It is of the utmost value to a nation, a human group-soul, to preserve its language and to make of it a strong and living cultural instrument. A nation, race or people which loses its language, cannot live its whole life or its real life."[1]

We have to ask ourselves what are the requirements of a national language and which language of India meets best these requirements. Firstly, a national language should be national in the true sense, that is, it should have taken birth in the country and be capable of expressing its special ethos and genius. It cannot be a foreign language, even though the foreign language may be widely spoken. Therefore, straight away we cannot consider English as the national language of India, though it is spoken all over the country and may even have a special role to play in the future. The national language of India has to be a language of and from India.

The national language has to express the many facets of the genius, culture and heritage of the country in diverse fields. And without doubt, one can say that no other Indian language has such a rich treasure of noblest thoughts, highest achievements in religion and philosophy, in art and literature, in science and technology, in dance and music, architecture and sculpture, than Sanskrit. It is for the sake of this knowledge and wisdom that, through the centuries, travellers and seekers from all over have come to India. Even in the present times scholars from the West and the East are studying and translating Indian texts, a majority of which are in Sanskrit. But unfortunately, most Indians now come into contact with our ancient wisdom not by studying them in the original but through English translations. So much so that "English lexicons, and English histories of Sanskrit language and literature, English estimates of our writers and expositions of our texts, secular and religious – these are our standard authorities and references." This has also inevitably led to many distortions and misinterpretations and if we want to find the roots of our culture, its greatness and its living force, we have to go once again to Sanskrit. It will not be an exaggeration to say that if India has to rise, Sanskrit will have to rise once again.

A third requirement of a national language is that it must not be too closely identified with any particular region of the country. Every Indian language we may think of, whether it is Gujarati, Bengali, Tamil, Telegu, Malayalam, Punjabi or Assamese, is closely identified with one state or region. Hindi alone is perhaps not identified with a particular province but still it is regional in the sense that it belongs to the north of India. Sanskrit alone is non-regional. No province or state or people can claim it as its own. It has not sprung up in one area. It belongs to the whole of India and has been used in the whole of India for centuries.

Recent archeological and historical researches have shown that it was the link language from ancient times for the entire Indian subcontinent. Jean Filliozat, the well known French Indologist observes, "While Middle-India dialects and other languages were local, Sanskrit was universal throughout India. It was fully known by a few people only, but everywhere; and it was superficially known by more numerous people mixing it with local language."[2]

Sanskrit alone, even if it was the mother tongue of a limited number of groups or families, and in spite of its sophisticated shape, was regularly taught everywhere in traditional schools.[3] In fact, Sanskrit has always been the binding force except for a short period when it was replaced by Pali and the Prakrits. However, it soon regained its importance during the middle ages. It became a sort of common link language among the speakers of different mother tongues. Thus, in his *Naiṣadhīyacarita*, Sriharsha describes the kingly suitors of Damayanti, from all parts of India, as speaking to each other in Sanskrit to avoid unintelligibility. Rajashekhara, in his *Kāvyamīmāṁsā*, written in the 10th century A.D., says that the Magadha king Sisunaga and the Ujjain ruler Sahasanka insisted that the royal women should speak only in Sanskrit. Another poet, Bilhana, in the 11th century, mentions in his *Vikramāṅkadevacarita* that in Kashmir, in every house Sanskrit was spoken like the mother tongue. Shankara, born in the Southern state of Kerala, travelled and debated with scholars all over the country and established *maṭhas* in the four corners of this land. This became possible only through Sanskrit, the link language, which was understood in all parts of the country.[4]

Sanskrit and other Indian Languages

If Sanskrit was so widespread over the whole of India and was the common language of communication, it no doubt had a very special relation with and a great influence on all Indian languages. "The ideas, the literary forms and even the themes of the literature of our great regional languages are predominantly derived from Sanskrit.

For proper use of a large percentage of words, even in Dravidian languages, an understanding of Sanskrit is necessary; the great classics of India, not only the *Rāmāyaṇa* and the *Mahābhārata*, but the masterpieces from which everyone in India draws his inspiration from the simple *Pañcatantra* to *Śakuntalā*, are in Sanskrit, and it is on their translations and their vulgarisations that our minds are fed and nourished from childhood."[5]

The relation of Sanskrit with North Indian languages is obvious. Sanskrit is universally accepted as the mother of all North Indian languages – Hindi, Bengali, Assamese, Oriya, Rajasthani, Gujarati, Marathi, Punjabi, Kashmiri, Maithali, Sindhi etc. They are all derived from and rooted in Sanskrit in their vocabulary, syntax and grammatical structure. These languages belong to the Indo-Aryan group and contain four types of words:

1. *Tatsama* – words which are the same as in Sanskrit
2. *Tadbhava* – words which are derived from Sanskrit
3. *Deśya* – words peculiar to the language and the region
4. *Vaideśika* – words borrowed from foreign languages

A proper study of all North Indian languages would show that more than 70 percent of the words in these languages are *Tatsama* and *Tadbhava*, that is, they have been taken directly from Sanskrit or are derived from Sanskrit. This is why there are a very large number of words like हस्त, पाद, करुणा, दान, महान् (*hasta*, *pāda*, *karuṇā*, *dāna*, *mahān*) found in all North Indian languages. We find that when a person speaks in one North Indian language it is often possible for another North Indian to understand even though he may not know that language. This is because, along with the vocabulary, there is a very great similarity in the sentence structure.

In fact all the North Indian languages have basically the same alphabet, similar classifications and the same grammar. So much so that when Hemachandra wrote the first non-Sanskrit grammar his concluding remark was "...Whatever you cannot find in this *apabhraṁśa* grammar, is the same as it is in the Sanskrit grammar."

The situation is slightly different with the South Indian languages – Telugu, Kannada, Malayalam and Tamil. These languages belong to what is known as the Dravidian group and there is a feeling among some that they do not have a close relationship with Sanskrit. This again is a misconception. If we take the example of Telugu, out of forty thousand words in a modern Telugu dictionary, nearly twenty-five thousand, that is 65 percent of the words, would be derived from Sanskrit. A large number of important literary works in Sanskrit have been adapted or translated into Telugu and often the Sanskrit vocabulary has been retained and Telugu endings added.

The same applies to Kannada and Malayalam in slightly different degrees. An interesting point to note is that many of the early grammars for Kannada, Malayalam and Telugu were written in Sanskrit, with commentary and explanatory notes in Sanskrit and modelled on the Paninian system. And in Kerala an entire poetical sytle came into existence, with its own literature, freely employing a large number of Sanskrit words with Malayalam endings, and a strong influence of Sanskrit metres and figures of speech. This special literary dialect came to be called *Maṇipravālam*, meaning a necklace strung with 'pearls and corals'. But what about Tamil? Even here we find a close relationship when we look at the alphabet, the syntax and even the vocabulary, though it may be to a lesser degree. In fact the cultural and historical bond between the Dravidian languages and Sanskrit has been very strong. The four great Acharyas who wrote major *Bhāṣya*s or commentaries on the *Bhagavadgītā* – Shankara, Ramanuja, Vallabha and Madhva – were all from the South. These commentaries are all in Sanskrit and are studied as authoritative interpretations of the *Gītā* by seekers and scholars from all over India. Sanskrit has been the language of prayer and worship in the temples all over the South from times immemorial.

The great Sayana, who wrote the well-known commentary on the *Vedas*, lived in the Vijayanagara Empire. The other two Vedic commentators, Venkatamadhava and Bharatasvamin, were under the

Cholas and the Hoysalas. Mallinathasuri, who commented on the works of Kalidasa, was a Telugu speaker. Kumarila Bhatta and Appaya Dikshita were great scholars from the South and enriched Sanskrit language by their works.

Although early Tamil literature, for example the *Saṅgam* texts, shows certain special characteristics that are perhaps unique to Tamil, it is fully within the ambit of Sanskrit. As Sivajnana-munivar has said in his commentary on the *Tolkāppiyam*, the oldest extant grammar of Tamil: "The nature of Tamil will not be clear to those who have not learnt Sanskrit". Tamil of the oldest *Saṅgam* texts shows a very good number of Sanskrit words, and the number goes on increasing with the centuries.

There was a time when the Mayapith Empire was established by the Tamil kings in Cambodia, Thailand, Vietnam and Malaya by Emperor Vijay. In the 12th century A.D. these Tamil kings made Sanskrit the state language of these countries. The Andhra people established the Moan Empire in Burma, which extended from Pegu to Mandalaya. The state language of this Empire was Sanskrit and it remained so up to the 12th Century A.D. Take the case of Malayasia, where people from both Tamil and Andhra nationality dwelled. Malaya's last king was Parameswaran. He adopted the Arabic script but the state language continued to be Sanskrit till about 150 years ago.

It is significant to read what the great Tamil poet Subramania Bharati wrote under the title '*Oḷir Maṇi Kovai*' for *Swadesha Mitran,* which was later on reproduced in the June 1942 issue of *Kalaimagaḷ*: "Elders such as Gandhiji are of the opinion that Hindi may be offered as the common language for India. But Aurobindo Ghose, who may be rightly called the greatest of the Indian patriots, and many others speak of Sanskrit as the common language of India. They say that it is not a new status to be conferred upon Sanskrit; it has enjoyed it from ancient times. For instance, before the advent of the British rule in this country, in which language would a king from Tamil Nadu have written to a king in Gujarat if he wanted to communicate with him? If it were in Tamil the Gujarati king would not have understood it, and it would not have been possible for the Tamil king to write in Gujarati. Hence their communication had to be in Sanskrit, a language in which the pandits, the Rajagurus and the chief ministers of both the States were equally well-versed. Is that not evident?

Some people state that it will not be practical to keep Sanskrit as the common language for the whole country, since it is difficult to learn Sanskrit and acquire proficiency in it. This is perhaps true if we were to follow the old way of learning. But we do not need to do that any more. Now Shri Bhandarkar, a pandit from Bombay, has written primers through which one can learn Sanskrit in seven or eight months without the help of a teacher. Of these, the first book has already been translated into Tamil. This method can be even further simplified. In fact, anyone who reads the *Pañcatantra* three times with an understanding of its meaning and learns it by heart, should acquire the ability to speak Sanskrit fluently. It may take some more time to be familiar with the strenuous style of Bana and Bhatti; but for a common use, works like the *Pañcatantra* which are written in a simple style are sufficient."[6]

If such are the views and feelings of a poet and a patriot like Subramania Bharati, then why has there been recently such a strong opposition to Sanskrit in the South? We must first realise that this is a relatively recent phenomenon and for centuries Sanskrit and Tamil have not only lived together but enriched one another. The opposition has never come from persons who were educated in the true sense of the word, who had the necessary catholicity and depth of vision. In fact the eminent Tamil scholar, Dr. V. Raghavan who has written several books on Sanskrit, claims that it is possible to speak in Tamil sentences made entirely of Sanskrit words and to be understood.

The reasons for the recent divide are to be found in human folly and ignorance. One of the historical aberrations that has fuelled this controversy is the widely accepted idea of the Aryan invasion into India by which the original Dravidian inhabitants were driven down into the South, leading to a constant conflict and opposition. Fortunately, now more and more historians are realising that this theory has no factual basis and was wrongly propounded by some Western historians, and Aryan and Dravidian, North and South are two aspects of the same Indian culture.

A Capacity to Grow

It is obvious that there is no language apart from Sanskrit which has such a close relationship with all the other languages of India. But there is another characteristic of Sanskrit that is of great importance. A national language must have at its command a storehouse of a very large vocabulary to meet the demands of a vast range of subjects and disciplines, from science to spirituality, art to animals, from philosophy to information technology. Sanskrit fulfills these requirements admirably. "Look at the wonderful pageant of Sanskrit literature, in arts, crafts, science and politics, in concrete spheres and in realms of abstractions and speculations. Its *Śilpa*, *Gaṇita*, *Rasāyana*, *Āyurveda*, *Jyotiṣa*, *Arthaśāstra* and *Dharmaśāstra* literature forms a mine of technical terms which can assist efficiently in the rendering into an Indian medium all kinds of knowledge now known and learnt from English."[7]

But this vocabulary can be static, while the demand of the changing times and the explosion of information and knowledge in every field require that the language should have within itself sufficient growing power or vitality, to put forth fresh forms to tackle the new and vastly expanded needs. As has been pointed out by several reputed scholars, the wonderful grammatical structure of Sanskrit is such that the language has an eternal fecundity and an incredible capacity to widen itself without losing its genius and individuality.

Therefore, apart from its own vitality, growth and adaptability, Sanskrit can serve and has been serving as a feeder language for other Indian languages. "The reason for this lies in the linguistic structure of Sanskrit language which possesses high potentiality in affixation and word-compounding and richness in abstract concepts and discursive terms, besides being a rich store-house of knowledge."[8]

In the words of the noted Indologist Monier Williams, "India, though it has, as we have seen, more than 500 spoken dialects, has only one sacred language and only one sacred literature, accepted and revered by all... however diverse in race, dialect, rank and creed. That language is Sanskrit and that literature is Sanskrit literature... the only quarry whence the requisite materials may be obtained for improving the vernaculars or for expressing important religious and scientific ideas."[9]

A Source of Unity and Pride

A vast and diverse country like India needs a national language that can unify and harmonise. We have seen that Sanskrit was this great unifying force for centuries. Even when India was not a single political unit, Sanskrit made the Indian people one in spirit, heart and culture.

Now when India has attained political unity, but is being torn apart by various divisive forces, the role of Sanskrit becomes even more important. Any other language will add to the divisive tendencies. It is only Sanskrit which can help India and Indians to rise above narrow regional and linguistic factionalism and to grow in oneness and unity.

A national language must not only unite but give its people a sense of pride in their past, a sense of belonging to the present, a sense of hope and confidence for the future. It must bring to them a feeling of fulfillment in their achievements and have the power to mould their character and to inspire them to greater endeavours, attainments and heights.

"Sanskrit is a language which through its contents, sonority and mellifluousness, has the power to lift us up above ourselves – it is, as thousands of people would say from their own experience, a potent aid to the formation of character and sense of exaltation, in addition to ensuring a sense of pan-Indian cultural as well as political unity."[10]

Through Sanskrit every Indian can feel a oneness and belonging with every other Indian and with every part of India. We can feel proud of a great and magnificent heritage, which can compare with the best in the world in every field, and to which every region of India has contributed. We can look to the future with the confidence that this mighty nation will rise again and attain a glory far greater than ever attained in the past, and in which every Indian has a role to play.

some doubts and questions

Some Doubts and Questions

Is Sanskrit a Hindu Language?

It would be good at this stage to look at some of the objections that have been raised against Sanskrit becoming the national language of India. One argument, which is often used nowadays, is that Sanskrit is predominantly a Hindu language – and with India being a multi-religious country, how is it possible for the Muslims and the Christians to accept Sanskrit?

This argument has no basis, as a language cannot be Hindu. Just because the Ganga or the Himalayas are worshipped by Hindus, it does not make them 'Hindu'. Even though the Taj Mahal was built by Shah Jahan it does not become a 'Muslim' monument, and similarly Urdu is not a Muslim language simply because many Muslims use it.

All these are the heritage and the pride of the whole of India. We must also realise that all literature in Sanskrit can by no means be considered purely religious or sectarian in character. There is in Sanskrit a considerable amount of technical, scientific and secular literature. Works on polity like the *Arthaśāstra* of Kautalya or on architecture like the *Mānasāra*, the *Samarāṅgaṇa-sūtradhāra* and the *Aparājitāpṛccha*, as also many other treatises relating to the *Kalās*, can certainly not be characterised as religious. We must not forget, in this context, the pure literature embodied in the various types of Sanskrit drama and poetry.

It must be further pointed out that the large mass of literature in Sanskrit was not produced by any particular community. Several instances can be quoted of non-brahmin and non-Hindu authors who have made significant contributions to Sanskrit literature.*[1] It is definitely misleading to assume that Sanskrit represents only the religious literature of the Hindus.

This aspect of Sanskrit not being exclusively religious, was appreciated even by some of the Muslim rulers of India, who patronised Sanskrit literature, and, in some cases (as in Bengal and Gujarat), had their epigraphic records inscribed in Sanskrit. It was the scientific and secular aspect of Sanskrit literature that made the Arabs welcome Indian scholars to Baghdad to discourse on sciences like medicine and astronomy, and to translate books in these subjects into Arabic. The *Āyurveda* system of medicine, until recently, was the truly national Indian system, which was practised everywhere, and access to this was through Sanskrit books, which even Muslim practitioners of the *Āyurveda* in Bengal studied.

Or we can take the case of Kashmir. A large majority of people there are converts to Islam. But the language of Kashmir was the

* To give only one instance: Khan Khanan Nawab Abdur Rahim was an important officer in the court of Akbar. He had a genuine love for Sanskrit. Not only was he a Sanskrit lover, he wrote some scholarly books in Sanskrit. His *Kheṭakautukam* is an astrological work dealing with the influence of the planets on human beings. *Rahima Kāvyam* is another work of his, in which he writes about the Hindu-Muslim unity of the time. Daraf Khan Gazi was a Sanskrit scholar who lived towards the end of the 13th century A.D. He wrote eight beautiful verses on Ganga called '*Gaṅgāṣṭakam*', which were published in the 16th issue of the "Journal of Asiatic Society of Bengal', in 1847.

language of *Loka Prakash* for centuries, including the Moghul period. This book was written in Sanskrit and had been current in the society from the 5th century B.C. up to the 16th century A.D. for more than 2000 years. Of course during the time when the rule of Islam was established in Kashmir, a few words of Arabic and Persian entered in *Loka Prakash* but its language remained the same, namely Sanskrit.[2]

Even in modern times there have been Muslim scholars and lovers of Sanskrit. It is significant that when the bill on the National Language of India was being discussed in the Constituent Assembly, soon after independence, it was a Muslim, Shri Najiruddin Ahmed, who proposed that the national language of India should be Sanskrit. He asked rhetorically, "If you have to adopt a language, why should you not have the world's greatest language?" He also quoted Dr. Shaidullah, Professor of Dhaka University and a great Sanskrit scholar, as saying, "Sanskrit is the language of every man, to whatever race he may belong."[3]

Is Sanskrit a Dead and Difficult Language?

Whenever there is a demand for Sanskrit as the national language it is met with the opposition: 'How can a dead language be the national language of a country?'

In the words of Professor Lakshmikanta Maitra, "I know it will be said that it is a dead language. But dead to whom? Dead to you, because you have become dead to all sense of grandeur. You have become dead to all that is great and rich in your own culture and civilisation. You have been chasing the shadow and never tried to grasp the substance which is contained in your great literature. If Sanskrit is dead, may I say that Sanskrit is ruling us from her grave. Nobody can get away from Sanskrit in India."[4]

"To call Sanskrit dead is only to utter a cheap slogan. Even *Saṅgam* Tamil is dead, even Tulasi's Hindi is dead; Sanskrit is not so dead as even these. It can be denied only by one who makes bold to deny the roots of a tree, the ether that pervades us on every side, or our inner being, merely because these are not visible to the eyes. When the great philologists and scholars of computational linguistics whole-heartedly accept Sanskrit as the best and most scientific language of the world, on what basis can one say that Sanskrit is a dead language? One should always remember that a natural language never dies. It is the artificially created language that dies. Sanskrit being a natural language, there is no question of its death. It is alive in the heart and mind of the people of India." As Professor Sampurnananda has said, 'Sanskrit is not merely alive, it is also a medicine to make the dead alive.'[5]

To be an official language it is not necessary that the language should be the language of the masses. Today we have English as an official language of India and we have fought for it. It is the language of only the intelligentsia, and has been accepted in the Constitution as the official language of the Union. In that way Sanskrit has always been the language of the intelligentsia in India. Sir William Jones carried out extensive researches in 1786 and came to the conclusion that for a long time Sanskrit was the language of administration for courts and used for other official purposes. The University Education Commission presided over by Dr. S. Radhakrishnan, later the President of India, came to the conclusion that "Sanskrit was all the time the lingua-franca of the world of learning in India, and this position it has held all the time in India."[6]

There are thousands of Sanskrit institutions in India and abroad engaged in research in Sanskrit and in its propagation. Almost all universities in India have departments of Sanskrit. There are special Sanskrit universities, colleges and schools where Sanskrit is taught through Sanskrit only. Most of the high schools in India offer Sanskrit as an optional subject. Every year hundreds of research theses are prepared by Sanskrit scholars. Sanskrit magazines and journals are being published by many institutions, and number over a thousand at present. Thousands of people use this language as their mother tongue. The news in Sanskrit is broadcast by All India Radio and by Delhi Doordarshan and has many listeners.

There are some villages like Matur in Shimoga district in Karnataka where several people from all walks of life communicate in Sanskrit only. A number of original writings in Sanskrit are created every year. The Sanskrit scholars of this country are tirelessly engaged in bringing out original works in Sanskrit in every field. Every year many prestigious awards are given to the outstanding scholars in the field of research, translations and original writings in Sanskrit. How then can one say that Sanskrit is dead?

Hebrew appeared to be a dead language for a long time in Israel. It was mainly the language of study and prayer. The people of Israel realized its value and made efforts to revive it. And due to their deep love and interest, it successfully became their national language in a short time. Now Hebrew is a language of the day-to-day life of the people of Israel. This should be our spirit as regards Sanskrit. Sri Aurobindo warns that "...it will not be a good day for India when the ancient tongue ceases entirely to be written or spoken."[7]

As for the difficulty of learning, this is not something peculiar to Sanskrit. "To decry it as difficult is to practice a *vibhīṣaka* [scarecrow] before the young and unthinking. There is no language whose learning is easy. People in Tamil Nadu know how difficult it is to learn Hindi. To them Sanskrit is much easier. If they can learn the broken syllables of Hindi, why can they not, with less labour, learn the fuller, and more perfect Sanskrit itself! There is an illuminating passage in Tagore's *Reminiscences*, where the poet records the reactions to his teaching Bengali to Scot girls, and says with reference to the erratic nature of English pronunciation, that the difficulties of one language are the same as those of another and that habit blinds one to those of his own. In a recent address Professor S.K. Belvelkar pointed out that considering the success that a totally foreign language like English, with all its tricks of pronunciation, had in India, it should be very easy for Sanskrit to succeed."[8]

Furthermore, Sanskrit itself provides us many clues and possibilities of simplification, which can make it very easily a language of daily use and mass communication. It is not necessary to enter into the details of this work here, but there is already a vast amount of literature available on this subject. It is therefeore both strange and sad to see the lack of understanding about the importance and value of Sanskrit in India itself, and the lack of interest in its study and learning.When Prof. Sheldon Pollock of the University of Chicago was asked why one should study Sanskrit, he replied, "It is indicative of the appalling quality of the public discourse on Sanskrit in India today that you even ask this question."[9] And Prof. Richard Gombrich who holds the Boden chair at Oxford says, "The reasons for studying Sanskrit today are the same as they ever were: that the vast array of Sanskrit texts preserves for us a valuable part of the cultural heritage of mankind, including much beautiful literature and many interesting, even fascinating, ideas."[10]

the language of india's soul

The Language of India's Soul

A Common National Inheritance

So deeply is Sanskrit ingrained in its national consciousness, that when India became free and tried to express its aspirations in every field, it looked to Sanskrit for inspiration and fulfilment. It gave itself the ancient Sanskrit name, *Bhārata*. India's national motto is the wonderful exhortation from the *Taittirīya Upaniṣad*, सत्यमेव जयते (*satyameva jayate*) –'Truth alone triumphs'.The national anthem and the national song of India, *Jana Gaṇa Mana* composed by Rabindranath Tagore and *Vande Mātaram* by Bankim Chandra Chatterjee, are 90 percent Sanskrit and 10 percent Sanskritic, and hence are understood all over India. The motto of the Lok Sabha, the lower house of the Indian Parliament, is धर्मचक्रप्रवर्तनाय (*dharmacakrapravartanāya*) – 'For the promulgation of the Wheel of Law'. All India Radio has adopted as its guiding principle and motto the Sanskrit expression बहुजनहिताय बहुजनसुखाय (*bahujanahitāya bahujanasukhāya*) – 'For the good of the many and for the happiness of the many'. The Life Insurance Corporation's motto, योगक्षेमं वहाम्यहम् (*yogakṣemaṁ vahāmyaham*), is a quotation from the *Bhagavadgītā* meaning 'I take responsibility for access and security'. The Indian Navy has accepted as its motto the Vedic invocation शं नो वरुणः (*śaṁ no varuṇaḥ*), meaning 'May Varuna, the god of the waters, be auspicious for us'.

Indeed, the soul of India has spoken through Sanskrit. "Sanskrit is the one common national inheritance of India. The South and the North, the West and the East have equally contributed to it. No part of India can claim it as its exclusive possession."[1] And the subjects and topics covered too range from religion to mathematics, philosophy to drama, politics to architecture, horses and elephants. So great has been the identity between Sanskrit and India's life, thought and culture, that the Russian linguist, Professor V.V. Ivanov, was led to exclaim, "The very notion of India is hardly conceivable without Sanskrit, which has symbolised and cemented the unity of Indian culture throughout several millennia."[2]

Unity in Diversity

India is a continent in itself. The people of India come from different racial stock, profess different religions, adhere to different languages and follow different customs and manners. In the midst of all this diversity they possess, however, certain common ideas, cherish certain common ideals, conform to certain common codes of conduct in secular and religious life, and thus feel and cultivate a sense of unity. This fundamental unity has been possible because all Indians are inheritors of the same unique culture and the principal language of this culture is Sanskrit.[3]

The noted historian K.M. Panikkar says, "When we talk of our national genius being unity in diversity, of the fundamental oneness of the Indian mind, what we really mean is the dominance of Sanskrit, which overrides the regional differences and linguistic peculiarities and achieves a true national character in our thoughts and emotions and even gives form and shape to the languages. So far as I know there has never been an instance in world history when a language was able to establish its unchallenged authority over a whole subcontinent and be its permanently unifying factor for over a thousand years. Sanskrit is India's one national language...and the unity of India will collapse if it ceases to be related to Sanskrit or breaks away from the Sanskrit tradition. Sanskrit alone has that pre-eminence over the great regional languages, enabling her to maintain and uphold in every region of India the supreme claim of Indian unity. It may indeed be said that one who knows Sanskrit is a better Indian for he is in a position to appreciate what every part of India has contributed to it.

With Vyasa he can roam about in the forests and pilgrimage centres of the whole country, with Valmiki he can visit Lanka, with Kalidasa see the glories of Ujjain, walk in the Himalayan valleys, or follow the cloud from Ramagiri to Kailash, with Bhartrihari contemplate on the vanities of the world, with the merchants of Somadeva travel to Dvipantaras and even to Kanakapuri, with Shudraka live the life of a gay *nāgarika*. Kalhana makes us live with the kings of Kashmir. With Jonaraja we share in the glory of Prithviraja. We take from Jayadeva some of his ecstasy, from Hemachandra Suri his gift of being able to illumine almost anything. With queen Gangadevi of Vijaynagar we march on Madura. With Bhavabhuti we sport on the Godavari. With Dandin we are at the Pallava court at Kanchi. With Narayana Bhatta we are in Kerala. With Jagannatha Pandit we taste a little of the magnificence of Shah Jahan." [4]

The concept of the unity of all India, from the Himalayas to the sea, हिमवत् सेतुपर्यन्तम् (*himavat setuparyantam*), has existed from ancient times. It finds expression in the *Viṣṇupurāṇa*, where this country and its people are described:

उत्तरं यत् समुद्रस्य हिमाद्रेश्चैव दक्षिणम् ।
वर्षं तद् भारतं नाम भारती यत्र सन्ततिः ॥ [5]

> The land which is north to the ocean, south to the Himalaya, and where the inhabitants are called Bharati, know that to be the land of Bharatavarsha.

Who does not know the stupendous passage with which Kalidasa begins his *Kumārasambhavam.* To be in the Himalayan region and to gaze at the sublimity of the tremendous peaks is to remember, with a thrill, how our poet nearly two thousand years ago had spoken of the Himalayas as constituting the backbone of the earth. The living experience of the fundamental unity of India finds expression in several ancient texts. We find it in the concept of the 'seven rivers' situated in different parts of the country:

> गङ्गे च यमुने चैव गोदावरि सरस्वति ।
> नर्मदे सिन्धुकावेरि जलेऽस्मिन् सन्निधिं कुरु ॥[6]

> O Ganga! O Yamuna! O Godavari! O Saraswati! O Narmada! O Sindhu and Kaveri! Come altogether and be present in this water!

The concept of the 'seven places of pilgrimage', the concept of the 'seven hills', the concept of oneness led to the setting up of *Śaiva* and *Vaiṣṇava* sacred sites, from Amarnath, Kedarnath and Badrinath in the North to Kanyakumari in the South, from Kamakhya and Chandranath in the East to Dwaraka and even Hinglaj (Baluchistan) in the West.

Sanskrit literature teaches us that not only did this land have a geographical unity but a life of its own, which demanded the love of its people. This love is enshrined in the *Rāmāyaṇa* couplet where Rama tells Lakshman: जननीजन्मभूमिश्च स्वर्गादपि गरियसी (*jananī janmabhūmiśca svargādapi garīyasī*), 'The mother and the motherland are greater than heaven'. This is by no means an exceptional statement, for in the *Mahābhārata* we are told of this *Bhārata* being श्रेष्ठ (*śreṣṭha*) –'the greatest', the land where one should dedicate oneself to work, कर्मभूमि (*karmabhūmi*), an idea repeated in the *Rāmāyaṇa* where one is directed to do one's duty even in difficult conditions, in this land where we are born for work that is aimed at welfare: कर्मभूमिमिमां प्राप्य कर्तव्यं कर्म यत् शुभम् (*karmabhūmimimām prāpya kartavyam karma yat śubham*) .

Beyond Indian Borders

But the extent and reach of Sanskrit was not confined to the borders of India. With the spread of Indian culture and specially the spread of Buddhism, Sanskrit became a medium of communication with foreign countries too. Says Jean Filliozat, "Sanskrit was the only link-language from Afghanistan up to Kanyakumari between the Indian communities. So the post-vedic religions were able to compose their scriptures directly in Sanskrit.

Almost all Indian epigraphy outside India is in Sanskrit. The most ancient Indian inscription in Indochina, the epigraph of Vocanh on the Eastern Coast, a document from about the 3rd century A.D. is in Sanskrit. The seals discovered in Low Cochin China by Dr.Malleret, and documents of a little later date, are chiefly in Sanskrit. In Indochina, particularly in Cambodia, we can trace many influences from South India, from Tamil countries, and that through Sanskrit inscriptions. In South India itself, the inscriptions of the important dynasty of the Pallavas, after having been at first in *Prākṛt*, are in Sanskrit. Tamil people themselves, though preserving their own splendid literary tradition side by side with cultivating Sanskrit literature, wrote frequently in Sanskrit as well as in Chentamil, that is to say, literary Tamil. Barring the period of Muslim invasion, in all parts of India and in countries abroad receiving Indian influences, Sanskrit became till the Muslim invasion, and remained later, the chief language of broad communication."[7]

India's Gift to the World

If Sanskrit can find its true place in India it will also help India find its true place in the world. For among all the languages of India, it is Sanskrit that is identified the most with Indian civilisation and culture, with all that is priceless and is India's gift to the world.

The *Upaniṣads* and the *Gītā* have been sources of inspiration for spiritual seekers and philosophers; Panini is admired by grammarians the world over. The *Rāmāyaṇa* and *Mahābhārata* are being translated in numerous languages. Books on Buddhism are becoming increasingly popular and people are looking for new insights into Indian sciences, arts, dance and music. Says Professor Max Mueller: "We can hardly understand how, at so early a date, the Indians had developed ideas which to us sound decidedly modern. Some of the riddles of the future find their solution in the wisdom of the past."[8]

More and more universities are offering courses in Sanskrit as part of their programmes on Indology. It is by far the most famous of all Indian languages, studied the world over by those who want to understand India and its culture. The French scholar Dr. Lui Reno asserts, "There is not a living culture without a living tradition. If India is beloved and cherished among the elite of the West, it is on account of her traditional culture. And this culture is embedded above all in the treasures of Sanskrit. Sanskrit and India are inseparably connected in spite of all the transitory harangues of the politicians."[9]

In fact Sanskrit is related not only to all Indian languages but has a close link with most Western languages as well. In the large family tree of the world's languages, Sanskrit belongs to the Indo-European branch and occupies a central position there. Nearly all European languages belong to this branch, with a few exceptions such as Finnish, Hungarian and Basque. Some of the more well-known Sanskrit relatives are Greek, Latin, French, Italian, Russian, English and German. All of these tongues have developed from the so-called Proto-Indo-European, which was spoken thousands of years ago, according to the assumption of some linguists who have reconstructed this language with sophisticated methods.

About the eminence of Sanskrit in this family, we may quote some scholars of repute. Says Dr. Ballantyne: "All languages of the Indo-European family have been derived from Sanskrit."[10] Sir William Jones remarks: "The study of comparative philosophy tends to show that Sanskrit is the mother of all Indo-European languages. From the Sanskrit were derived the original roots and the essentially necessary words which form the basis of all these languages. In other words, the part that is common to all or most of the languages of this group is supplied to each language by Sanskrit."[11]

Not only in the West, but in the countries of South-East Asia closer to India, Sanskrit has made a significant contribution. After a pioneering research Jean Filliozat wrote: "Sanskrit has played in India and around India the same role that Latin played in the old Europe or Persian for a time, and above all the role English today plays.

Though the propagation of Sanskrit has been very large through the continent of Asia, its influence and its adaptation in South-East Asia has been much greater. There, it has not merely been imported and translated: it has flourished. More than one thousand Sanskrit inscriptions, often very long and in *kāvya* style, have been found in Champa, Cambodia and Indonesia, from the 3rd till the 13th century. They give a clear evidence of the high level of Indian culture in those countries... It is also well-known that Shaivism and Buddhism, with Sanskrit texts, have been preserved till today in Bali Island (where the name for 'religion' is the Sanskrit word *āgama*) as well as in Java and in the modern Indonesian language.

There is a strong evidence, during the long centuries, of the use of literary Sanskrit in the inscriptions. Sanskrit was not confined to literary circles and had echoes in the colloquial and ordinary languages. Otherwise, how can one explain the popular languages of Champa, Cambodia, Burma, Thailand, Laos, Malaysia and Indonesia, which have incorporated many Sanskrit words?"[12]

The Language of India's Soul

What has been the place of Sanskrit in ancient India? What role has it played in its development? And what is its significance for the future? To find an answer to these questions we have to turn to those who have loved India and entered deep into its culture, its ethos and its history. And there is no better person to begin than Jawaharlal Nehru, the first Prime Minister of free India and the author of the famous book *The Discovery of India.* He says in most categorical terms: "If I was asked what is the greatest treasure which India possesses and what is her finest heritage, I would answer unhesitatingly – it is the Sanskrit language and literature, and all that it contains. This is a magnificent inheritance, and so long as this endures and influences the life of our people, so long the basic genius of India will continue."[13] He adds, "India built up a magnificent language, Sanskrit, and through this language, and its art and architecture, it sent its vibrant message to far away countries. It produced the *Upanishads*, the *Gita* and the Buddha. Hardly any language in the world has probably played as vital a part in the history of a race as Sanskrit has. It was not only the vehicle of the highest thought and some of the finest literature, but it became the uniting bond for India, even though there were political divisions. The *Ramayana* and the *Mahabharata* were woven into the texture of millions of lives in every generation for a thousand years. I have often wondered if our race forgot the Buddha, the *Upanishads* and the great epics, what then would it be like?"[14]

Furthermore Dr. Rajendra Prasad, the first President of India, said, "Sanskrit is the language of Indian culture and inspiration, the language in which all her past greatness, her rich thought and her spiritual aspirations are enshrined... Sanskrit has not only been the treasure-house of our past knowledge and achievements in the realm of thought and art, but it has also been the principal vehicle of our nation's aspirations and cultural traditions, besides being the source and inspiration of India's modern languages."[15]

We are compelled to only one conclusion: Sanskrit is the one language that can play the role of the national language of India. We have seen the various criteria needed for such a language and found that no other language comes close to Sanskrit in fulfilling simultaneously all these criteria. Why? Because Sanskrit meets all our needs and conditions perfectly. Because it is the language of India's soul, the only fit vehicle for its expression, the only language that can bind India into one nation and people – emotionally, culturally and spiritually. Because it alone can help India to rise again as a "leader in the ways of the spirit and a friend and helper of all the peoples." It is for us to aspire and to work so that the day may soon arrive.

We started this book by invoking Shiva and Parvati through a well-known verse from Kalidasa. We may end the book by once again invoking the Supreme God through another verse of Kalidasa, the opening verse of *Vikramorvaśīyam*:

वेदान्तेषु यमाहुरेकपुरुषं व्याप्य स्थितं रोदसी
यस्मिन्नीश्वर इत्यनन्यविषयः शब्दो यथार्थाक्षरः ।
अन्तर्यश्चमुमुक्षुभिर्नियमितप्राणादिभिर्मृग्यते
स स्थाणुः स्थिरभक्तियोगसुलभः निःश्रेयसायास्तु वः ॥[16]

He in the Vedanta by the Wise pronounced
Sole Being, who the upper and the under world
Pervading overpasses, whom alone
The name of God describes, here applicable
And pregnant – crippled else of force, to others
Perverted – and the Yogins who aspire
To rise above the human death, break in
Breath, soul and senses passionately seeking
The immutable, and in their own hearts find –
He, easily by work and faith and love
Attainable, ordain your heavenly weal.

References

Introduction

1. *India, What Can It Teach Us,* p.14
2. Quoted in *Janaśikṣā O Samskṛta*, Dhyanesh Narayan Chakraborty, p.44
3. *Journal of Royal Asiatic Society*, Vol. II
4. Quoted in *Devavāṇī* – A Collection of Essays, Articles and Quotes on Sanskrit, The American Sanskrit Institute, p.8a
5. Sri Aurobindo, *Sri Aurobindo Birth Centenary Library (SABCL)*, Vol. 14, pp.255-56
6. *Devavāṇī*, p.13
7. *Raghuvaṁśam* of Kalidasa, 1.1

Sanskrit Grammar

1. Dr. Venkatasubramania Ayre, *The Outlook on Sanskrit Grammar*, Oriental Journal, Venkateswar University, Tirupati, Vol. xxi-xxii, Jan - Dec, 1978 - 1979, p.1
2. *The Language*, L. Bloomfield, New York, 1933, p.11
3. From the Preface to Boethlingk's *Panini's Grammatik*, cited by Barend Faddegon in *The Mnemotechnics of Panini's Grammar*, Acta Orientalia, Gottingen, Vol. vii, 1929
4. *The Study of Hindu Grammar and the Study of Sanskrit*, American Journal of Philology, Vol. v, 1884
5. *Bhagavadgītā*, 2.29
6. *The Study of Hindu Grammar and the Study of Sanskrit*, American Journal of Philology, Vol. v, 1884
7. *Sanskrit: Essays on the value of the Language and the Literature*, Madras, 1972, p.23
8. *Ibid.*, p.26
9. *Sri Aurobindo Mandir Annual,* Calcutta, 1976, p.17
10. *Praṇavopaniṣad*
11. Quoted in *Constituent Assembly of India*, 12th September, 1949, pp.1333-34
12. *Pāṇinīya Śikṣā*, 1.6

Interesting and Amazing Creations in Sanskrit

1. Quoted in *Sarasvatī Kaṇṭhābharaṇam* of Bhoja, 2.263
2. *Kāvyādarśa* of Dandi, 3. 93 and *Sarasvatī Kaṇṭhābharaṇam* of Bhoja 2.260

3. *Śiśupālavadham* of Magha, 19.66
4. *Kirātārjunīyam* of Bharavi, 15.15
5. *Śiśupālavadham* of Magha, 19.114
6. *Ibid.*, 19.3
7. *Sarasvatī Kaṇṭhābharaṇam* of Bhoja, 2.275
8. *Ibid.*, 2.278
9. *Ibid.*, 2.276
10. *Pādukāsahasram* of Shri Deshikan, Verse No. 936
11. *Sarasvatī Kaṇṭhābharaṇam* of Bhoja, 2.201
12. *Ibid.*, 2.149
13. *Ibid.*, 2.299
14. *Ibid.*, 2.300
15. *Ibid.*, 19.33
16. *Ibid.*, 19.34
17. *Rāmakṛṣṇakāvyam* of Surya kavi, Verse No.1
18. *Sarasvatī Kaṇṭhābharaṇam* of Bhoja, 2.324
19. *Ibid.*, 2.320
20. *Ibid.*, 2.310
21. *Pādukāsahasram* of Shri Deshikan, Verse No. 929-30
22. *Subhāṣita Ratnabhāṇḍāgāram*, 4.5
23. *Ibid.*, 4.28
24. *Ibid.*, 4.13
25. *Ibid.*, 4.25
26. *Kṛṣṇakarṇāmṛtam*, 2.81
27. *Subhāṣita Ratnabhāṇḍāgāram*, 1.191
28. *Ibid.*, 6.16
29. *Ibid.*, 2.52
30. *Bhoja Prabandha*, 94
31. *Ibid.*, 326
32. *Ibid.*, 327

Sanskrit in Arts, Sciences and Daily Life

1. Sri Aurobindo, *SABCL*, Vol. 14, p.185
2. *Artificial Intelligence Magazine*, Vol. 6, No.1, p.32, 1985
3. *Baudhāyana Śulbasūtram*, ch. 1:48
4. *Kātyāyana Śulbasūtram*, 2:13
5. *Āryabhaṭīyam* of Aryabhatta, 1
6. *Ibid.*
7. *Ibid.*

The Beauty and Charm of Sanskrit Poetry

1. Prema Nandakumar, *Beauty*, *Truth*, *Sublimity*, p.1, (unpublished)
2. *Ibid.*
3. Sri Aurobindo, *SABCL*, Vol. 14, p.285

4. *Ibid.*, p. 290-91
5. *Ibid.*, p.290
6. Prema Nandakumar, *Beauty,Truth, Sublimity*, pp.2-3
7. *Ibid.*, p.5
8. Sri Aurobindo, *SABCL*, Vol. 3, p.156
9. The *Rāmāyaṇa, Bālakāṇḍa*, 34:15-18
10. Sri Aurobindo, *SABCL*, Vol. 3, p.158
11. *Ibid.*, p.147
12. *Ibid.*, pp.150-51
13. The *Mahābhārata, Vanaparva*, 63:3-12
14. Sri Aurobindo, *SABCL*, Vol. 3, pp.160-61
15. The *Mahābhārata*, *Vanaparva*, 294:27
16. Sri Aurobindo, *SABCL*, Vol. 3, pp.223-24
17. Translated by Sri Aurobindo, *SABCL*, Vol. 8, p.113
18. Prema Nandakumar, *Beauty*, *Truth*, *Sublimity*, p.7
19. *The Wonder that was India* by A.L. Basham, pp.423-24
20. Quoted in *History of Indian Literature*, by M. Winternitz, Vol. 3, p.120
21. Sri Aurobindo, *SABCL*, Vol. 3, pp.245-46
22. *Meghadūtam* of Kalidasa, 1:10
23. *Ibid.*, 1:59
24. *Ibid.*, 2:45
25. Quoted in *History of Indian Literature* by M. Winternitz, Vol. 3, P.238
26. *Abhijñānaśākuntalam* of Kalidasa, 1:18
27. *Ibid.*, 4:12
28. *Ibid.*, 4:14
29. *Ibid.*, 4:9
30. *Ibid.*, 4:6
31. *Vikramorvaśīyam* of Kalidasa, 4:20
32. Sri Aurobindo, *SABCL*, Vol. 3, p. 257
33. *Ṛtusaṁhāram* of Kalidasa, 1:25
34. *Harṣacaritam* of Bana, iii
35. *Gītagovindam* of Jayadeva, 1:27
36. *Ibid.*, 1:38
37. *Śivatāṇḍava Stotram*, 1
38. *Ibid.*,13
39. *Ślokas* reproduced by Dr. V.S.Vishnu Potty

A Language of Upliftment and Enlightenment

1. Swami Paramarthananda, *Sanskrit*, Vishva Samskrita Pratishtanam, Feb.85, p.1
2. Sri Aurobindo, *SABCL*, Vol. 27, p.143
3. The *Mahābhārata*, *Śāntiparva*, 330.21
4. *Ibid.*, *Udyogaparva*, 39.84
5. *Ibid.*, *Bhīṣmaparva*, 26.11

6. *Ibid., Udyogaparva*, 34.42
7. *Ibid., Udyogaparva*, 40.6
8. *Ibid., Vanaparva*, 313.116
9. *Rāmāyaṇamañjarī* of Kshemendra, *Bālakāṇḍa*, 5.27
10. *Hitopadeśa* of Narayana, Mitralabha, 71
11. *Subhāṣita Ratnabhāṇḍāgāram*, p.30
12. *Vairāgyaśatakam* of Bhartrihari, 12
13. *Nītiśatakam* of Bhartrihari, 19
14. *Ibid.*, 27
15. *Ibid.*, 4
16. This whole passage is based on the talk given by H. N. Mukherjee, titled: *The glory of Sanskrit and its relevance to our life today* published in *Vyākhyāna Vallarī*
17. *Aitareya Brāhmaṇa*, 7.15.5
18. Based on H.N. Mukherjee's talk *The glory of Sanskrit*
19. *Hanumannāṭakam* of Hanuman, 1:1
20. *Mahābhārata, Śāntiparva*, 15:14
21. H. N. Mukherjee, *The glory of Sanskrit*
22. *Dhammapada*, 4:7
23. *Ibid.*, 25:2
24. *Ibid.*, 10:13
25. *Ibid.*, 10:14
26. *Ibid.*, 8:1
27. *Ibid.*, 8:4

Sanskrit – A Sacred and Spiritual Language

1. Sri Aurobindo, *SABCL*, Vol. 18, p.46
2. *Devavāṇī*, p.20
3. *Ibid.*, p.14
4. *Ibid.*, p.30
5. *Language of the Gods*, p.15-16
6. Sri Aurobindo, *SABCL*, Vol. 11, p.449
7. *Ibid.*, Vol. 9, p.17
8. *Ṛgveda*, 3-62.10
9. *Bṛhadāraṇyaka Upaniṣad*, 1.3.28
10. *Collected Works* of Nolini Kanta Gupta, Vol. 7, p.108
11. *Devavāṇī*, p.11
12. Sri Aurobindo, *SABCL*, Vol. 14, p.266
13. *Ṛgveda*, 1.113, 1-2, 4, 16,
14. *Ibid.*, 10.191, 2-4
15. Sri Aurobindo, *SABCL*, Vol. 14, p.269
16. *Collected Works* of Nolini Kanta Gupta, Vol. 2, p.37-39
17. *Kenopaniṣad*, 1:9
18. *Chāndogyopaniṣad*, 7.23.1

19. *Śvetāśvataropaniṣad*, 3:9
20. *Muṇḍakopaniṣad*, 2.2.4
21. *Kaṭhopaniṣad*, 2:10
22. *Ibid.*, 3:3
23. *Īśopaniṣad*, 7
24. *Kaṭhopaniṣad*, 4:12
25. *Ibid.*, 3:4
26. *Śvetāśvataropaniṣad* 2:1.12-13
27. *Kaṭhopaniṣad* 1:20
28. *Ibid.*, 1:21
29. *Ibid.*, 1:22
30. *Ibid.*, 1:23-24
31. *Ibid.*, 1:25
32. *Ibid.*, 1:26-29
33. *Ibid.*, 2:1-5
34. *Ibid.*, 5:15
35. Sri Aurobindo, *SABCL*, Vol. 13, pp.9-10
36. *Bhagavadgītā,* 2:20
37. *Ibid.,* 4:7-8
38. *Ibid.,* 5:18
39. *Ibid.,* 12:17
40. *Ibid.,* 11:18
41. *Ibid.,* 11:19
42. *Ibid.,* 11:20
43. *Ibid.,* 11:31
44. *Ibid.,* 18:65-66
45. *Bhavānyaṣṭakam,* 1-3

Sanskrit as the National Language of India

1. Sri Aurobindo, *SABCL,* Vol. 15, pp.492-93
2. *Annals of Bhandarkar Oriental Research Institute*, Poona, Vol. xxxvi, July- Oct, 1955, Pts. iii-iv, p.188
3. Jean Filliozat, *Cultural Forum*, p.12
4. H.S. Ananta Narayana, *Vishweshwarananda Indological Journal*, Hoshiarpur Vol. xxii, Pts, 1-2, June-Dec. 1989, pp.160-61
5. K. M. Panikkar, *Bhavan's Journal*, Bombay, July 15, 1994, p.31
6. Subramania Bharati, *Kalaimagal*, June, 1942,
7. Dr. V. Raghavan, *Sanskrit*, p.18
8. H. S. Ananthanarayan, *Vishweshwarananda Indological Journal*, Vol. xxii, pts 1-2, June, Dec, 1984, p.161
9. Monier Williams, *Hinduism*, p.13
10. Based on the *Sanskrit Commission Report*, p.84

Some Doubts and Questions

1. a. *Sanskrit Commission Report*, p.79
   b. A Companion to Sanskrit Literature, by S.C. Banerji, pp.610-13
2. *Janaśikṣā O Samskṛta*, Dhyanesh Narayan Chakraborty, p.91
3. Debate on National Language, *Constituent Assembly of India*, 12th September, 1949, pp.1333-34
4. *Ibid.*, p.1354
5. *Samsara*, 2nd November, 1948
6. *Janaśikṣā O Samskṛta*, Dhyanesh Narayan Chakraborty, p.68
7. Sri Aurobindo, *SABCL*, Vol. 17, p.299
8. Dr. V.Raghavan, *Sanskrit*, Madras. 1972, p.22
9. *Indian Express*, 17th June, 2001
10. *Ibid.*

Sanskrit - The Language of India's Soul

1. K. M. Panikkar, *Bhavan's Journal*, July 15, 1994, p.35
2. *Sanskrit*, Moscow, 1968, pp.26-27
3. K.R. Pisharoti, *Sanskrit: Its place in Free India*, Vedantakeshari, p.388
4. K. M. Panikkar, *Bhavan's Journal*, July 15, 1994, p.35
5. *Viṣṇupurāṇa*, 3.2.1
6. Well-known shloka from an ancient text
7. J. Filliozat, *Annals of Bhandarkar Oriental Research Institute*, Vol. xxxvi, 1955, p.188
8. *Janaśikṣā O Samskṛta*, Dhyanesh Narayan Chakraborty, p.43
9. *Ibid.*, p.17
10. *Samskṛta aur Videśī Vidvān*, Sarvabhauma Samskrit Karayalaya, Varanasi, p.2
11. *Ibid.*, p.17
12. See J. Filliozat, *Cultural Forum*, 1972, p.13
13. *The Hindu*, 13th Feb. 1949
14. Azad Memorial Address by Jawaharlal Nehru
15. Janashiksha O Samskrita, by DhyaneshNarayanaChakraborty, p.17
16. *Vikramorvaśīyam* of Kalidasa, 1:1

Transliteration of Shlokas

CHAPTER-1

Page-8

Vāgarthāviva samprktau vāgarthapratipattaye
Jagataḥ pitarau vande pārvatīparameśvarau.

CHAPTER-2

Page-17

Āścaryavat paśyati kaḥ cit enam
Āścaryavat vadati tathā eva ca anyaḥ
Āścaryavat ca enam anyaḥ śṛṇoti
Śrutvā api enaṁ veda na ca eva kaḥ cit.

Āścaryavatpaśyati kaścidenamāścaryavadvadati tathaiva cānyaḥ
Āścaryavaccainamanyaḥ śṛṇoti śrutvāpyenaṁ veda na caiva kaścit.

Page-19

Rāmo rājamaṇiḥ sadā vijayate rāmaṁ rameśaṁ bhaje
rāmeṇābhihatā niśācaracamū rāmāya tasmai namaḥ
Rāmānnāsti parāyaṇaṁ parataraṁ rāmasya dāso'smyahaṁ
rāme cittalayaḥ sadā bhavatu me he rāma māmuddhara.

Page-31

Alpākṣaram asandigdhaṁ sāravad viśvato mukham
Astobham anavadyaṁ ca sūtraṁ sūtravido viduḥ.

CHAPTER-3

Page-36

Kaḥ khagaughāṅacicchaujā jhāñjño'ṭauṭhīḍaḍaṇḍhaṇaḥ
Tathodadhīn papharbābhīrmayo'rilvāśiṣāṁ sahaḥ.

Devānāṁ nandano devo nodano vedanindinām
Divaṁ dudāva nādena dāne dānavanandinaḥ.

Bhūribhirbhāribhirbhīrābhūbhārairabhirebhire
Bherīrebhibhirabhrābhairabhīrubhiribhairibhāḥ.

Page-37

Na nonanunno nunneno nānā nānānanā nanu
Nunno'nunno nanunneno nānenā nunnanunnanut.

Dādado duddaduddādī dādado dūdadīdadoḥ
Duddādaṁ dadade dudde dādādadadado'dadaḥ.

Jajaujojājijijjājī
taṁ tato'titatātatut
Bhābho'bhībhābhibhūbhābhū-
rārārirarirīraraḥ.

Page-38
Agā gāṅgāṅgakākākagāhakāghakakākahā
Ahāhāṅka khagāṅkāgakaṅkāgakhagakākaka.

Kṣitisthitimitikṣiptividhivinnidhisiddhiliṭ
Mama tryakṣa namaddakṣa hara smarahara smara.

Uruguṁ dyuguruṁ yutsu cukruśustuṣṭuvuḥ puru
Lulubhuḥ pupuṣurmutsu mumuhurnu muhurmuhuḥ.

Page-39
Yāyāyāyāyāyāyāyāyāyāyāyāyāyāyāyā
Yāyāyāyāyāyāyāyāyāyāyāyāyāyāyāyā.

Page-40
Bakulakalikālalāmani kalakaṇṭhīkalakalākule kāle
Kalayā kalāvato'pi hi kalayati kalitāstratāṁ madanaḥ.

Sabhāsamānāsahasāparāgāt sabhāsamānā sahasā parāgāt
Sabhāsamānā sahasāparāgāt sabhāsamānā sahasāparāgāt.

Page-41
Vāraṇāgagabhīrā sā sārābhīgagaṇāravā
Kāritārivadhā senā nāsedhāvaritārikā.

Niśitāsirato'bhīko nyejate'maraṇā rucā
Cāruṇā ramate janye ko bhīto rasitāśini.

Page-42
Vāhanājani mānāse sārājāvanamā tataḥ
Mattasāragarājebhe bhārīhāvajjanadhvani.

Nidhvanajjavahārībhā bheje rāgarasāttamaḥ
Tatamānavajārāsā senā mānijanāhavā.

Taṁ bhūsutāmuktim udārahāsaṁ vande yato bhavyabhavaṁ dayāśrīḥ
Śrīyādavaṁ bhavyabhatoyadevaṁ saṁhāradāmuktim utāsubhūtam.

Bhūsutāmuktim udārahāsaṁ bhavyabhavaṁ yato dayāśrīḥ taṁ vande.

Page-43
Bhavyabhatoyadevaṁ saṁhāradāmuktim uta asubhūtaṁ śrīyādavaṁ vande.

Kāṅkṣanpulomatanayāstanapīḍitāni
vakṣaḥsthalotthitarayāñcanapīḍitāni
Pāyādapāyabhayato namucipraharī
māyāmapāsya bhavato'mbumucāṁ prasārī.

Page-45
Sā senā gamanārambhe rasenāsīdanāratā
Tāranādajanā mattadhīranāgamanāmayā.

Page-46
Devākānini kāvāde vāhikāsvasvakāhi vā
Kākārebhabhare'kākā nisvabhavyavyabhasvani.

Page-47
Sthirāgasāṁ sadārādhyā vihatākatatāmatā
Satpāduke sarāsā mā raṅgarājapadaṁ naya.

Sthitā samayarājatpāgatarā mādake gavi
Duraṁhasāṁ sannatādā sādhyātāpakarāsarā.

Page-48
Tiṣṭhārjunādya saṅgrāme tvāṁ haniṣyāmyahaṁ śaraiḥ
Tiṣṭhāmi karṇa kiṁ mūḍha mṛgāt siṁhaḥ palāyate.

Page-49
Rāmābhiṣeke madavihvalāyā hastāccyuto hemaghaṭastaruṇyāḥ
Sopānamāsādya karoti śabdaṁ ṭhaṭhaṇṭhaṭhaṇṭhaṇṭhaṭhaṭhaṇṭhaṭhaṇṭha.

Hanūmati hatārāme vānarā harṣanirbharāḥ
Rudanti rākṣasāḥ sarve hā hārāmo hato hataḥ.

Page-50
Kṛṣṇamukhī na mārjārī dvijihvā na ca sarpiṇī
Pañcabhartrī na draupadī yaḥ jānāti sa paṇḍitaḥ.

Kastvaṁ bāla balānujaḥ tvamiha kiṁ manmandirāśaṅkayā
buddhaṁ tannavanītakumbhavivare hastaṁ kathaṁ nyasyasi
Kartuṁ tatra pipīlikāpanayanaṁ suptāḥ kimudbodhitā-
bālā vatsagatiṁ vivektumiti sañjalpan hariḥ pātu vaḥ.

Page-51

Aṅgulyā kaḥ kapāṭaṁ praharati viśikhe
mādhavaḥ kiṁ vasanto
no cakrī kiṁ kulālo na hi dharaṇidharaḥ
kiṁ dvijihvaḥ phaṇīndraḥ
Nāhaṁ ghorāhimardo kimuta khagapatir
no hariḥ kiṁ kapīndraḥ
ityevaṁ satyabhāmā prativacanajitaḥ
pātu vaścakrapāṇiḥ

Page-52

Svayaṁ pañcamukhaḥ putrau gajānanaṣaḍānanau
Digambaraḥ kathaṁ jīved annapūrṇā na cet gṛhe.

Svayaṁ maheśaḥ śvaśuro nageśaḥ
sakhā dhaneśaḥ tanayo gaṇeśaḥ
Tathāpi bhikṣāṭanameva śambhoḥ
balīyasī kevalamīśvarecchā.

Page-53

Kāvyaṁ karomi nahi cārutaraṁ karomi
yatnāt karomi yadi cārutaraṁ karomi
Bhūpālamaulimaṇimaṇḍitapādapīṭha
he bhojarāja kavayāmi vayāmi yāmi.

Adya dhārā nirādhārā nirālambā sarasvatī
Paṇḍitāḥ khaṇḍitāḥ sarve bhojarāje divaṁ gate.

Page-54

Adya dhārā sadādhārā sadālambā sarasvatī
Paṇḍitāḥ maṇḍitāḥ sarve bhojarāje bhuvaṁ gate.

CHAPTER-4

Page-60

Dīrghacaturasrasyākṣṇayā rajjuḥ
pārśvamānī tiryaṅmānī ca
yatpṛthagbhūte kurutastadubhayaṁ karoti.

Karaṇīṁ tṛtīyena vardhayettacca
svacaturthenātmacatustriṁśonena saviśeṣa iti viśeṣaḥ.

Caturadhikaṁ śatamaṣṭaguṇaṁ dvāṣaṣṭistathā sahasrāṇām
Ayutadvayaviṣkambhasyāsanno vṛttapariṇāhaḥ.

Page-61

Vargākṣarāṇi varge'varge'vargākṣarāṇi kāt ṅmau yaḥ
Khadvinake svarā nava varge'varge navāntyavarge vā.

CHAPTER-5

Page-77

Akardamamidaṁ tīrthaṁ bharadvāja niśāmaya
Ramaṇīyaṁ prasannāmbu sanmanuṣyamano yathā.

Page-78

Pāpānāṁ vāśubhānāṁ vā vadhārhāṇāṁ plavaṅgama
Kāryaṁ karuṇamāryeṇa na kaścinnāparādhyati.

Niṣpandāstaravaḥ sarve nilīnā mṛgapakṣiṇaḥ
Naiśena tamasā vyāptā diśaśca raghunandana.
Śanairviyujyate sandhyā nabho netrairivāvṛtam
Nakṣatratārāgahanaṁ jyotibhiravabhāsate.
Uttiṣṭhati ca śītāṁśuḥ śaśī lokatamonudaḥ
Hlādayan prāṇināṁ loke manāṁsi prabhayā svayā.
Naiśāni sarvabhūtāni vicaranti tatastataḥ
Yakṣarākṣasasaṅghāśca raudrāśca piśitāśanāḥ.

Page-80

Uttiṣṭhottiṣṭha kiṁ śeṣe bhīmasena yathā mṛtaḥ
Nāmṛtasya hi pāpīyān bhāryāmālabhya jīvati.

Hā nātha hā mahārāja hā svāmin kiṁ jahāsi mām
Hā hatāsmi vinaṣṭāsmi bhītāsmi vijane vane.
Nanu nāma mahārāja dharmajñaḥ satyavāgasi
Kathamuktvā tathā satyaṁ suptāmutsṛjya māṁ gataḥ.
Paryāptaḥ parihāso'yametāvān puruṣarṣabha
Bhītāhamatidurdharṣa darśayātmānamīśvara.
Dṛśyase dṛśyase rājanneṣa dṛṣṭā'si naiṣadha
Āvārya gulmairātmānaṁ kiṁ māṁ na pratibhāṣase.
Nṛśaṁsa bata rājendra yanmāmevaṅgatāmiha
Vilapantīṁ samāgamya nāśvāsayasi pārthiva.
Na śocāmyahamātmānaṁ na cānyadapi kiñcana
Kathaṁ nu bhavitāsyeka iti tvāṁ nṛpa rodimi.
Kathaṁ nu rājanstṛṣitaḥkṣudhitaḥ śramakarṣitaḥ
Sāyāhne vṛkṣamūleṣu māmapaśyanbhaviṣyasi.

Page-82

Dīrghāyurathavālpāyuḥ saguṇo nirguṇo'pi vā
Sakṛdvṛto mayā bhartā na dvitīyaṁ vṛṇo'myaham.

Page-83

Astyuttarasyāṁ diśi devatātmā
himālayo nāma nagādhirājaḥ
Pūrvāparau toyanidhī vagāhya
sthitaḥ pṛthivyā iva mānadaṇḍaḥ.

Sthitāḥ kṣaṇaṁ pakṣmasu tāḍitādharāḥ
payodharotsedhanipātacūrṇitāḥ
Balīṣu tasyāḥ skhalitāḥ prapedire
cireṇa nābhiṁ prathamodabindavaḥ.

Page-84

Āgāmidaityāśanakelikāṅkṣiṇī
kupakṣiṇāṁ ghoratarā paramparā
Dadhau padaṁ vyomni surārivāhinīr
uparyuparyetya nivāritātapāḥ.

Muhurvibhagnātapavāraṇadhvajaś
caladdharādhūlikalākulekṣaṇaḥ
Dhūtāśvamātaṅgamahārathākarān
avekṣeṇo'bhūt prasabhaṁ prabhañjanaḥ.

Page-85

Sadyo vibhinnāñjanapuñjatejaso
mukhairviṣāgniṁ vikiranta uccakaiḥ
Puraḥ patho'tītya mahābhujaṅgamā
bhayaṅkarākārabhṛto bhṛśaṁ yayuḥ.

Tviṣāmadhīśasya puro'dhimaṇḍalaṁ
śivāḥ sametāḥ puruṣaṁ vavāśire
Surārirājasya raṇāntaśoṇitaṁ
prasahya pātuṁ drutamutsukā iva.

Page-86

Mandaṁ mandaṁ nudati pavanaścānukūlo yathā tvāṁ
vāmaścāyaṁ nadati madhuraṁ cātakaste sagandhaḥ
Garbhādhānakṣaṇaparicayānnunamābaddhamālāḥ
seviṣyante nayanasubhagaṁ khe bhavantaṁ balākāḥ.

Śabdāyante madhuramanilaiḥ kīcakāḥ pūryamāṇāḥ
saṁraktābhistripuravijayo gīyate kinnarībhiḥ
Nirhrādaste muraja iva cetkandareṣu dhvaniḥ syāt
saṅgītārtho nanu paśupatestatra bhāvī samagraḥ.

Page-87

Tvāmālikhya praṇayakupitāṁ dhāturāgaiḥ śilāyām-
ātmānaṁ te caraṇapatitaṁ yāvadicchāmi kartum
Asraistāvan muhurupacitairdṛṣṭirālupyate me
krūrastasminnapi na sahate saṅgamaṁ nau kṛtāntaḥ.

Kāvyeṣu nāṭakaṁ ramyaṁ tatra ramyā śakuntalā
Tatra ramyaścaturtho'ṅkastatra ślokacatuṣṭayam.

Page-88

Sarasijamanuviddhaṁ śaivalenāpi ramyaṁ
malinamapi himaṁśorlakṣmalakṣmīṁ tanoti
Iyamadhikamanojñā valkalenāpi tanvī
kimiva hi madhurāṇāṁ maṇḍanaṁ nākṛtīnām.

Udgalitadarbhakavalā mṛgyaḥ parityaktanartanā mayūrāḥ
Apasṛtapāṇḍupatrā muñcantyaśrūṇīva latāḥ.

Yasya tvayā vraṇaviropaṇamiṅgudīnāṁ
tailaṁ nyaṣicyata mukhe kuśasūcividdhe
Śyāmākamuṣṭiparivarddhitako jahāti
so'yaṁ na putrakṛtakaḥ padavīṁ mṛgaste.

Page-89

Pātuṁ na prathamaṁ vyavasyati jalaṁ
yuṣmāsvapīteṣu yā
nādatte priyamaṇḍanāpi bhavatāṁ
snehena yā pallavam
Ādye vaḥ kusumaprasūtisamaye
yasyā bhavatyutsavaḥ
seyaṁ yāti śakuntalā patigṛhaṁ
sarvairanujñāyatām.

Yāsyatyadya śakuntaleti hṛdayaṁ
saṁspṛṣṭamutkaṇṭhayā
kaṇṭhaḥ stambhitabāṣpavṛttikaluṣaś
cintājaḍaṁ darśanam
Vaiklavyaṁ mama tāvadīdṛśamidaṁ
snehādaraṇyaukasaḥ
pīḍyante gṛhiṇaḥ kathaṁ nu tanayā-
viśleṣaduḥkhairnavaiḥ.

Page-90

Sarasi nalinīpatreṇāpi tvamāvṛtavigrahāṁ
nanu sahacarīṁ dūre matvā virauṣi samutsukaḥ

Iti ca bhavato jāyāsnehāt pṛthak sthitibhīrutā
mayi ca vidhure bhāvaḥ kāntāpravṛttiparāṅmukhaḥ.

Siteṣu harmyeṣu niśāṣu yoṣitāṁ
sukhaṁ prasuptāni mukhāni candramāḥ
Vilokya nūnaṁ bhṛśamutsukaściraṁ
niśākṣaye yāti hriyeva pāṇḍutām.

Sasīkarāmbhodharamattakuñjaras
taḍitpatāko'śaniśabdamardalaḥ
Samāgato rājavaduddhatadyutir
ghanāgamaḥ kāmijanapriyaḥ priye.

Balāhakāścāśaniśabdamardalāḥ
surendracāpaṁ dadhatas taḍitgaṇam
Sutīkṣṇadhārāpatanograsāyakais
tudanti cetaḥ prasabhaṁ pravāsinām.

Page-91
Jvalati pavanavṛddhaḥ parvatānāṁ darīṣu
sphurati paṭuninādaiḥ śuṣkavaṁśasthalīṣu
Prasarati tṛṇamadhye labdhavṛddhiḥ kṣaṇena
glapayati gṛhavargaṁ prāntalagno davāgniḥ.

Paścādaṅghriṁ prasārya trikanativitataṁ
drāghayitvāṅgamuccair
āsajyā bhugnakaṇṭho mukhamurasi saṭā
dhūlidhūmrā vidhūya
Ghāsagrāsābhilāṣādanavaratacalat
prothatuṇḍasturaṅgo
mandaṁ śabdāyamāno vilikhati śayanād
utthitaiḥ kṣmāṁ kṣureṇa.

Kurvannābhugnapṛṣṭho mukhanikaṭakaṭiḥ
kandharāmātiraścīṁ
lolenāhanyamānaṁ tuhinakaṇamucā
cañcalā keśareṇa
Nidrākaṇḍūkaṣāyaṁ kaṣati niviḍita
śrotraśuktistaraṅgās
tvaṅgatpakṣmāgralagnapratanubusakaṇaṁ
koṇamakṣṇaḥ kṣureṇa.

Page-92
Lalitalavaṅgalatāpariśīlanakomalamalayasamīre
Madhukaranikarakarambitakokilakūjitakuñjakuṭīre.

Candanacarcitanīlakalevarapītavasanavanamālī
Kelicalanmaṇīkuṇḍalamaṇḍitagaṇḍayugasmitaśālī.

Page-93
Jaṭākaṭāhasambhramabhramannilimpanirjharī
vilolavīcivallarīvirājamānamūrdhani
Dhagad dhagad dhagajjvalallalāṭapaṭṭapāvake
kiśoracandraśekhare ratiḥ pratikṣaṇaṁ mama.

Kadā nilimpanirjharīnikuñjakoṭare vasan
vimuktadurmatiḥ sadā śiraḥsthamañjalim vahan
Vilolalolalocano lalāmabhālalagnakaḥ
śiveti mantramuccaran kadā sukhī bhavāmyaham.

Snigdhatvaṁ pallavebhyo mṛginayanamina-
syāṅghritaḥ sadvilāsam
asraṁ tāvat tuṣārādaticapalayutaṁ
sādhvasaṁ śāśamevam
Māyūraṁ garvabhāvaṁ madhuramatha madhu-
bhyastathā vyāghrato'pi
krauryaṁ kāṭhinyamevaṁ kuliśagatamath-
auṣṇyañca vahnestaśca.

Page-94
Svīkṛtyaitacca sarvaṁ militamatha ca saṁ-
pīḍya pārāvatānāṁ
kūṅkārañcaivamalpetaramapi vihitā
sā vidhatrā ca nārī
Viśvasyotpattisamyaksthitigativilaya-
prāptaye sādareṇa
tasmai martyāya dattaṁ varamatimahitaṁ
sundarañcopahāram.

CHAPTER-6
Page-97
Anto nāsti pipāsāyāstuṣṭistu paramaṁ sukham.

Yat pṛthīvyāṁ brīhi yavaṁ hiraṇyaṁ paśavaḥ striyaḥ
Nālamekasya tat sarvaṁ ....

Page-98
Gatāsūnagatāsūṁśca nānuśocanti paṇḍitāḥ.

Ya īrṣuḥ paravitteṣu rūpe vīrye kulānvaye
Sukhasaubhāgyasatkāre tasya vyādhiranantakaḥ.

Sukhārthī vā tyajed vidyāṁ vidyārthī vā tyajet sukham.

Ahanyahani bhūtāni gacchantīha yamālayam
Śeṣāḥ sthāvaramicchanti kimāścaryamataḥ param.

Yathā caturbhiḥ kanakaḥ parīkṣyate
nigharṣaṇacchedanatāpatāḍanaiḥ
Tathā caturbhiḥ puruṣaḥ parīkṣyate
kulena śilena guṇena karmaṇā.

Page-99
Ayaṁ nijaḥ paro veti gaṇanā laghucetasām
Udāracaritānāṁ tu vasudhaiva kuṭumbakam.

Na caurahāryaṁ na ca rājyahāryaṁ
na bhrātṛbhājyaṁ na ca bhārakāri
Vyaye kṛte vardhata eva nityaṁ
vidyādhanaṁ sarvadhanapradhānam.

Bhogā na bhuktā vayameva bhuktāḥ
tapo na taptaṁ vayameva taptāḥ
Kālo na yāto vayameva yātāḥ
tṛṣṇā na jīrṇā vayameva jīrṇāḥ.

Page-100
Keyūrāṇi na bhūṣayanti puruṣaṁ
hārā na candrojjvalā
na snānaṁ na vilepanaṁ na kusumaṁ
nālaṅkṛtā mūrdhajāḥ
Vāṇyekā samalaṅkaroti puruṣaṁ
yā saṁskṛtā dhāryate
kṣīyante khalu bhūṣaṇāni satataṁ
vāgbhūṣaṇaṁ bhūṣaṇam.

Prārabhyate na khalu vighnabhayena nīcaiḥ
prārabhya vighnavihatā viramanti madhyāḥ
Vighnaiḥ punaḥ punarapi pratihanyamānāḥ
prārabhya cottamaguṇā na parityajanti.

Page-101
Prasahya maṇimudhdarenmakaravaktradaṁṣṭrāntarāt
samudramapi santaret pracaladūrmimālākulam
Bhujaṅgamapi kopitaṁ śirasi puṣpavaddhārayet
na tu pratiniviṣṭamūrkhajanacittamārādhayet.

Caran vai madhu vindati caran svādumudumbaram
Sūryasya paśya śromāṇaṁ yo na tandrayate caran.
Caraiveti caraiveti.

Page-105
Yaṁ śaivāḥ samupāsate śiva iti brahmeti vedāntino
bauddhā buddha iti pramāṇapaṭavaḥ karteti naiyāyikāḥ
Arhannityatha jainaśāsanaratāḥ karmeti mīmāṁsakāḥ
so'yaṁ no vidadhātu vāñchitaphalaṁ trailokyanātho hariḥ.

Page-106
Nācchitvā paramarmāṇi nākṛtvā karma dāruṇam
Nāhatvā matsyaghātīva prāpnoti mahatīṁ śriyam.

Page-107
Na paresaṁ vilomāni na paresaṁ katākatam
Attano va avekkheyya katāni akatāni ca.

Kāyena saṁvaro sādhu sādhu vācayā saṁvaro
Manasā saṁvaro sādhu sādhu sabbattha saṁvaro
Sabbattha saṁvuto bhikkhu sabbadukkhā pamuccati.

Na naggacariyā na jaṭā na paṅkā
nānāsakā thaṇḍilasāyikā vā
Rajovajallaṁ ukkuṭikappadhānaṁ
sodhenti maccaṁ avitiṇṇakaṅkham.

Alaṅkato cepi samaṁ careyya
santo dantā niyato brahmacārī
Sabbesu bhūtesu nidhāya daṇḍaṁ
so brāhmaṇo so samaṇo sa bhikkhu.

Page-108
Sahassamapi ye vācā anatthapadasaṁhitā
Ekam atthapadaṁ seyyo yaṁ sutvā upasammati.

Yo sahassaṁ sahassena saṅgāme mānuse jine
Ekaṁ ca jeyyamattānaṁ sa ve saṅgāmajuttamo.

CHAPTER-7

Page-113
Om bhūr bhuvaḥ svaḥ tat saviturvareṇyam
Bhargo devasya dhīmahi
Dhiyo yo naḥ pracodayāt.

Page-114
Om asato mā sad gamaya
Tamaso mā jyotir gamaya
Mṛtyor mā'mṛtaṁ gamaya
Om śāntiḥ śāntiḥ śāntiḥ.

Page-115
Etadālambanaṁ śreṣṭham etadālambanaṁ param
Etadālambanaṁ jñātvā brahmaloke mahīyate.

Dukheṣvanudvignmanāḥ sukheṣu vigataspṛhaḥ

Page-116
Idaṁ śreṣṭhaṁ jyotiṣāṁ jyotirāgāccitraḥ
praketo ajaniṣṭa vibhvā
Yathā prasūtā savituḥ savāyaṁ evā
rātryuṣase yonimāraik.

Page-117
Ruśadvatsā ruśatī śvetyāgādāraigu kṛṣṇā sadanānyasyāḥ
Samānabandhū amṛte anūcī dyāvā varṇa carata āmināne.

Bhāsvatī netrī sūnṛtānāmaceti citrā vi duro na āvaḥ
Prārpyā jagadvyu no rāyo akhyaduṣā ajīgarbhuvanāni viśvā.

Kṣatrāya tvaṁ śravase tvaṁ mahīyā iṣṭaye tvamarthamiva tvamityai
Visadṛśā jīvitābhipracakṣa uṣā ajīgarbhuvanāni viśvā.

Udīrdhvaṁ jīvo asurna āgādapa prāgāt tama ā jyotireti
Āraik panthāṁ yātave sūryāyāganma yatra pratiranta āyuḥ.

Page-118
Saṁ gacchadhvaṁ saṁ vadadhvaṁ saṁ vo manāṁsi jānatām
Devā bhāgaṁ yathā pūrve sañjanānā upāsate.
Samāno mantraḥ samitiḥ samānī
Samānaṁ manaḥ saha cittameṣām
Samānaṁ mantramabhi mantraye vaḥ
Samānena vo haviṣā juhomi.
Samānī va ākūtiḥ samānā hṛdayāni vaḥ
Samānamastu vo mano yathā vaḥ susahāsati.

Page-119
Na sandṛśe tiṣṭhati rūpamasya na cakṣuṣā paśyati kaścanainam

Yat prāṇena na prāṇiti yena prāṇaḥ praṇīyate tadeva brahma...

Page-120
Nālpe sukhamasti bhūmaiva sukhaṁ yo vai bhūmā tadamṛtamatha yadalpaṁ tanmartyam

Vṛkṣa iva stabdho divi tiṣṭhatyekaḥ

Śaravat tanmayo bhavet

Na hyadhruvaiḥ prāpyate hi dhruvaṁ tat

Ātmānaṁ rathinaṁ viddhi śarīraṁ rathameva tu
Buddhiṁ tu sārathiṁ viddhi manaḥ pragrahameva ca.
Indriyāṇī hayānāhur viṣayāṁsteṣu gocarān
Ātmendriyamanoyuktaṁ bhoktetyāhurmanīṣiṇaḥ.

Page-121
Kaḥ śoka ekatvam anupaśyataḥ

Aṅguṣṭhamātraḥ puruṣo madhya ātmani tiṣṭhati...
...Īśāno bhūtabhavyasya sa evādya sa u śvaḥ.

Uttiṣṭhata jāgrata prāpya varānnibodhata
Kṣurasya dhārā niśitā duratyayā
durgaṁ pathastat kavayo vadanti.

Na tasya rogo na jarā na mṛtyuḥ
prāptasya yogāgnimayam śarīram

Page-122
Yeyaṁ prete vicikitsā manuṣye'stītyeke nāyamastīti caike
Etadvidyāmanuśiṣṭastvayā'haṁ varāṇāmeṣa varastṛtīyaḥ.

Devairatrāpi vicikitsitaṁ purā
na hi suvijñeyamaṇureṣa dharmaḥ
Anyaṁ varaṁ naciketo vṛṇīṣva
mā moparotsīrati mā sṛjainam.

Devairatrāpi vicikitsitaṁ kila
tvaṁ ca mṛtyo yanna sujñeyamāttha
Vaktā cāsya tvādṛganyo na labhyo
nānyo varastulya etasya kaścit.

Page-123
Śatāyuṣaḥ putrapautrān vṛṇīṣva
bahūn paśūn hastihiraṇyamaśvān
Bhūmermahadāyatanaṁ vṛṇīṣva
svayaṁ ca jīva śarado yāvadicchasi.

Etattulyaṁ yadi manyase varaṁ
vṛṇīṣva vittaṁ cirajīvikāṁ ca
Mahābhūmau naciketastvamedhi
kāmānāṁ tvā kāmabhājaṁ karomi.

Ye ye kāmā durlabhā martyaloke
sarvān kāmāñśchandataḥ prārthayasva
Imāḥ rāmāḥ sarathāḥ satūryā
nahīdṛśā lambhanīyā manuṣyaiḥ
Ābhirmatprattābhiḥ paricārayasva
naciketo maraṇaṁ mānuprākṣīḥ.

Śvobhāvā martyasya yadantakaitat
sarvendriyāṇāṁ jarayanti tejaḥ
Api sarvaṁ jīvitamalpameva
tavaiva vāhāstava nṛtyagīte.

Page-124
Na vittena tarpaṇīyo manuṣyo
lapsyāmahe vittamadrākṣma cettvā
Jīviṣyāmo yāvadīśiṣyasi tvaṁ
varas tu me varaṇīyaḥ sa eva.

Ajīryatāmamṛtānāmupetya
jīryanmartyaḥ kvadhaḥsthaḥ prajānan
Abhidhyāyanvarṇaratipramodān
atidīrghe jīvite ko rameta.

Yasminnidaṁ vicikitsanti mṛtyo
yatsāmparāye mahati brūhi nas tat
Yo'yaṁ varo gūḍhamanupraviṣṭo
nānyaṁ tasmānnaciketā vṛṇīte.

Anyacchreyo'nyadutaiva preyas
te ubhe nānārthe puruṣaṁ sinītaḥ
Tayoḥ śreyaḥ ādadānasya sādhu
bhavati hīyate'rthādya u preyo vṛṇīte.

Śreyaśca preyaśca manuṣyametas
tau samparītya vivinakti dhīraḥ
Śreyo hi dhīro'bhi preyaso vṛṇīte
preyo mando yoga kṣemādvṛṇīte.

Sa tvaṁ priyān priyarūpāñśca kāmān
abhidhyāyan naciketo'tyasrākṣīḥ
Naitāṁ sṛṅkāṁ vittamayīm avāpto
yasyāṁ majjanti bahavo manuṣyāḥ.

Dūramete viparīte viṣūcī
avidyā yā ca vidyeti jñātā
Vidyābhīpsinaṁ naciketasaṁ manye
na tvā kāmā bahavo'lolupanta.

Avidyāyāmantare vartamānāḥ
svayaṁ dhīrāḥ paṇḍitaṁ manyamānāḥ
Dandramyamāṇāḥ pariyanti mūḍhā
andhenaiva nīyamānā yathāndhāḥ.

Page-125
Na tatra sūryo bhāti na candratārakaṁ
nemā vidyuto bhānti kuto'yam agniḥ
Tameva bhāntamanubhāti sarvaṁ
tasya bhāsā sarvamidaṁ vibhāti.

Page-126
Na jāyate mriyate vā kadācin
nāyaṁ bhūtvā bhavitā vā na bhūyaḥ
Ajo nityaḥ śāśvato'yaṁ purāṇo
na hanyate hanyamāne śarīre.

Yadā yadā hi dharmasya glānir bhavati bhārata
Abhyutthānamadharmasya tadātmānaṁ sṛjāmyaham.

Paritrāṇāya sādhūnāṁ vināśāya ca duṣkṛtām
Dharmasaṁsthāpanārthāya sambhavāmi yuge yuge.

Page-127
Vidyāvinayasampanne brāhmaṇe gavi hastini
Śuni caiva śvapāke ca paṇḍitāḥ samadarśinaḥ.

Yo na hṛṣyati na dveṣṭi na śocati na kāṅkṣati
Śubhāśubhaparityāgī bhaktimān yaḥ sa me priyaḥ.

Tvamakṣaraṁ paramaṁ veditavyaṁ
tvamasya viśvasya paraṁ nidhānam
Tvamavyayaḥ śāśvatadharmagoptā
sanātanas tvaṁ puruṣo mato me.

Anādimadhyāntamanantavīryam
anantabāhuṁ śaśisūryanetram
Paśyāmi tvāṁ dīptahutāśavaktraṁ
svatejasā viśvamidaṁ tapantam.

Page-128
Dyāvāpṛthivyoridamantaraṁ hi
vyāptaṁ tvayaikena diśaśca sarvāḥ
Dṛṣṭvādbhutaṁ rūpamugraṁ tavedaṁ
lokatrayaṁ pravyathitaṁ mahātman.

Ākhyāhi me ko bhavānugrarūpo
namo'stu te devavara prasīda
Vijñātumicchāmi bhavantamādyaṁ
na hi prajānāmi tava pravṛttim.

Manmanā bhava madbhakto madyājī māṁ namaskuru
Māmevaiṣyasi satyaṁ te pratijāne priyo'si me.

Sarvadharmān parityajya māmekaṁ śaraṇaṁ vraja
Ahaṁ tvā sarvapāpebhyo mokṣayiṣyāmi mā śucaḥ.

Page-129
Na tāto na mātā na bandhur na bhrātā
na putro na putrī na bhṛtyo na bhartā
Na jāyā na vidyā na vṛttir mamaiva
gatis tvaṁ gatis tvaṁ tvamekā bhavāni.

Na jānāmi dānaṁ na ca dhyānayogaṁ
na jānāmi tantraṁ na ca stotramantram
Na jānāmi pūjāṁ na ca nyāsayogaṁ
gatis tvaṁ gatis tvaṁ tvamekā bhavāni.

Na jānāmi puṇyaṁ na jānāmi tīrthaṁ
na jānāmi muktiṁ layaṁ vā kadācit
Na jānāmi bhaktiṁ vrataṁ vā'pi mātar
gatis tvaṁ gatis tvaṁ tvamekā bhavāni.

CHAPTER-10
Page-155
Uttaraṁ yat samudrasya himādreścaiva dakṣiṇam
Varṣaṁ tad bhārataṁ nāma bhāratī yatra santatiḥ.

Page-156
Gaṅge ca yamune caiva godāvari sarasvati
Narmade sindhukāveri jale'smin sannidhiṁ kuru.

Page-161
Vedānteṣu yamāhur ekapuruṣaṁ vyāpya sthitaṁ rodasī
yasminnīśvara ityananyaviṣayaḥ śabdo yathārthākṣaraḥ
Antaryaścamumukṣubhirniyamitaprāṇādibhir mṛgyate
sa sthāṇuḥ sthirabhaktiyogasulabhaḥ niḥśreyasāyāstu vaḥ.

Glossary

Abhinavagupta: A great Kashmiri, famous in poetics, dramaturgy and the Shaiva philosophy of Kashmir. His celebrated commentaries on the *Dhvanyāloka* and the *Nāṭyaśāstra* are respectively the *Kāvyālokalocana* (popularly known as *Locana*) and the *Abhinavabhāratī*. In the *Locana*, he refers to a commentary by himself on Bhatta Tauta's *Kāvyakautuka*. He was the author of several works like: *Tantrāloka, Paramārthasāra, Tantrasāra, Mālinīvijayavārtika, Parātriṁśikā-vivṛti, Bodhapañcadaśikā, Tantravaṭadhānikā, Īśvarapratyabhijñāvimarśinī* etc. He can be assigned to a period between the last quarter of the tenth century and first quarter of the eleventh. His interpretation, called *Abhivyaktivāda*, of Bharata's well-known dictum on *Rasa* was very popular and profoundly influenced later writers.

Amarakoṣa: A standard lexicon, by Amarasimha, arranged in three books, viz. *Svargādikāṇḍa*, *Bhūmyādikāṇḍa* and *Sāmānyakāṇḍa*. The work presents synonyms, and its last part contains an appendix on homonyms, indeclinables and genders.

Amarasimha: Author of the celebrated lexicon, entitled *Nāmaliṅgānuśāsana*, popularly called *Amarakoṣa*. Supposed to have flourished in the fourth century A.D. He was a Buddhist. Tradition makes him one of the nine distinguished men (*navaratna*) who adorned the court of King Vikramaditya.

Anandavardhana: According to the *Rājataraṅgiṇī*, he was the court-poet of Avantivarman (855–84 A.D.), king of Kashmir. The *Dhvanyāloka*, a celebrated work on poetics, is generally attributed to him. Some scholars think that he wrote the *Vṛtti* portion of the above work, while the *Kārikā* portion was composed by another writer, usually referred to as *Dhvanikāra*. To Anandavardhana is attributed also the devotional poem called *Devīśataka*. The Prakrit poem, *Viṣamabāṇalīlā*, and the Sanskrit *Arjunacarita* are ascribed to Anandavardhana by his commentators. He himself refers to his work, entitled *Dharmottama*, a commentary on the *Pramāṇa-viniścaya* of Dharmakirti. He, for the first time, succeeded in establishing that *Dhvani* or suggested sense is the soul of poetry.

Apastamba: One of the traditional writers on original *Smṛti*. Author of a *Gṛhya-sūtra*, *Dharma-sūtra* and *Pitṛmedha-sūtra*. *Āpastamba-sūtra* is supposed to have been written by him sometime between 600–300 B.C.

Appaya Dikshita: Also called Apya or Appa, Appaya Dikshita appears to have flourished in third and fourth quarters of the 16th century. Author of three works on poetics, called *Kuvalayānanda*, *Citramīmāṁsā* and *Vṛttivārtika*. Besides these, he also wrote *Lakṣaṇaratnāvalī*, a work on dramaturgy.

Arthaśāstra: Attributed to Kautilya or Kautalya (also called Vishnugupta or Chanakya), the *Arthaśāstra* is the most well-known earlier extant text on politics and statecraft. Some scholars think that it is not a work of Kautilya, but rather of a school that followed his views.

Aryabhatta I: Aryabhatta, an Indian mathematician and astronomer, was born in 476 A.D. at Pataliputra (Patna) during the Gupta era. He maintained the theory of rotation of earth round its axis and explained the cause of eclipses of sun and moon. His only work *Āryabhaṭīya* treated of astronomy and mathematics (including quadratic equations, table of signs, and other rules of Algebra and trigonometry).

Aṣṭādhyāyī: The oldest and most authoritative grammar by Panini. Divided into eight *Adhyāyas* (chapters) each of which is subdivided into four sections called *Pādas*. The total number of aphorisms is nearly 4000. It consists of aphorisms by Panini and supplementary rules, called *Vārtikasūtras*, by Katyayana. This work, besides dealing with classical Sanskrit, gives rules for the Vedic language as well as Vedic accents.

Banabhatta: Author of the prose works called *Kādambarī* and *Harṣacarita*. A devotional lyric, entitled *Caṇḍīśataka*, is also attributed to him. From the autobiographical account contained in the introductory portions of the *Kādambarī* and the *Harṣacarita* we have some information about his personal history. His patron was King Harshavardhana (606–647 A.D.) of Thaneswar.

Baudhayana: The author of the *Baudhāyana-kalpa-sūtra* (comprising *Śrauta*, *Gṛhya* and *Dharma-sūtras*) and *Śulva-sūtra*. His *Dharma-sūtra* is supposed to have been written by him not later than 600 B.C. A *Pitṛmedha-sūtra* by Baudhayana is also well-known.

Bharata: Supposed author of the earliest work on dramaturgy, called *Nāṭya-śāstra*. Date controversial. Probably flourished earlier than the fourth or fifth century A.D. Sometimes referred to as Adi-Bharata. Bharata appears to have propounded, for the first time, the theory of *Rasa* in connection with drama. A work on music, called *Gitālaṅkāra*, is also attributed to Bharata.

Bhartrihari: Author of the lyric poems entitled *Nītiśataka, Vairāgyaśataka* and *Śṛṅgāraśataka*. A *Puruṣārthopadeśa* is also attributed to him. Identified by some with Bhartrihari, author of the grammatico-philosophical work called *Vākyapadīya*. Bhatti, author of the *Rāvaṇavadha*, popularly known as *Bhaṭṭi-kāvya*, is identified by some scholars with the author of the *Vākyapadīya*. The grammarian Bhartrihari is supposed to have written also the *Mahābhāṣyadīpikā*, a commentary on the *Mahābhāṣya*.

Bhavabhuti: Author of the dramas entitled *Uttararāmacarita*, *Mālatīmādhava* and *Mahāvīracarita*. From the autobiographical account contained in his works we learn that he was born in a Brahmin family of *Kāśyapagotra* in Padmapura situated probably in Vidarbha. He had the title of *Śrīkaṇṭha* and is mentioned in the *Rājataraṅgiṇī* as a court–poet of King Yashovarman of Kanauj (725–753 A.D.)

Bhoja: Bhoja, also known as Bhoja-raja and Dharadhisha, was born around 11th century A.D. in the family of Paramar Kings who ruled in the Central and Western part of India. He ruled in the Malva territory from 933–1051 A.D. and was well-known as a scholar-king. Bhoja is credited to have written about 84 books of which only 38 (most in Sanskrit, and a few in Prakrit language) are available. His work *Śṛṅgāraprakāśa*, a treatise on Rhetorics, is widely known for its comprehensive treatment of the subject. His other well-known works include *Sarasvatī-kaṇṭhābharaṇa* and *Campū Rāmāyaṇa*.

Bilhana: A famous Kashmirian poet who was born at Konamukha near *Pravarapura*. He wrote *Vikramāṅkadevacarita* in honor of his patron, the Chalukya king Tribhuvanamalla or Vikramaditya VI (1076–1123 A.D.), who conferred on him the title 'Vidyapati'. Besides this he composed also the well-known erotic lyric called the *Caurapañcāśikā* or *Caura(Cauri)suratapañcāśikā*.

Boehtlingk (1815–1904): His first publication was *Panini's Eight Books of Grammatical Rules* and it appeared in 1839 with Indian commentaries. His other works are a first attempt at explaining the accent in Sanskrit, declension in Sanskrit, The Unadi affixes etc. He also translated and edited two Sanskrit Dramas, Kalidasa's *Ring-Śakuntalā* and *Mṛcchakaṭika*, *Chāndogya Upaniṣad* and Dandin's *Kāvyādarśa*. He was the first to give a specimen of the original accentuation in the *Ṛgveda*.

Buddha (c. 563-483 B.C.): Gautama the Buddha, one of the greatest spiritual personalities of India, was born in the Lumbini Grove near the ancient town of Kapilavastu in the now dense terai region of Nepal. He was a prince and at 29, he left his palace and everything else and wandered into the forests in quest of a solution to all sufferings. After six years of rigorous spiritual practices, he came to be known as Buddha, the Enlightened One. According to the teachings of the Buddha the world is a field of suffering and the cause of this suffering is desire. By following the Eight-fold path one can abolish desire and enter into *Nirvāṇa*, an eternal peace.

Dandin: One of the earliest writers on poetics, the name of his work being *Kāvyādarśa.* Supposed to have flourished in the first half of the 18th century A.D. The prose-romance, entitled *Daśakumāracarita,* is generally believed to have been written by him. Some scholars think that the work called *Avantisundarīkathā* is also by Dandin, and constitutes the lost earlier portion of *Daśakumāracarita.*

David Frawley: David Frawley is the director of the American Institute of Vedic Studies and an Ayurvedic Specialist. His field of study includes Ayurvedic medicine, Vedic astrology, *Tantra*, *Yoga* and Vedantic philosophy. His books include *Gods, Sages & Kings*, *From the River of Heaven*, and *Hymns of the Ṛg Veda* etc.

Devīcandragupta : A drama, attributed to Vishakhadeva who is probably identical with Vishakhadatta, from which passages are quoted in the *Nāṭyadarpaṇa* of Ramachandra and Gunachandra (12th cent. A.D.). Abhinavagupta quotes the work, without the author's name in his commentary on the *Nāṭyaśāstra.* It is also quoted in Bhoja's *Śṛṅgāraprakāśa.*

Dharmakirti: A Buddhist logician of the seventh century. Author of the well-known *Nyāyabindu* and *Pramāṇavārtika.* A *Pramāṇaviniścaya* exists in Tibetan, the original Sanskrit text being lost.

Dinnaga: Chief of the early Buddhist logicians. Probably lived before 400 A.D. and wrote the *Pramāṇasamuccaya*, the *Nyāyapraveśa*, and other texts most of which are preserved only in translations. The work, entitled *Prajñāpāramitā-piṇḍārtha*, epitomizing in 58 verses the *Aṣṭasāhasrikāprajñāpāramitā*, is also attributed to Dinnaga. I-Tsing ascribed eight other philosophical works to him.

Filliozat, J.: Dr. J. Filliozat, an Indologist, was actively associated with the Institute of Indian Civilization at Sorbonne in Paris and did pioneering work in archaeology and Indian culture. He was a student of Prof. Sylvain Levi.

Friedrich Engels (1820–1895) : Friedrich Engels, social philosopher and businessman, the closest collaborator of Karl Marx, was born at the Rhineland industrial town of Barmen. His formal education terminated with the Gymnasium, after which he continued to study and write in his free time while he was a commercial apprentice. At the age of 49 he devoted himself to political activities and writing. He was the author of *Dialectics of Nature, Ludring Feuerback and The End of classical German Philosophy, The origin of the Family, Private Property and the State, The present war in Germany* etc.

Friedrich Schlegel (1772 –1829): Professor Schlegel began his academic career in law but soon turned to philosophy, art and the classics, which he studied at

Goettingen and Leipzig. He studied Sanskrit for two years in Paris. His books *On Language*, *On Philosophy* and *Historical Ideas* are the first attempt at Indo-Germanic linguistics and the starting point of the study of Indian language and comparative philology. He published some metrical translations of Indian works, including (1) *The Beginning of Ramayana* (2) *Indian cosmology from the first book of the laws of Manu* (3) *On the Bhagavadgita* (4) *Extracts from the history of Shakuntala according to Mahabharata.*

Gangadevi: Author of *Madhurāvijaya.* Wife of Kampana or Kamaparaya who was the son of Rukka I (c. 1343–79 A.D.) of Vijayanagara.

Gautama: One of the traditional writers on original *Smṛti.* He is also known as Akshapada. Three texts - *Gautama-dharma-sūtra*, *Pitṛmedha-sūtra* and *Śrāddha-kalpa* - are attributed to him. A Gautama or Gotama (c. 500 B.C.) is supposed to have founded the *Nyāya* philosophy. The work *Nyāya-sūtras* is ascribed to him.

Gītagovinda: Composed by Jayadeva. It is a devotional lyric dealing with the amorous play of Krishna at Vrindavan, Radha's separation, Krishna's play with the gopis, Radha's anguish, yearning for union and jealousy, Krishna's return, penitence and appeasement of Radha and finally the blissful reunion. The *Gītagovinda* has received unstinted praise not only from Indian critics, but also from eminent Western scholars like Lassen, Jones, Levi, Pischel and Schroeder.

Harṣacarita: A prose composition of the *Ākhyāyikā* type by Banabhatta, written in eight chapters. It deals with the activities of Harsha's father, Prabhakaravardhana and the expedition of Harsha's brother Rajyavardhana against the Hunas, but chiefly with the important incidents of the reign of Harshavardhana. In the introductory portion of this work we get references to some earlier poets and dramatists and information about the personal history of the author.

Hemachandra Suri: Originally known as Changadeva. Born at Dhanduka (in Ahmedabad) he became a Jaina monk and wrote the grammatico-historical poem *Kumārapālacarita* or *Dvyāśrayakāvya*, partly in Sanskrit and partly in Prakrit, in honour of Kumarapala, the Chalukya king of Anhilvad. Author also of the philosophical work *Pramāṇamīmāṁsā*, and of the grammatical work called *Śabdānuśāsana.* He wrote also the *Kāvyānuśāsana*, a work on poetics and the *Abhidhānacintāmaṇi*, a lexicon.

Hitopadeśa: The Bengal version of the *Pañcatantra.* In place of the five books of the original *Pañcatantra*, it contains only four. Besides, it has made many additions to, and alterations in the original treatise. Many gnomic verses of the *Kāmandakīya Nītisāra* occur in it. Its author is Narayana.

Ivanov, V.V.: Prof. V.V. Ivanov is a distinguished Russian linguist.

Jagannatha Pandita: Author of the *Rasagaṅgādhara,* the celebrated work on poetics. He received the title of *Paṇḍitarāja* from Shah Jahan (1628–58 A.D.), emperor of Delhi. After crticising the views of the earlier writers he defines poetry as a linguistic composition which brings a charming idea into expression. Jagannatha's *Citramīmāṁsā* is another work on poetics. His other works include the erotico-didactic poem *Bhāminīvilāsa*, the euologistic works called *Āsaphavilāsa, Jagadābharaṇa* and *Prāṇābharaṇa*, the last three being eulogies respectively of Asaph Khan, brother of Nur-Jahan, queen of emperor Jahangir, king Jagatsimha of Udaipur and king Prananarayana of Kamarupa.

Jānakīharaṇa: A *mahākāvya* by Kumaradasa. Twenty cantos of the work are available. According to a Sinhalese commentary the original work appears to have consisted of 25 cantos. It is based on the *Rāmāyaṇa* story. The subject matter runs beyond *Jānakīharaṇa* (abduction of Janaki) and appears to have dealt with the incidents up to the re-installation of Rama on the throne.

Jawaharlal Nehru (1889–1964)**:** Jawaharlal Nehru, Indian Nationalist leader, was born in Allahabad on 14th Nov. 1889, of a prosperous Brahmin family from Kashmir. After his education for 7 years at Harrow and Cambridge absorbing the culture of the West, he returned to India but was disgusted by the general attitude of the ruling Britishers against Indians which provoked him to join the freedom struggle. Anointed early by Mahatma Gandhi, he advanced steadily through the ranks of Congress, eventually to preside over it 3 times. He was a superb orator and writer, and greatly loved by his countrymen. After India gained her Independence, he became its first Prime Minister. His writings include *An Autobiography*, *The Unity of India* and *The Discovery of India.*

Jayadeva: Author of the *Gītagovinda*, a well-known lyric poem. He flourished in 12th century A.D. He was an inhabitant of Kenduvilva which is identified by some with a village called Kenduli in the district of Puri, Orissa.

Jonaraja: A Kashmirian writer. He wrote the *Dvitīyarājataraṅgiṇī* as a continuation of the *Rājataraṅgiṇī* which was left incomplete due to Kalhana's death. His patron was Sultan Zain-ul-Abidin (14th century A.D.). Jonaraja's work ends abruptly due to his death in 1459 A.D.

Judith M. Tyberg: Judith Tyberg was born on 17th May, 1902, to Danish parents who were Theosophists. Educated at the Theosophical Society's Point Lama Raja Yoga school, she received here M.A. in Religion and Philosophy from the Theosophical University, with a specialisation in Oriental Thought. Here she also obtained another graduate degree in Sacred Scriptures and Ancient Civilizations and her doctorate in Sanskrit studies. She is the founder of East-West Cultural Centre and author of many books like *Sanskrit keys to the wisdom Religion*, *The Language of Gods*, *First Lessons in Sanskrit.*

Kalhana: Author of the well-known historical poem entitled *Rājataraṅgiṇī*. He was the son of Champaka who was a minister of King Harsha of Kashmir (1089–1101 A.D.). He mentions Jayasimha (1127–59 A.D.) as the reigning sovereign.

Kalidasa: The greatest poet and dramatist in Sanskrit literature. Author of the *mahākāvyas* called *Raghuvaṁśa* and *Kumārasambhava*, the lyric poem entitled *Meghadūta* and the dramas *Abhijñānaśākuntalam, Vikramorvaśīya* and *Mālavikāgnimitra*. The lyric poem *Ṛtusaṁhāra* is attributed by some scholars to Kalidasa. Nearly a score of other *Kāvyas* are traditionally attributed to Kalidasa. The well-known among them are the *Nalodaya* and the *Śṛṅgāratilaka*. Tradition makes him a court poet of Vikramaditya. According to a legend, Kalidasa was a great fool in his early age, and acquired prodigious learning and poetic skill through the grace of goddess Kali whom he propitiated by severe penance.

Kāmasūtra: The earliest extant work on erotics, ascribed to Vatsyayana. It consists of 1250 verses divided into seven *Adhikaraṇas*, 14 *Prakaraṇas* and 36 *Adhyāyas*. The work incidentally mentions 64 arts, particulary to be learnt by women. These include dance, music, art of decoration, skill in houshold work etc. The life of a *Nāgaraka* (man about town) has been depicted in detail.

Kapila: Sage Kapila is considered to be the father of Sankhya system of philosophy. His two works, *Tattva-samāsa* and *Sāṅkhya-sūtra*, which formed the basis of his philosophy are not available to us now. Traditionally he is held to be the fifth *avatāra* of God Vishnu. He is believed to have flourished several generations before the Buddha, and the birth place of Buddha - Kapilavastu - is said to have derived its name from him.

Karl Marx (1818–1883): Karl Marx, a German political philosopher, was born on May 5, 1818, at Treves, Prussia. He made his mark first as a journalist when he accepted the editorship of the newspaper "Rheinische Zeitung" where he displayed a fearlessness and ruthlessness that made striking impression on the readers, earning him the reputation of being the first German journalist of note. He devoted his outstanding literary powers to pressing for reform of many Prussian laws but his attacks on the government resulted in his permanent exile from his homeland. Later, he formed an international Communist League where the Communist groups in all countries might collaborate, and presented to it a *Communist Manifesto* with the help of Friedrich Engels. From then onwards he devoted all his energies to promoting Communism and was instrumental in the foundation of International Working Men's Association. In 1867 he published his great work *Das Kapital* (in 3 vols.) in which he set out his doctrine in full.

Katyayana: Author of the *Vārtika-sūtras* or supplementary rules in Panini's *Aṣṭādhyāyī*. Believed to have flourished some time between 500 and 350 B.C. in South India. Vararuci appears to have been his other name.

Kautalya: Also known as Kautilya, Vishnugupta or Chanakya. Author of the celebrated *Arthaśāstra*, the oldest extant work on politics and statecraft. Believed to have been Prime Minister of the Maurya King Chandragupta (c. 324–300 B.C.).

Kāvyamīmāṁsā: A work on poetics by Vagbhatta, who is to be distinguished from the author, bearing the same name, of the *Vāgbhaṭṭālaṅkāra.*

Kshemendra (surnamed **Vyasadasa**)**:** The Kashmirian polygrapher who flourished in the eleventh century A.D. He wrote on a variety of subjects. His two works on poetics are the *Kavikaṇṭhābharaṇa* and the *Aucityavicāracarcā.* His work on prosody is called *Suvṛttatilaka.* Among his satirical and didactic works the following are noteworthy: *Kalāvilāsa, Samayamātṛkā, Sevyasevakopadeśa, Narmamālā, Darpadalana, Cārucaryā.* His *Rāmāyaṇamañjarī* and *Bhārata-mañjarī* are poetical works based respectively on the *Rāmāyaṇa* and *Mahābhārata.* His *Bṛhatkathāmañjarī* is a metrical version of the *Bṛhatkathā.*

Kumārasambhava: A famous court epic by Kalidasa in 17 cantos. It opens with a fine picture of the Himalayas. Uma, the daughter of Himalaya, is keen upon having Shiva as her spouse. The gods, persecuted by the demon Taraka, approach Brahma at whose behest they depute the Cupid to break the deep meditation of Shiva. This is necessary to bring about the wedding of Shiva and Uma, as only a son born of their union can rescue the gods from the demon's oppression. The Cupid succeeds initially in his mission, but the enraged Shiva burns him to ashes. Uma then begins hard penance to win the hand of Shiva. Shiva, convinced of the sincerity of her love, marries her. In course of time, a son named Kumara (Kartikeya) is born to them. This son is the future saviour of the gods. Some of the finest portions of Sanskrit poetry are found in this poem.

Kumarila Bhatta: Founder of Bhatta school of *Mīmāṁsā*, he was a native of South India and wrote perhaps around 700 A.D. His works are *Ślokavārtika, Tantravārtika* and *Ṭupṭīkā.*

Lakshmikanta Maitra: An M.P. who participated in the Constituent Assembly Debate on National Language in India.

Leonard Bloomfield (1887–1949)**:** Leonard Bloomfield, an American philologist, was born on April 1 at Chicago Bloomfield, taught successively at the Universities of Wisconsin (Madison) Cincinnati and Illinois (Urbana), Ohio State University (Columbus), the University of Chicago and Yale University, where he was a steering Professor of Linguistics from 1940 until his death. His book *Language* is famous for its treatment of linguistics.

Madhva: Also known as Purnaprajna and Anandatirtha, he founded the *Dvaita* school of *Vedānta* which sought to demolish the *Advaita* doctrine of Shankara. His standpoint is called unqualified dualism. Born in 1199 or 1197 A.D. in a village near Udipi, South Canara district, early in life he became proficient in Vedic learning, and renounced the world. His preceptor was Achyutapreksha. He died at the age of 79. He commented on seven of the important *Upaniṣads*, the *Bhagavadgītā*, the *Brahmasūtra* and the *Bhāgavatapurāṇa*. He wrote also a number of independent tracts including the *Anuvyākhyāna* and *Tattvasaṅkhyāna (Tattva-nirṇaya)*. His epitome of the *Mahābhārata*, called *Bhāratatātparyanirṇaya,* and gloss on the *Bhāgavatapurāṇa* help to elucidate his philosophy. He wrote a commentary on the first 40 hymns of the *Ṛgveda*. His *Gītā-tātparya*, in prose and verse, gives the essence of the *Gītā*.

Magha: Author of the *mahākāvya* entitled *Śiśupālavadha* which shows deep influence of Bharavi's *Kirātārjunīya*. Mentioned by the rhetoricians Vamana and Anandavardhana in the 8th – 9th century A.D. Magha himself says, at the end of his work, that his grandfather was the minister of a king named Varmala. Varmala is identified by some with king Varmalata, an inscription of whom is dated 625 A.D.

Mahābhārata: The second of the two great Indian epics, *Mahābhārata* is the work of Rishi Vyasa. The epic most powerfully brings out the representative characters of the age, their ideals and culture in a most profound and dramatic way. It describes the battle between two royal families – the Pandavas and the Kauravas – culminating in the victory of the Pandavas. Over time a large body of subsidiary stories dealing with every imaginable subject of worth were added to it and the traditional count of the verses now stands at about 100,000. This epic contains the famous discourse, the crowning synthesis of Indian philosophy, known as the *Bhagavad Gita,* between Sri Krishna and Arjuna on the battlefield when Arjuna is caught in a dilemma as to the nature of his duty. *Mahābhārata*, because of its universal appeal, is hailed as the fifth *Veda*.

Mahābhāṣya: The Great Commentary; the oldest extant commentary by Patanjali on Panini's *Aṣṭādhyāyī*. Patanjali comments on 1228 rules of Panini in the order of the *Aṣṭādhyāyī*. His commentary on each *pāda* of the *Aṣṭādhyāyī* is divided into several parts called *Āhnikas*. There are 85 such *Āhnikas*.

Mahatma Gandhi (1869–1948): Mohandas Karamchand Gandhi, whom the world called *mahatma* (the great soul), was a political leader of recent times to achieve a major revolution by means of the movement of civil disobedience through the policy of non-violence against the British government in India. He was born at Porbandar, Kathiawar, and obtained a Degree in Law from England. He went to South Africa to practice Law and there he founded the Natal Indian Congress and successfully fought against the racial discrimination shown to the Indians living there, through non-violent means. After returning to India, he applied the same methods to the freedom struggle and soon became the President of the Indian National Congress. He was arrested by the Britishers several times, and finally in 1947 when Britain agreed for the transfer of power, Gandhi fearlessly traveled the length and breadth of India, trying to create peace and goodwill among the rioting Hindus and the Muslims. He wrote a few books, the most famous being his autobiography entitled *My Experiments with Truth.*

Mālavikāgnimitra: A drama in five acts by Kalidasa. King Agnimitra falls in love with princess Malavika in disguise. The youngest queen, Iravati, is incensed when she sees them embracing and insults the king. The eldest queen, Dharini, keeps Malavika confined with the help of the clever Vidushaka. The king and Malavika meet again, but the meeting does not last owing to Iravati's hostility. Eventually the true identity of Malavika is revealed. Dharini, delighted at the news of her son's victory over the Yavanas, fulfills her promise of reward by giving consent to the king's marriage with Malavika. Iravati's wrath is also appeased. Thus the drama has a happy denouement.

Mallinatha Suri: A famous commentator on the poetical works of Kalidasa, Bharavi, Bhatti, Magha, Sriharsha and on some works on poetics, lexicography and grammar. The *Udārakāvya, Raghuvīracaritakāvya, Vaidyakalpataru* and *Vaidyaratnamālā* are the original works attributed to Mallinatha. The great commentator Mallinatha appears to have flourished in the later half of the 14th century or in the earlier half of the 15th century.

Mānasāra: A well-known work on *Vāstuvidyā*, the science of Architecture. The extant work, which appears to be a later version, perhaps came into being some time between the 11th century and the 15th. The original work may have been composed in the Gupta period.

Manu: Manu is one of the fourteen progenitors of mankind and rulers of earth. Each of them is supposed to rule the earth for one *manvantara* (age of Manu) extending over 4,320,000 years. The starting of *kali-yuga* is taken to represent the beginning of the age of the present Manu - the seventh one - known as Vaivasvata Manu. It is held that the Great Deluge occurred during this time and all but Manu are said to have perished, he having been rescued by a fish which he reared up from its infancy. In *Ṛgveda*, Manu is spoken of as the father of mankind, and is traditionally regarded as the author of the *Manusmṛti*. He is considered the foremost among the twenty great writers of original *Smṛti.*

Max Mueller (1823–1900): A Professor of Comparative Linguistics at Oxford, Max Mueller studied classical philology and philosophy at Leipzig University and was induced by Hermann Brockhaus to take up Sanskrit. He published the *Rigveda with Sayana's Commentary* in 1849. He was also the author of *Sacred*

Books of the East, History of Ancient Sanskrit literature, Science of Languages, Science of Religion, Origin and Growth of Religion etc.

Meghadūtam: A love lyric (or rather a monody) by Kalidasa. It is divided into two parts called *Pūrvamegha* and *Uttaramegha*. The total number of verses varies from 110 to 121 in the different versions. A *Yakṣa*, banished to Ramagiri for a year for dereliction of duty, pines for his beloved in Alaka. At the advent of the monsoons he becomes disconsolate and chooses a cloud to carry his tidings to his beloved. In the first part of the lyric the *Yakṣa* gives the cloud a detailed description of the path he has to follow. In the second part he describes the supernatural beauty of Alaka and gives the cloud the message to be delivered to his sweet-heart.

Monier Williams: Sir Monier Williams, a British Sanskrit scholar, was born in 1819 at Bombay. In 1860 he became the Professor of Sanskrit at Oxford. He died in 1899. His works include *Practical Grammar of Sanskrit Language* and *The study of Sanskrit in relation to missionary work in India*. He also compiled a Sanskrit- English dictionary.

Mṛcchakaṭika: A ten-act drama by Shudraka. It is unique in the sense that it breaks away from the usual theme and describes the brahmin Charudatta – once very rich but now improverished, nevertheless large-hearted – and the rich courtesan Vasantasena. It describes their love and how, through the vicissitudes of life, they are united in wedlock. Parallel to this love-story runs the political story of how the bad king Palaka is dethroned and slain by Aryaka. This social drama, breathing as it does a plebian atmosphere, is regarded as the most Shakespearean of all Sanskrit plays. The drama has taken its name from a toy earthen cart (*mṛcchakaṭika*), with which Rohasena, Charudatta's son, plays.

Mudrārākṣasa: A seven-act drama by Vishakhadatta. The main plot is the winning over, through astute diplomacy, by Chanakya, minister of the Maurya king Chandragupta, of Rakshasa, the faithful and efficient minister of the Nandas. It has certain features that distinguish it from other classical Sanskrit dramas. Contrary to the usual practice, it is written on a purely political theme. Secondly, it is practically devoid of female characters.

Mukherjee, H.N: Prof. H.N. Mukherjee is an eminent Sanskrit scholar from West Bengal.

Nagarjuna: The Buddhist philosopher of this name, who probably flourished in the latter part of the 2nd century A.D., was author of the *Mādhyamikakārikās*. According to his biography, translated into Chinese by Kumarajiva (c. 405 A.D.), he was a Brahmin born in South India, was versed in various branches of knowledge including the *Vedas*. He is stated to have embraced Buddhism and propagated it .

He is described also as a great magician and as well-versed in astronomy, medicine etc. Nagarjuna was the founder of the *Mādhyamika* school of *Mahāyāna.*

Naiṣadhīyacarita: A *mahākāvya,* in 22 cantos, by Sriharsa who is different from Sriharsha, the author of the dramas called *Ratnāvalī*, *Priyadarśikā* and *Nāgānanda.* Based on the story of Nala and Damayanti in the *Mahābhārata*, it describes the events up to the marriage of Nala and Damayanti and the arrival of Kali in the capital of Nala. Among departures from the original, a notable one is the character of Nala. The poet is traditionally praised by Indian critics for *Pada-lālitya* (gracefulness of words) in this poetical composition. There are more than 20 commentaries on this work.

Najiruddin Ahmed: Md. Najiruddin Ahmed was an M.P. who participated actively in the Constituent Assembly Debate for National Language in India and spoke strongly in favour of Sanskrit.

Narayana: Author of the *Hitopadeśa.* His patron was Dhavalacandra. He is believed to have flourished sometime in the period between 900 and 1373 A.D.

Nāṭyaśāstra: The earliest extant work on dramaturgy, attributed to Bharata. The treatise, in its present form, is considered to be the result of additions by later hands. It is an elaborate work, dealing as it does with the theatre, the religious rites to be performed at every representation, the dress and equipment of actors, the music, dance, movements and gestures of actors, the different classes of drama and the emotions and sentiments which constitute the vital element in the drama. It anticipates many of the concepts elaborated in later works on poetics. It states the nature of *Rasa* and enumerates eight sentiments.

Pañcatantra: The only Sanskrit work on fables, ascribed to Vishnusharman by some scholars. It consists of five books: *Mitrabhedha* (separation of friends); *Mitraprāpti* (acquisition of friends); *Sandhivigraha* (peace and war); *Labdhanāśa* (loss of what is acquired); and *Aparīkṣitakāritva* (rash action).

Panikkar, K.M.: Sardar K.M. Panikkar, lived an illustrious life devoted with equal passion to public service and creative work. Born in the year of 1893, he was a poet, writer, historian, educationist, administrator, statesman and diplomat. He wrote about 52 Books in English and 45 in Malayalam. He was the Chairman of Kerala Sahitya Academy in 1955.

Panini: Author of the celebrated grammatical work called *Aṣṭādhyāyī.* Two *Kāvyas* called *Pātālavijaya* and *Jāmbavatīvijaya* are traditionally attributed to Panini. He is generally placed in the 4th century B.C. According to some, he flourished in the 6th or 7th cent. B.C., if not earlier. In later literature, Panini is referred to as *Śālātūrīya*, an inhabitant of Salatura, identified with the present Lahore in the Yusufzai Valley.

Pargiter, F.E.: Pargiter was the first to make a bold attempt to coordinate the varying details of the royal dynasties before the Great War of Mahabharata (which is held to have occurred between 1500–1000 B.C.) into a skeleton of political history. He has authored the books *The Purana Text of the Dynasties of the Kali Age* (London, Oxford University Press, 1913) and *Ancient Indian Historical Tradition* (London, Oxford University Press, 1922).

Patanjali: Author of the *Mahābhāṣya,* the Great Commentary on the *Aṣṭādhyāyī.* He appears to have been a contemporary of the Sunga King Pushaymitra who highly honored him for his learning. He is regarded by some as identical with Patanjali, author of the *Yogasūtra*. The date of Patanjali is controversial. He is, however, generally assigned to the second century B.C. Patanjali, the grammarian, is believed by some to have been a Kashmirian. The epithets *Gonardīya* and *Goṇikāputra*, mentioned in the *Mahābhāṣya*, are supposed by some to refer to Patanjali himself. Thus his mother appears to have been named Gonika, and Gonarda seems to be his native place.

Plato (427–347 B.C.)**:** A Greek philosopher whose influence on thought has been continuous for more than 2,400 years. He founded the Academy - an institute for the systematic pursuit of philosophical and scientific research - which was to function as a society for the prosecution of both exact and human sciences. He authored 36 works arranged in nine tetralogies (groups of four), which include the famous works *Symposium*, *Phaedo* and *Republic*.

Pūrvamīmāṁsā: Attributed to Jaimini. Written in twelve chapters, it describes the various sacrifices and their purposes, the theory of *Apūrva* as well as some philosophical propositions. The first chapter discusses the sources of knowledge and the validity of the *Vedas*.

Pythagoras (c. 530 B.C.)**:** The Greek philosopher Pythagoras gave his name to an order of scientific and religious thinkers through a widespread organization which was, in its origin, more of a religious brotherhood than a philosophical school. In his later years, the political reaction against him brought about a forced retirement to Metapontum where he remained until his death at the end of the 6th or the beginning of the 5th Century B.C.

Rabindranath Tagore (1861–1941)**:** Rabindranath Tagore, a Poet and mystic, was born in Calcutta. He started writing poetry in Bengal and soon captivated the readers with the high lyrical beauty and the lilting sound rhythm of words in his poems that breathed a fresh vigour into the very language itself. In 1912 he established a school in the traditional *gurukula* style at Shantiniketan, near Bolpur, which developed into an international University called Vishwabharati. Besides being a poet, he was also an accomplished writer and wrote many stories and plays. His earlier works were entirely in Bengali, but later when he felt the need to reach out to a wider audience, he started translating his own works into English. His translation *Gitanjali*, an anthology of Poems, won him the Nobel Prize in Literature in 1913. He has authored about 60 poetical works besides volumes of stories, such as *Mashi*, *Broken Ties*, plays including *The Post Office*, *Sacrifice*, *Red Oleander*, novels including *The Home and The World*, *Gora*. His best known poems are *Gitanjali*, *Songs of Kabir*, *Stray Birds* etc.

Radhakrishnan, S. (1888–1975) **:** Dr. S. Radhakrishnan, a world famous scholar, philosopher and statesman, was born in Chittoor district, Madras Presidency. He was educated at Madras Christian College. At the age of 20, he published his first book on Vedanta. Soon he became a prolific writer and his works covered a wide variety of topics including religion, philosophy, education, politics, sociology, literature and culture. He assumed Professorship in various Universities of India and was the leader of the Indian delegation to the United Nations Educational, Scientific and Cultural Organisation and also was elected as the Chairman of UNESCO's executive board for 1948–49. In 1952, he took up his appointment as Vice-president of the Republic of India and in 1962, was elected as President of India. His works include *Indian Philosophy*, *The Philosophy of the Upaniṣads*, *An Idealist View of Life*, *Eastern Religions and Western Thought*, *East and West: Some Reflections*, *Religion in a Changing World.*

Raghavan, V. (1908–1979)**:** An eminent Sanskrit Scholar from South India. He was the Head of the Sanskrit Dept., Madras University for about 13 years (1955–68). He was tirelessly engaged in New Catalogue Catalogaram and several other projects, since he joined the University of Madras in 1935. He has authored nearly 100 books and monographs, besides having about 900 research papers and 100 creative writings in Sanskrit to his credit.

Raghuvaṁśa: A *mahākāvya*, in 19 cantos, by Kalidasa. It describes the activities of the kings of *Ikṣvāku* race from Dilipa to Agnivarma. It takes its name from the famous King Raghu, son of Dilipa and is known for its fine specimens of poetry. It is based chiefly on the Ramayana.

Rajashekhara : Author of the Prakrit drama *Karpūramañjarī*, the Sanskrit dramas *Bālarāmāyaṇa, Viddhaśālabhañjikā* and the *Kāvyamīmāṁsā*, a work dealing with miscellaneous matters relating to poets and poetry. In the *Bālarāmāyaṇa* he refers to six earlier works. In the *Kāvyamīmāṁsā* he refers to his work called *Bhuvana-koṣa*. He probably flourished in the period covering the last quarter of the 9th century and the first quarter of the 10th.

Rājataraṅgiṇī: The most famous historical poem by Kalhana. Consisting of eight chapters and drawing upon earlier sources, notably the *Nīlamatapurāṇa*, it deals, in the earlier part, with the legendary kings of Kashmir. In the later part, it gives an account of the Kashmiri kings of its historical period. It is a valuable work for the political and social history of Kashmir as well as the topography of that land.

Raman, C.V. (1888–1970): Dr. C.V. Raman, an Indian physicist, was born at Trichinopoly (Tiruchirapalli). He graduated from Presidency College in Madras and received a master's degree in 1907. From 1917 to 1933 he was Professor at Calcutta University. In 1930 he received the Nobel Prize in Physics for his work on the diffusion of light popularly known as "Raman Effect". He contributed to the building up of many research organisations in india. He founded the 'Indian Journal of Physics' and the 'Indian Academy of Science' and helped train hundreds of students. In 1947 he was named Director of the Raman Research Institute at Bangalore. He gave the much needed thrust in the scientific fields to the modern India and he was finally conferred "Bharat Ratna," the highest civilian award of the nation. He had published many scientific papers during the course of his research.

Ramanuja: A famous philosopher who founded the *Viśiṣṭādvaita* (qualified monism) school of *Vedānta* philosophy. Son of Keshava and Kantimati, He was born in Sriperumbudur in 1017 A.D., studied at first under Yadavaprakasha and then under Yamunacharya whom he succeeded as the Head of a *Vaiṣnava* sect. He became a *Sannyāsin* and died in about 1137 A.D. Author of the *Śrībhāṣya* on the *Brahmasūtra*. Among other works, he wrote a *Gītābhāṣya, Vedārthasaṅgraha and Vedāntadīpa.*

Rāmāyaṇa: One of the two great Indian epics, traditionally ascribed to Valmiki who is a legendary figure. *Rāmāyaṇa* is held as the earliest poem, the *ādikāvya*, the first metrical composition after the *Vedas*. It deals with the story of Rama of Ikshvaku dynasty, the theme being the triumph of righteousness over evil by the hero, Rama the God incarnate, who defeats in battle the *asura* king Ravana who was oppressing mankind with his immense power and inordinate lust and who had abducted his wife Sita. This book of about 25000 *shlokas* has been a constant source of inspiration to the people of India in maintaining the ideals of character and conduct. Even to this day the very name Rama is a *mantra* and a solace to many devout Indians.

Rāmāyaṇamañjarī: A poetical work by Kshemendra. It gives us an abridged version of the entire story of Rama. All the seven books of the ***Rāmāyaṇa***, with the same titles, are found in this work. Kshemendra, however, has altered the contents to a considerable extent.

Rick Briggs: Rick Briggs is a NASA Researcher & Scientist working in the field of Artificial Intelligence.

Samarāṅgaṇasūtradhāra: A work on architecture, ascribed to Bhojadeva (11th century A.D).

Sankuka: He is supposed to have lived during 9th Century A.D. at the time of King Ajitapida of Kashmir. He is famous for his interpolation - known as *Anumiti-vāda* - of the renowned *Rasa-sūtras* of Bharata. May be identical with a Sankuka the poet who and whose poem *Bhuvanābhyudaya* are mentioned by Kalhana of 12th Century A.D.

Sayana : Author of commentaries on the *Veda Saṁhitās*. He commented also on some *Brāhmaṇa* texts, notably the *Taittirīya, Aitareya* and *Śatapatha*. The *Smṛti* work, *Prāyaścittasudhānidhi*, and the anthology called *Subhāṣitasudhānidhi* are also attributed to him. Son of Mayana and Srimati, and brother of Madhava, he was a contemporary of king Bukka (14th cent.) of Vijayanagara.

Śākuntalam: The most famous Sanskrit drama. Written by Kalidasa in seven acts, it deals with the Dushyanta-Shakuntala legend that occurs in the *Mahābhārata* as well as in the *Padmapurāṇa* (*Svargakhāṇḍa*). Kalidasa has introduced many changes into the original story, the most prominent of which are the curse of Durvasa and the Ring episode. Some scholars point out the similarity of the theme of the drama with the story of the Katthahan-jataka.

Shankaracharya: A great philosopher who founded the *Advaita* (non-dualistic) school of *Vedānta* philosophy. He belonged to the Nambudiri sect of Brahmins of Malabar, and is believed to have been born at Kaladi on the Western coast. Quite early in life he is said to have mastered Vedic learning. He described himself as a pupil of Govinda. According to tradition, he renounced the world at an early age, became a sannyasi and established four *Maṭhas* or monasteries, one each at Sringeri in Mysore in the South, Puri in the East, Dvaraka in the West and Badrinath in the Himalayas. He is said to have died at Kedarnath in the Himalayas at the age of 32. Supposed to have flourished between the last quarter of the 8th century and the first quarter of the 9th. Author of a commentary (*Bhāṣya*) on the *Vedāntasūtra*. He wrote also commentaries on ten *Upaniṣads*, viz. *Īśa, Kena, Kaṭha, Praśna, Muṇḍaka, Māṇḍūkya, Aitareya, Taittirīya, Chāndogya* and *Bṛhadāraṇyaka*. He commented also on the *Bhagavadgītā*. Also attributed to him are the following works: *Advaitānubhūti, Āgamaśāstravivaraṇa, Aparokṣānubhūti, Ātmabodha, Ātmajñānopadeśa, Ātmānātmaviveka, Ātmopadeśavidhi, Cidānandastavarāja, Dṛgdṛśyaprakaraṇa, Gaudapādīyabhāṣya, Hastāmalaka, Laghuvākyavṛtti, Mantraśāstra, Mohamudgara, Pañcīkaraṇaprakriyā, Prauḍhānubhūti, Sarvadarśanasidhāntasaṅgraha, Śataślokī, Tattvopadeśa, Upadeśasāhasrī, Vākyavṛtti, Vivekacūḍāmaṇi.*

Shankaravarman (883–902 A.D.): A Kashmirian king mentioned in *Rājataraṅgiṇī*, the historical poem-text of the 12th Century A.D. Kashmirian poet Kalhana.

Shudraka: Author of the celebrated drama *Mṛcchakaṭika*. From the introductory portion of the drama we learn that the author was a Brahmin king versed in various branches of learning and that he immolated himself in fire at the age of one hundred and ten years. Some think that it is really a work of Bhasa, while others think that it was composed by court poet of a certain king Shudraka with whose name it was associated as a token of gratitude. The drama is assigned by different scholars to different dates ranging from the second century B.C. to the sixth century A.D. The one–act play *Padmaprabhṛtaka* is also attributed to Shudraka. He is supposed, by some scholars, to have been the author also of the play called *Vīṇāvāsavadattā*.

Somadeva: A Brahmin poet in the court of King Ananta of Kashmir (1029–1064 A.D.), Somadeva wrote his work, called *Kathāsaritsāgara,* a version of the *Bṛhatkathā*, between 1063 and 1082 A.D.

Sri Aurobindo (1872–1950)**:** Poet, scholar, writer, literary critic, philosopher, social thinker, revolutionary, nationalist, commentator on Indian culture and the scriptures, visionary, Yogi and Rishi Sri Aurobindo was born in Calcutta on the 15th of August 1872. He had his education in England where he mastered not only English and French but also Greek and Latin, and after his return to India, Sanskrit and other Indian languages also. In 1906 he became the first Principal of the Bengal National College, but resigned it soon after to participate openly in India's freedom struggle. Within a few years he was able was able to fix in the national consciousness the goal of complete and absolute independence, gave a new political programme to the country and a new direction to the freedom movement itself. In 1910 in answer to an inner call, he withdrew from the political field and sailed for Pondicherry where he devoted himself entirely to a *Yoga* which aimed at a total transformation and perfection of life upon earth. His works include *Life Divine* (his major philosophical work), *Synthesis of Yoga, Essays on the Gita* and *The Secret of the Veda*. His magnum opus *Savitri - A Legend and a Symbol*, a mystical poem of nearly 24000 lines in blank verse, sums up his vision and philosophy.

Sriharsha: Two authors of this name are found in the history of Sanskrit literature. One is the author of the three dramas, entitled *Ratnāvalī, Priyadarśikā* and *Nāgānanda* and usually referred to simply as Harsha. The other is the author of the *mahākāvya* called *Naiṣadhīyacarita* and the philosophical treatise named *Khaṇḍanakhaṇḍakhādya.* The author of the dramas is identified by some scholars with Harshavardhana, King of Thanesvara, who flourished in the first half of the seventh century A.D. He probably flourished in the second half of the twelfth century A.D. during the reign of Vijayachandra and Jayachandra of Kanyakubja.

Subramania Bharati (1882–1921)**:** Bharati is hailed as the greatest Tamil poet of the modern era. He was a fiery poet-patriot, a writer as well as a speaker, and his songs and writings were the source of the outburst of national fervour in South India during the years 1905-08 which was also a period of great political awakening of India. He sought to give literary form and poetic expression to the national craving for freedom. In 1908 he took political refuge in the French occupied Pondicherry and it was here that he composed most of his literary and philosophical works. His epic *Pāñcāli Sapatam* and his lyrical poems *Kuyil Pāṭṭu* and *Kaṇṇan Pāṭṭu* are appreciated for their fresh vigour, beauty of phrases and poetic quality.

Vallabha: Author of the commentary, called *Anubhāṣya*, on the *Vedāntasūtras*. He lived from 1376 to 1430 A.D. He offers a theistic interpretation of the *Vedānta*, which is different from those of Shankara and Ramanuja. His view is called *Śuddhādvaita*.

Valmiki: Author of the *Rāmāyaṇa*. The legend goes that a bandit, Ratnakara by name, gave up his vile means of livelihood at the instance of sage Narada and started a long and arduous penance. While seated for long years at the same spot, he was covered all over with an anthill which is called *Valmīka* in Sanskrit; hence his name Valmiki. Having completed his penance, he was one day moved to pity at the sight of one of a pair of curlews, killed with an arrow by a fowler. This scene made him utter a verse (*mā niṣāda pratiṣṭhā tvamagamaḥ* etc.) cursing the fowler. This verse was the first piece of poetry; hence Valmiki is designated as *Ādikavi* (the first poet). Thereafter he wrote the *Rāmāyaṇa* at the bidding of God Brahma.

Vārtikasūtras: By Katyayana. Such *sūtras* are intended to be supplements to the rules of the *Aṣṭādhyāyī*.

Vatsyayana: The author of the well-known *Kāmasūtra*. His date is uncertain, but he appears to have been earlier than Kalidasa and is generally assigned to different periods from third century A.D. to the sixth. According to some, he flourished about the fourth century A.D. Supposed by some to have belonged to Pataliputra; according to others, he belonged to Avanti.

Vikramāṅkadevacarita: A historical pgoem, in 18 cantos, by Bilhana. It deals with the Calukyas of Kalyana, particularly with the history of king Vikramaditya VI (11th–12th century). Along with historical facts it contains fanciful accounts and exaggerations also.

Vishakhadatta: Author of the drama called *Mudrārākṣasa*. Scholars associate the author with Chandragupta II (4th–5th cent. A.D.) of the Gupta dynasty.

Vishnusharman: The author of the *Pañcatantra*. In the introduction to this work, he is described as relating the stories to the sons of King Amarashakti of Mahilaropya or Mihilaropya in the Deccan. The original *Pañcatantra*, now lost, appears to have been written prior to 531 A.D.

Vyas Houston: Dr. Vyas Houston, an American Sanskrit scholar, is presently working as the Director of American Sanskrit Institute, New York. He has made a major contribution in the propagation of Sanskrit through various means. He was in India for about 15 years and had the opportunity of learning Sanskrit directly from Swami Brahmananda.

Vyasa: Author of the *Mahābhārata*. Often referred to as Vedavyasa. The legend goes that he was born out of the union of sage Parasara and Matsyagandha or Satyavati. Having been born in an island (*dvīpa*) he is also called Dvaipayana. On account of his dark complexion he is sometimes styled Krishna Dvaipayana. He is said to have compiled the Vedas for the first time, and written the *Purāṇas* besides an excellent commentary on the philosophical work of Patanjali. While he composed the *Mahābhārata*, God Ganesha is said to have acted as his scribe. The stipulation between the author and the scribe was that the former would not stop dictating the verses till the completion of the book and the latter would not write without understanding the meaning of the verses. Vyasa at intervals dictated extremely difficult verses known as *Vyāsakūṭas*. During the time Ganesha took to comprehend the import of these verses, Vyasa composed new stanzas.

Whitney (1827–1894)**:** As a philologist, he made notable contributions in the study of Sanskrit and was Editor in chief of '*The Century Dictionary*'. Although he was at first interested in Natural Science, after 1848 he devoted himself with enthusiasm to Sanskrit, at that time a little-explored field. In 1854 he was appointed Professor of Sanskrit at Yale and in 1869 Professor of Comparative Philology also. He received the first Bopp prize from the Berlin Academy of Sciences for the most important contribution to Sanskrit. He was the author of *Taittirīya Prātiśākhya* (Journal of the American Oriental Society, vol. ix), *Atharva-veda saṁhitā, Atharvaveda Prātiśākhya, Sanskrit grammar, language and the study of language, Oriental and linguistic studies, The life and growth of Language* etc.

William Jones (1746–1794)**:** Sir William Jones was an English orientalist and jurist. He was educated at Oxford. From 1783 to 1794 he was a judge of the High Court at Calcutta. He founded the Bengal Asiatic Society in 1784. His notable works include a version of the Arabic '*Muallaqat*', a dissertation on the *Orthography of Asiatic Words in Roman Letters*, and translations of *Hitopadeśa* and *Śākuntalam* in the field of Sanskrit.

Will Durant: Will Durant was an American educator and writer, born on 5th Nov. 1885 in North Adams, Mass. He was educated at St. Peter's college, Jersey city, N.J., and at Columbia University, from which he received a doctorate in philosophy in 1917. He was the Director of Labor Temple School, New York city in 1914. In 1935 he was the professor of philosophy at the University of California at Los Angeles.

Yajnavalkya: One of the traditional writers on original *Smṛti*. The extant *Yājñavalkya-smṛti* is supposed to have been composed by him during the first two centuries of the Christian era or even earlier.

Bibliography

Primary Sources

1. *Aitareya Brāhmaṇa* of the *Ṛgveda*, Martin Haug, Bombay, 1863
2. *Āryabhaṭīya* of Aryabhatta, Vol. 1, K. Sambasiva Sastri, 1930
3. *Āryabhaṭīya* of Aryabhatta, Vol. 2, K. Sambasiva Sastri, 1931
4. *Baudhāyana Śulbasūtram*, Dr. Satyaprakash & Pt. Ram Swarup Sharma, New Delhi, 1968
5. *Bhartṛhari-śatakatrayam*, P. Gopinath, Delhi, 1989
6. *Bhoja-prabandha*, Kedarnath Sharma, Varanasi, 1961
7. *Bṛhadāraṇyaka Upaniṣad*, Sri Ramakrishna Math, Madras, 1979
8. *Chāndogya Upaniṣad*, Swami Swahananda, Sri Ramakrishna Math, Madras, 1984
9. *Dhammapada*, The Mother, Ladnun, Rajasthan, 1997
10. *Eight Upanishads*, Vol. 1 & 2, Swami Gambhirananda, RamakrishnaMath, Calcutta, 1991–92
11. *Harṣacaritam* of Banabhatta, Pt. Jagannath Pathaka, Varanasi, 1972
12. *Hitopadeśa* of Narayana, Peter Peterson, Delhi, 1999
13. *Kāvyādarśa* of Dandi, Jeevananda Vidyasagara Bhattacharya, Madras, 1964
14. *Kirātārjunīyam* of Bharavi, Acharya Sesaraja Sarma Regmi, Varanasi, 1987
15. *Mahābhārata*, Pt. Ramachandra Shastri Kinjawadekar, Poona, 193–32
16. *Pādukāsahasram* of Sri Venkatanath Vedanta Deshikan, Madras, 1970
17. *Pāṇinīya Śikṣā*, Goswami Prahlad Giri, Varanasi, 1987
18. *Rāmakṛṣṇakāvyam* of Daivajna Suryakavi, B. Velanakara, Bombay, 1978
19. *Rāmāyaṇamañjarī* of Kshemendra, Pt. Bhavadatta Shastri. Delhi, 1985
20. *Rig Veda Sanhita*, Dr. R.L. Kashyap & Dr. S. Sadagopan, Bangalore, 1998
21. *Sarasvatī Kaṇṭhābharaṇam* of Bhoja, Pandita Kedara Natha Sarma & Vasudeva Sarma, Varanasi, 1987
22. *Śiśupālavadham* of Magha, Pt. Haragovinda Shastri, Varanasi, 1993
23. *Stotraratnāvali*, Gita Press, Gorakhpur, 1986
24. *Subhāṣita Ratnabhāṇḍāgāram*, Narayan Ram Acharya, Bombay, 1952
25. The *Gītagovindam* of Jayadeva, Barbara Stoler Miller, Delhi, 1984
26. *The Message of the Gita*, Anilbaran Roy, Pondicherry, 1993
27. The *Rāmāyaṇa*, Gita Press, Gorakhpur, 1995
28. *Viṣṇupurāṇa*, H.H. Wilson, Calcutta, 1972
29. *Vyākhyāna Vallarī*, Lal Bahadur Shastri Sanskrit Vidyapeeth, Delhi

30. *Works of Kalidasa*, Vol. 1, C.R. Devadhar, Delhi, 1999
31. *Works of Kalidasa*, Vol. 2, C.R. Devadhar, Delhi, 1993

Secondary Sources

1. *A Companion to Sanskrit Literature*, Sures Chandra Banerji, Delhi, 1989
2. *A Debate on National Language*, Constituent Assembly of India, Govt. of India, 1949
3. *A History of Sanskrit Literature*, A. Berriedale Keith, Delhi, 1993
4. *Collected Works of Nolinikanta Gupta*, Vol. 2, Pondicherry, 1971
5. *Collected Works of Nolinikanta Gupta*, Vol. 5, Pondicherry, 1974
6. *Collected Works of Nolinikanta Gupta*, Vol. 7, Pondicherry, 1978
7. *Devavāṇī - A Collection of Essays, Articles and Quotes on Sanskrit*, The American Sanskrit Institute, New York
8. *Encyclopaedia of Language and Linguistics*, R.E. Asher, Oxford, 1994
9. *Gleanings from the Upanishad*, M.P. Pandit, Madras, 1969
10. *Hinduism*, M. Monier Williams, Calcutta, 1951
11. *History of Indian Literature*, Vol. 1, Maurice Winternitz, Delhi, 1990
12. *History of Indian Literature*, Vol. 3, Maurice Winternitz, Delhi, 1985
13. *Janaśikṣā O Saṁskṛta*, Dhyanesh Narayana Chakraborty,Calcutta, 1961
14. *Japa*, M.P. Pandit, Pondicherry, 1977
15. *Language of the Gods*, Judith M.Tyberg, Los Angeles, 1970
16. *Samskṛta aur Videśī Vidvān*, Sarvabhauma Samskrit Karayalaya, Varanasi
17. *Samskṛta Vaṅmaya Koṣa*, Vol. 1&2, Dr. Shridhara Bhaskar Varnekar, Calcutta, 1988
18. *Sanskrit-English Dictionary*, M. Monier Williams
19. *Sanskrit Commission Report* 1956–957, Govt. of India, Delhi, 1984
20. *Sanskrit*, V.V. Ivanov, Moscow, 1968
21. *Sanskrit: Essays on the value of the Language and the Literature*, Dr. V. Raghavan, Madras, 1972
22. *Sri Aurobindo Birth Centenary Library*, Vol. 3, Pondicherry, 1972
23. " Vol. 8, " 1972
24. " Vol. 9, " 1972
25. " Vol. 11, " 1971
26. " Vol. 13, " 1970
27. " Vol. 14, " 1972
28. " Vol. 15, " 1971
29. " Vol. 17, " 1972
30. " Vol. 18, " 1972
31. " Vol. 27, " 1972
32. *The Language*, L. Bloomfield, New York, 1933

33. *The Wonder that was India*, A.L. Basham, Fontana, 1971
34. *Upaniṣad Vākya Mahākoṣa*, Vol. 1&2, S. Gajanan Shambhu-Sadhale, Delhi, 1987
35. *Vedic Concordance*, Maurice Bloomfield, Delhi, 1990

Index

CD-ROMs on "The Wonder that is Sanskrit"

Along with this book we have also prepared two CD-ROMs under the same title "The Wonder that is Sanskrit".

The first CD-ROM is '*Devabhasha* - the Language of the Gods'. It contains the entire text of this book along with images, illustrations and graphics and an audio for the *shlokas* and the quotes.

The second CD-ROM is titled '*Ashtavadhanam* – Eight-fold Concentration'. Through this CD-ROM we present an art form so rare that few have witnessed it. But once seen, it is both unbelievable and unforgettable. We witness the amazing power of Concentration which is the very basis of all realisation and success in the material and spiritual fields.

We see in these CD-ROMs not just the immense possibilities of the human mind in its faculties of concentration, memory, imagination, poetic creativity, aesthetic sensitivity and quick thinking, but also the fecundity and the priceless nature of Sanskrit... the language that shaped India's past and, one hopes, will once again help create its future.

Some Books, CD-ROMs, CDs, Video and Audio cassettes prepared by Sri Aurobindo Society related to Sanskrit and Indian Culture

Books

1. Bhartrihari Nitishatakam –The Century of Life
   (A rendering in English verse by Sri Aurobindo along with original text.)
2. Chandovallari – A Handbook of Sanskrit Prosody
3. Sri Aurobindo and Sanskrit
4. Hāsyamañjarī
   (A book of humorous stories written in Sanskrit.)
5. Indian Sculpture and Iconography - Forms and Measurements
6. India is One
7. The Gita for the Youth
8. A Call to the Youth of India
9. India's Contribution to Management
10. India and the World Scene

CD-ROMs, Video Tapes, Audio Tapes, CDs

1. The Wonder that is Sanskrit
   a. Devabhasha
   b. Ashtavadhanam
   (These two CD-ROMs present the beauty, charm and perfection of Sanskrit language and literature as well as the amazing capacities of the human mind, through a typically Indian art form which is both unbelievable and unforgettable.)

2. Alaap - A Discovery of Indian Classical Music
   (A set of 20 CDs introducing and explaining the deeper spiritual dimensions as well as the technical aspects of Indian Classical Music - both North Indian (Hindustani) and South Indian (Carnatic) / Audio-cassettes, with a book.)

3. Ashtavadhanam
   (A Video presentation of about 30 minutes introducing an Ashtavadhanam or Eight-fold Concentration practised in Sanskrit.)

4. Chandovallari – Illustration of major Chandas in Sanskrit.
   (These are two audio-cassettes illustrating the major Chandas in Sanskrit through musical renderings. These are companion cassettes to the book Chandovallari.)

Sri Aurobindo Society

Sri Aurobindo Society is a non-profit, international, spiritual, educational and cultural organisation. Inspired by the vision of Sri Aurobindo and the Mother, it strives for individual perfection, social transformation and human unity, beyond all divisions of nationality, religion, caste, creed or sex.

The Society has members, centres and branches all over India and in many countries of the world. It is deeply involved in several projects in Education, Health, Indian Culture and Management, Youth and Women. It regularly organises conferences, seminars and workshops on a variety of topics.

It has published a large number of books on diverse subjects, in Indian and foreign languages. It has prepared documentary films that have been telecast by the Indian national TV network.

It lays a very special emphasis on India and Indian culture and has taken up several projects in various fields, which include the publication of Books and preparation of Films and CD-ROMs.

<www.sriaurobindosociety.org.in>